THE BREAK-UP OF CZECHOSLOVAKIA: AN IN-DEPTH ECONOMIC ANALYSIS

The Break-up of Czechoslovakia: An In-depth Economic Analysis

OLDRICH DEDEK et al.
Institute of Economics of the Czech National Bank
Prague
Czech Republic

Avebury
Aldershot • Brookfield USA • Hong Kong • Singapore • Sydney

Published by
Avebury
Ashgate Publishing Limited
Gower House
Croft Road
Aldershot
Hants GU11 3HR
England

Ashgate Publishing Company
Old Post Road
Brookfield
Vermont 05036
USA

British Library Cataloguing in Publication Data

The break-up of Czechoslovakia : an in-depth economic
analysis
1. Czechoslovakia - Economic conditions - 1945-1992
2. Czechoslovakia - Economic policy - 1945-1992
I. Dědek, Oldřich
330.9'437'04

ISBN 1 85972 276 8

Library of Congress Catalog Card Number: 96-84033

Typeset by
Zdeňka Pfeiferová
Politických vězňů 7
110 00 Praha 1
Czech Republic

Printed and bound in Great Britain by
Ipswich Book Co. Ltd., Ipswich, Suffolk

Contents

Part Three
Fields of cooperation between the successor Republics of Czechoslovakia

Part Four
The Czech and Slovak Republics after the break-up of Czechoslovakia

Figures and tables

Authors

Oldřich Dědek, Editor

Alena Buchtíková (Chapter 2.4, 4.3), *Institute of Economics of CNB*

Aleš Čapek (Chapter 1), *Institute of Economics of CNB*

Oldřich Dědek (Introduction, Chapter 2.3.1, 2.3.2, 3.4), *Institute of Economics of CNB*

Aleš Gerloch (Chapter 1, 2.1), *Faculty of Law, Charles University of Prague*

Mojmír Hájek (Chapter 4.1, 4.2), *Institute of Economics of CNB*

Stanislava Janáčková (Chapter 3.2), *Institute of Economics of CNB*

Antonín Kotulan (Chapter 2.3.2), *Institute of Economics of CNB*

Josef Mervart (Chapter 3.1), *Institute of Economics of CNB*

Vladimír Nachtigal (Chapter 1, 2.2), *Institute of Economics of CNB*

Ladislav Prokop (Chapter 3.3), *Institute of Economics of CNB*

Pavel Soukup (Chapter 2.2, 3.3), *Institute of Economics of CNB*

Kateřina Šmídková (Chapter 3.4), *Institute of Economics of CNB*

Patricia Vlachová, Translator

Alexander Hajna, Translator (Chapter 3.1)

Gwendolyn Albert, English Language Editor

Introduction

If we were to analyze world history in order to determine which conditions typically accompany changes in the political map of the world, we would certainly find cases when political change was preceded and followed by chaos in the state administrative order, by growing hatred among national groups as well as war or other forms of violence. These cases would outnumber those in which old established orders fall, giving rise to new ones in a relatively quiet atmosphere without serious consequences for future relations and destructive effects on the economy. In other words, history has shown us that people and their political leaders tend not to be able to handle problems associated with changes in the political map rationally and without emotions running high.

The disintegration of the Soviet Union and, subsequently, of the entire Eastern bloc released an immense volume of energy which served not only constructive purposes, but, unfortunately, destructive ones as well. Instead of solving the numerous problems which had accumulated during the command economy period, the transition to democracy and market economy was left affected by escalated nationalism, economic demagogy and armed conflicts.

Similarly, Czechoslovakia, a country characterized by seventy-plus years of coexistence between two Slavic nations - the Czechs and the Slovaks - assumed its position next to those other post-Communist multinational states struggling to survive the political changes at the turn of the 1990s. The case of Czechoslovakia is, however, different in its own way. In 1989, Czechoslovakia taught the world about 'Velvet Revolution'. Three years later it again drew the world's attention, this time to the 'Velvet Separation'. The 'Velvet Separation' showed the world that it was possible to negotiate a peaceful split of the country as well as subsequently create healthy start-up conditions for the succeeding states.

Since the break-up of Czechoslovakia can be looked upon from different points of view and various possible causes, this book will examine several hypotheses of what happened and why it happened.

Firstly, the peaceful split of a highly integrated state did not come out of nowhere. In the background were the numerous clever, broad-minded and fine-tuned economic and political decisions made with impressive erudition by the people on lower decision making levels. Therefore, the authors find it worthwhile to survey thoroughly the often original policy measures taken to solve various problems and note them as a source of positive knowledge in our turbulent environment.

Secondly, each and every change has both its past as well as a logical consequence. This book thus focuses the reader's attention to the circumstances directly connected to the peaceful split of Czechoslovakia while attempting a deeper analysis of the history of Czech-Slovak relations, since this is where the origin of what subsequently happened later needs to be found. Because it seems interesting to compare the different visions of the future with later reality, this book also takes its readers partly beyond the horizon of a divided Czechoslovakia.

The authors of this book are economists, with all but one researchers in the Economic Institute of the Czech National Bank. Therefore the book is written mostly from the viewpoint of macroeconomists who are inclined to look at issues from financial perspective. This somehow narrower focus should not be to the detriment of the book since economic aspects or, more precisely, financial aspects were often the main agents of change.

Chronology offers itself as the most logical way to sort out the number of facts available. Based on this historic sequencing, this book is divided into four parts. The first part reviews the significant events which influenced the economic relations between the Czechs and the Slovaks from the year of the founding of Czechoslovakia until the fall of the Communist regime. To help the reader understand the contradiction in views which arose out of the formation of a common state, the authors strive to identify differences in the historical experience of both nations while co-existing in one state.

The second part surveys the most important economic and political events in Czechoslovak history after 1989. The democratization process unleashed a wide spectrum of political thoughts and inclinations which kept undermining the unity of the state. This period is rich in disagreements on the state set up, new concepts of economic reform, and other important questions. This lack of consensus finally resulted in an agreement to dissolve Czechoslovakia.

The third part represents the core of the book. It describes the major actions taken in order to minimize the trauma which resulted from the disintegration of a highly integrated economic system. During this period the authors find many examples of constructive cooperation and willingness to seek compromises acceptable for both parties as well as the disagreements intrinsic to any divorce. In an exceptionally short time, the Czech and Slovak policymakers formulated and introduced several unique measures such as the division of federal property, currency separation, clearing payment system and customs union, which substantially mitigated the distress caused by the split of Czechoslovakia.

The forth part attempts at answering a question of what economic consequences did the break-up of the state have for the succeeding Republics once they began a new life based on their own resources and ideas of how to manage their social and economic development.

Who might benefit from reading this book? Aside from the group of people who will be reminded of earlier as well as very recent history, the authors would recommend it to two categories of readers. The first are those students and teachers of economics whose focus is not only on national economic history but also on general macroeconomic analysis and policymaking. As a source offering a complete analysis of an important episode in the history of the Czech economy, this book features information which could very well disappear under the flow of new events.

In a wider context, a book about the break-up of a relatively small state in the heart of Europe can serve as a source of inspiration for those whom circumstances have brought face to face with similar problems. It remains up to the reader to synthesize the right message from the rich contents of this book.

The group of authors would like to extend their gratitude to those experts who supplied them with relevant information or who provided facts which were often stored only in the minds of these specialists. We would like thank Jiří Bruk, advisor to the Governor of the Czech National Bank; Ing. Marcela Dvořáková, Czech Postal Services General Headquarters; Vlastimil Gejdoš, department head, Ministry of Trade and Industry; Věra Hartlová, deputy Director, Czech National Bank; Zdeněk Hlaváč, department head, Ministry of Trade and Industry; Milena Horčicová, department head, Ministry of Finance of the CR; Vratislav Hubner, department head, Czech National Bank; Věra Churainová, Czech National Bank; Zdeněk Jičínský, former Vice Chairman of the Federal Parliament; Bibiana Jílková, department head, Czech National Bank; Jana Jirásková, Czech National Bank; Ota Kaftan, Director general, Czech National Bank; Pavel Klíma, deputy Director, Ministry of Finance of the CR; František Kubíček, department head, Academy of Sciences of the CR; Pavel Kysilka, Vice Governor, Czech National Bank; Ludmila Matznerová, department head, Czech National Bank; Jiří Novotný, head of Archive, Czech National Bank; Miloš Podrazil, department head, Ministry of Trade and Industry; Tomáš Potměšil, advisor to the Governor of the Czech National Bank; Ivan Rada, department head, Ministry of Transportation of the CR;

Ladislav Rusmich, Czech National Bank; Leopold Surga, department head, Czech National Bank; Vladimír Šlitr, department head, Ministry of Finance of the CR; Pavel Štěpánek, department head, Ministry of Finance of the CR; Oldřich Štětina, department head, Ministry of Transportation of the CR; Ota Švach, retired Colonel; Martin Švehla, department head, Czech National Bank; Pavel Trnka, department head, Czech Postal Services; František Vokatý, department head, Czech National Bank; Jan Vít, Vice Governor of the Czech National Bank; Vladimír Žďárský, advisor to the Governor of the Czech National Bank.

The authors would also like to thank Dana Rottová and the assistants of the Institute of Economics Jarmila Kadlasová, Zdeňka Pfeiferová, Ivana Saňová and Marcela Zemínová whose devoted work was of great help to them.

Part One
CHRONOLOGY OF THE CZECH AND SLOVAK COEXISTENCE IN ONE STATE (1918-89)

1 The founding of Czechoslovakia and its history between the two World Wars

The founding of the Czechoslovak Republic was one of the results of the disintegration of the Austro-Hungarian Empire which emerged from World War I a defeated power. Following the resolution of territorial disputes with Poland and Hungary, Czechoslovakia's borders were finally fixed in 1919 at the Versailles Treaty Conference which also approved the annexation of Subcarpathian Ruthenia to Czechoslovakia. This newly established state in Central Europe, which assumed about 21 per cent of the former Austro-Hungarian Empire and 25 per cent of its population, was composed of the territories of Bohemia, Moravia and Silesia (hereafter referred to as the Czech Lands), Slovakia and Subcarpathian Ruthenia.

After subsequent border rectifications, Czechoslovakia's territory totalled 140,394 km^2, out of which Bohemia was 52,064 km^2; Moravia 22,315 km^2; Silesia 4,423 km^2; Slovakia 48,936 km^2; and Subcarpathian Ruthenia 12,656 km^2. The Czechoslovakia of 1921 was home to 13.6 million inhabitants, more than a third of whom were ethnic minorities. The first census, dated 15 December 1921, shows that 65.5 per cent of the inhabitants declared themselves to be of Czech or Slovak origin (Slovak nationality less than 15 per cent); 23.4 per cent German; 5.7 per cent Hungarian; 3.4 per cent Ukrainian; 1.3 per cent Jewish; and 0.6 per cent Polish.[1]

The founding of Czechoslovakia substantially changed the position of the Czech Lands within the country, the nationals of which formed the most powerful force in the new political leadership of the country.[2] The position of the Slovaks changed greatly as well. Within the borders of the pre-war Austro-Hungarian Empire, the Slovaks were concerned mainly with maintaining their national identity in the face of what could be called forced Hungarization.[3] The economic differences between the Slovak and Hungarian territories were minor, with Slovakia maintaining a slightly higher level of industrial development. The creation of the Czechoslovak Republic not only removed the threats to the existence of the Slovak nation, but it also created unprecedented conditions for the development of its educational, cultural and political life which improved substantially compared to that under the Austro-Hungarian Empire. However, the noticeably lower level of Slovakia's economic development was to its disadvantage in the new Czechoslovak Republic and had a discernible effect in terms of its social relations. Slovaks perceived as belonging to a higher social class not only the non-Slovak (Czech and Hungarian) land owners and manufacturers but also Czech teachers, police and other government employees.

Czechoslovakia emerged as a union of two territories which were, prior to 1918, on a different level of economic development within the Austro-Hungarian Empire. The Czech Lands were part of the Austrian section of the empire and, after World War I, assumed about 70-75 per cent of its pre-war industrial potential. Slovakia, which used to belong to the Hungarian part of the empire, assumed less than 1/5 of the pre-war industrial potential. In the first years of its existence, the industrial and agrarian structure of Czechoslovakia was therefore determined by the character of the economy in the Czech Lands, which were not only more developed but also larger and more populated than the mostly agrarian Slovakia which was then in only the early stage of its industrial development.

The industrial development of Czechoslovakia between the world wars was influenced primarily by the progress in Bohemia, Moravia and Silesia which produced 92 per cent of the country's industrial output. Industrial development in Slovakia was complicated by several factors. Primarily, the Slovak domestic market was too small for large companies and efficient cooperation was hampered by the fragmented industrial structure. Many production units were obsolete and poorly concentrated. Trade between Slovakia and the Czech Lands was underdeveloped due to high and erratic transport tariffs. All these difficulties worsened the competitiveness of many branches of Slovak industry in the Czech and West European markets. Access to Slovakia's traditional markets in the south and southeast was further limited by the introduction of border control and other barriers restricting trade. Slovak companies experienced difficulties in obtaining loans and were charged higher interest rates and transportation fees. Most of the Slovak factories were unable to increase their competitiveness by using cheap labour, and consequently, in the years of economic slump, discontinued production or closed down forever.

Czechoslovakia acquired a major part (about 60 per cent of the pre-war potential) of the industrial capacity of the former Austro-Hungarian Empire. Before 1914, the empire's export level, given its industrial potential, was rather low (20 per cent), with most of its output consumed by its vast domestic market. The disintegration of the empire resulted in a loss of markets and forced a new reliance on exports. Many branches of industry (the textile, chemical and metallurgy industries) were dependent on imported raw materials. Post-war Czechoslovakia also suffered from a substantial scarcity of food. Therefore, from the beginning of the existence of Czechoslovakia, its economy intensively participated in international trade. For this reason it suffered from all the features of the world business cycles which troubled the world economy in the 1920s and 30s.

The first post-war crisis affected Czechoslovakia in 1921-23, a year later than it did the rest of the world. It badly hit the less competitive factories in Slovakia, particularly the steelworks and ore-mining plants.[4] Unlike in the Czech Lands, where the crisis did not slow down industrialization, the Slovak industrial base narrowed as a consequence of production decreases.

The positive trend following the economic revival of 1924-25 was interrupted in 1926 by a short recession, followed by a new period of growth which lasted until 1929. In that year, the pre-war output was exceeded by about 25 per cent. Slovakia suffered from the impact of the crisis longer than the western part of the country and its production base and the size of the industrial labour force had grown considerably slower. Despite the change in employment structure, by 1929 Slovakia's employment figures matched only the 1913 level.

Along with the rest of the world, Czechoslovakia experienced an economic crisis in the years of 1929-37. The crisis commenced in late 1929 and reached its peak in 1933, and was therefore longer than in the other developed European countries. In Slovakia, the 1930s depression developed later and had a slightly lesser impact. Export companies suffered worse, while production decreases in industries oriented at domestic markets were lower. Slovakia's production hit rock bottom in 1933, the most damaged being the ore-mining, timber and chemical industries. Less harmed were coal mining, metallurgy, electric energy, paper, cellulose and cement production.

The depression was strikingly long and ended only around 1936. Conversely, the subsequent period of economic recovery - 1936 to 1937 - was quite short. It was relieved by increased exports and the rearmament of the country as a reaction to the threat of Nazi Germany. This remarkable boom of the armament industry brought about an increase in the production of coal, machinery, chemical products, cement, clothes and shoes. With the exception of light industry, production levels surpassed those from before the crisis.

The Slovak post-depression recovery was more dynamic than in the Czech Lands. In 1937, production levels and employment figures exceeded those from before the depression. These increases were due mostly to the heavy industry output. The construction of new roads and the laying of about 200 kilometres of railway track had a stimulating effect on the economy. The locations of the newly built production facilities were often dictated by economic, military and strategic factors.

At the turn of 1937-38, a crisis emerged marking the beginning of a new industrial cycle. Its course was interrupted by the political developments of 1938, when Czechoslovakia lost 30 per cent of its territory as a result of the Munich Agreement. The next year it was completely dismembered and incorporated into the war-related economy of Nazi Germany.[5]

Table 1.1
Selected figures for the Czech Lands and Slovakia in 1937

	Czechoslovakia	Czech Lands	Slovakia
Population	100.0	75.5	24.5
National income	100.0	88.0	12.0
Industrial output	100.0	92.2	7.8
Agricultural output	100.0	77.7	22.4
National income per capita		100.0	41.9
Industrial output per capita		100.0	26.2
Agricultural output per capita		100.0	88.9

Note: Not including Subcarpathian Ruthenia
Source: Czech and Slovak Economic Relations, *Hospodarske noviny*, no. 24, 1991

After World War II, some critics blamed the Czechoslovak governments for not having done enough to close the gap between the economic levels of the Czech Lands and Slovakia. Nevertheless, the question remains of whether this could have been accomplished given the conditions of the 1920s and 1930s. Indeed, regional policies as well as financial support meant to assist the growth of the less developed areas became a subject of economic research and government decision making only after the World War II. Some of the government investment projects introduced prior to the Nazi occupation indicate a certain level of awareness of this problem as well as some attempts to address it, however, the political developments at the end of the 1930s put an end to any progress in that direction. The result were more profound economic differences between the western and eastern parts of the country (see Table 1.1).

2 The break-up of Czechoslovakia in 1938-39 and World War II

The seven year period of Fascist rule over Czechoslovakia remains a tragic phase in the history of the country. It commenced in Autumn 1938 following the Munich Agreement of 29 September 1938, where representatives of France, Italy and Great Britain agreed to yield to the demands of the Nazis for parts of the Czechoslovak territory. The Czechoslovak government complied with the dictate and surrendered the Czech borderlands to Germany. Poland followed suit with its own territorial demands (for Tesin and its vicinity, and small borderline corrections in northern Slovakia) and so did Hungary (asking for parts of southern Slovakia and Subcarpathian Ruthenia). The Czechoslovak government acceded to these demands as well, the Polish annexation taking place in October 1938, the Hungarian's in November 1938. The result was a reduction of Czechoslovak territory by 30 per cent and a population decrease of more than 1/3.

The annexed territories contained more than 40 per cent of the Czechoslovak industrial capacity (mainly coal mining and light industry), most of the forests and 1/3 of the farming land, including the Slovak grain-rich Wheat Island and the main areas producing corn, hops, grapes, tobacco and flax.

The Munich capitulation marked the onset of the so called Post-Munich Republic, a six month episode of the country's history which ended in the middle of March 1939. The worst social problem to come out of this period proved to be that of refugees, those people who were forced to leave their homes and often all of their possessions in the annexed territories. In 1938-39, what remained of the Czech and Slovak territories had to cope with 450,000 expatriates and the large increase in unemployment which resulted from their presence. In Slovakia this migration was remarkably lower than in the Czech Lands.

The secession of the borderlands to Germany, Hungary and Poland marked the beginning of the so called Second Republic. At the end of November 1938, what was left of the National Assembly passed a constitutional Act which gave Slovakia its autonomy and Czechoslovakia became the Czech-Slovak Republic.[6] The National Assembly also passed a separate Act determining the autonomy of Subcarpathian Ruthenia.

As subsequent developments showed, this autonomy served as the instigation for the complete separation of Slovakia from the Czech Lands. Nazi Germany deliberately encouraged tensions between the Czechs and the Slovaks for its own benefit. The Nazis induced the Slovak Assembly to proclaim an independent Slovak State on 14 March 1939. The next day, the German army occupied the central parts of the Czech Lands and established the Nazi Protectorate of Bohemia and Moravia (here after the Protectorate). Next, Subcarpathian Ruthenia was annexed by Horthy's Hungary. In the short period between the Munich Conference and 15 March 1939, former Czechoslovakia was broken into five parts which existed separately until 1945.

For Nazi Germany, gaining control of Czechoslovakia was a key strategic move both for its geographic position in Central Europe and for its economic potential. In contradiction to Slovakia, where the German interest initially focused on the exploitation of natural resources, the Protectorate was an important source of industrial and armament products. Militarisation of the Czech economy, stimulated by the newly introduced system of war-related production, began immediately after the establishment of the Protectorate with heavy industry gaining preference over light industry, construction and crafts.

In the Protectorate, production as a whole developed unevenly. There was a temporary decline from 1939-41 due to a decrease in light industry production as well as to the overall effect of re-organizing the economy to fit the needs of the German war machine. The increase of production following 1941 culminated in 1944, when the industrial production index (with the exception of the coal mining industry) climbed 18 per cent above the figure for 1939. The year 1941 saw a marked increase in industrial employment figures, surpassing those of 1939 by 35 per cent. The depth of structural changes in industrial production can be illustrated by employment figures in those areas which dominated pre-war Czechoslovak industry: the metallurgy and mining industry saw a rise of employment by 124 per cent after 1939; the aircraft industry saw an increase 25 times greater than that before the war; while, by 1945, textile employment had dropped by 43 per cent.

Slovak production figures indicate stronger war-related prosperity than in the Protectorate. The boom reached its peak in 1943 when industrial production surpassed the figures of 1937 by 63 per cent. The increase during the entire period of the independent Slovak State was about 50 per cent, about a 8.5 per cent annual increase between 1939-44 compared to the 3.4 per cent annual increase in the Protectorate. As of June 1944, the overall industrial employment in Slovakia reached 174,000 people, an increase of 66 per cent from 1937. About 30 per cent of this workforce operated in the metallurgy and mining industry.

The increase in Slovak industrial production from 1939-43 was influenced by a number of factors. Underemployment of production facilities in the 1930s permitted an expansion of production in a short period of time without the necessity of large investments. At the same time, the flow of competing goods from the Czech Lands decreased. The percentage of Czech goods imported into Slovakia fell from almost 50 per cent of the total imports in 1939 to about 35 per cent in 1940 (see Table 1.2). On the other hand, the data on Slovak exports to the Protectorate in the first two years following the split of Czechoslovakia in 1939 changed less dramatically. This factor played a specific role in the economic development of Slovakia and contributed to a temporary boom of some of the technologically outdated Slovak facilities.

Table 1.2
Protectorate share on Slovak foreign trade

	Import	Export
1939	49.9	51.1
1940	35.4	43.5
1941	31.2	43.3
1942	27.6	27.5
1943	23.3	25.9

Source: *Slovak National Bank Newsletter*, no. 9, 1943

Foreign outlets for Slovak products, low purchasing power of the domestic market and long geographic distance from the markets in Central Europe, ceased to be a problem during wartime. Slovakia was now successful in selling much of its output abroad and, now, instead of searching for markets, it actually faced the danger of overexploitation of its resources. Embargoes and intensive rearmament forced Germany to use raw materials, semi-finished goods and products of a lower quality and Slovakia reacted to this changing situation by renewing or expanding production, especially in mining industry and metallurgy. Slovakia's industrial structure which was based on domestic sources of raw materials was convenient for the Nazi's war-related objectives. The fact that Slovakia was spared aerial bombing and ground fighting until 1944 also helped the development of Slovak industry.

The economic development was considerably influenced by the Slovak National Uprising in 1944 which for many weeks interrupted the exploitation of the rebellious territories and exhausted the Nazi human and material resources. The uprising began exactly at the time the Nazis had planned to maximize Slovak war-related production. Transportation through Slovakia came to a halt, making deliveries to the front difficult. This had the effect of rescuing important equipment from being transported to Germany.

Although the Slovak war-related economy was unable to meet the demands of its population as it did in times of peace, the wartime period represents an era of economic and industrial boom of Slovakia. Undoubtedly, the brief existence of the independent Slovak State had positive consequences in the eyes of the Slovak population in terms of further strengthening the Slovak national consciousness as well as giving more weight to Slovak political and economic demands in later reunited Czechoslovakia.

3 The post-war restoration of Czechoslovakia and the period of the centrally planned economy

Czechoslovakia was reunited in 1945 following the end of World War II. With the exception of Subcarpathian Ukraine (former Subcarpathian Ruthenia), all annexed territories were again reincorporated. Subcarpathian Ukraine, in compliance with the Czechoslovak-Soviet agreement of 29 June 1945, was conceded to Ukraine. There were several minor border corrections with Hungary and Poland as well, thereby reducing the pre-war territory of 140,164 km^2 to 127,870 km^2. These territorial changes, combined with war casualties and the transfer of the German minority back to Germany, caused a decrease in population from a pre-war count of 15.3 million to 12.1 million in 1945. According to the treaties agreed upon by the Allies, Czechoslovakia fell into the Soviet sphere of influence, a condition that for the next forty five years would deeply affect all aspects of Czechoslovak political, social and economic development.

3.1 Economic reconstruction in 1945-46 and the Two-year Plan of 1947-48

Reunited Czechoslovakia entered post-war international politics on the side of the world antifascist front, a circumstance especially favourable to the Slovaks who, as one of the Nazi's war allies, had found themselves on the losing side. Towards the end of the war, representatives of the exiled Czechoslovak governments in London and in Moscow had agreed on a proclamation drafted by the Communists which, on 5 April 1945 in the Soviet-liberated town of Kosice in Slovakia, declared the official policy for the first Czechoslovak Government of the so called National Front of the Czechs and Slovaks.[7] The proclamation (hereafter called the Kosice Program) gave birth to the asymmetrical structure of state administration which was based on the existence of governmental (nationwide) agencies which had their Republic counterparts in Slovak agencies only (there were no Czech counterparts). The structure of the Communist party, which later acquired a monopoly power, was a case in point: the only counterpart to the Czechoslovak Communist Party was the Slovak Communist Party. In this asymmetry, we can find some of the roots of the differences in thinking and attitudes of the Czechs and Slovaks toward social, political and economic questions. Generally speaking, the attitudes of the Slovaks can be characterized as largely nationally oriented, while those of the Czechs as aligned more along Czechoslovak lines.

One of the first tasks of the post-war reconstruction was to remove, as quickly as possible, the consequences of the forced disintegration of Czechoslovakia and restore some unity to the national economy. This involved removing regional discrepancies in prices, wages and agrarian policies, and in the quality of supplies and social security administration. On 1 November 1945 a monetary reform was announced to accomplish the key objective of uniting the two currencies and overcoming the inflation inherited from the war period.[8] There were other signs of recovery, such as a revision of prices and stabilization of wages.

In May 1946, the first elections to the National Assembly and national councils (local governments) were held. The Communist parties of Czechoslovakia and Slovakia obtained 38 per cent of the vote, the Czechoslovak Social Democrats and Slovak Labour Party gained 12.8 per cent with the rest of less than half the country's other voters choosing other parties.[9] Klement Gottwald, a Communist, became the Prime Minister.

In keeping with one of the articles of the new government program, the Communist economists quickly drafted and, in October 1946, passed the Two-year Economic Plan. Its main objective was to complete the restoration of the economy and to achieve the pre-war standard of living. As for Slovakia, the Plan had in mind not only restoration but also deliberate industrialization. The planned investments represented about 20 per cent of the expected government revenues, 31.6 per cent of which were to be allocated in Slovakia, preferably into industry, transportation and the construction of housing.

As for its trade relations, the newly reunited Czechoslovakia was now in a more advantageous position than it had been upon its founding after World War I. Its successful industrial development in the 1920s and 1930s and its then good standing in world trade as one of the world leading exporters helped the country renew the numerous business contacts it had lost during the World War II.

One of Czechoslovakia's advantages, in a large part due to its pre-war industrial capacity, was its ability to offer attractive goods such as coal, metals, wood, machine products and sugar to the rest of Europe experiencing at that time a shortage in these products. With goods delivered by the

UNRRA, brought into the country outside the framework of international trade, Czechoslovakia was able to limit its import demand, thereby maintaining a healthy trade balance with imports reaching only 72 per cent of exports.

A major share of exports (approximately 80 per cent) was purchased by countries outside the Soviet sphere of influence. From 1946-47, Czechoslovakia's most important trade partner was Switzerland. Trade with Switzerland resulted in high surplus and enabled Czechoslovakia to cover its deficits with Dollar or Pound Sterling areas. Until the summer of 1947, Czechoslovak foreign trade assumed 1.5 per cent of the world trade, just a little bit less than in 1937.

The political parties assembled in the National Front, especially the Communist and Social Democrats on the one side and the non-Communists on the other, frequently clashed over ways of solving economic and political problems of the post-war development. In the middle of February 1948, the disputes resulted in a government crisis. Supported by organized unrest (national meetings of trade unions and agricultural committees, street demonstrations led by armed workers' action squads and mass demonstrations by the members of workers' political parties), the Communists assumed power and became the leading force in the country.

The Communists perceived the February events to be an important milestone in its history, for Czechoslovakia had now entered a new phase of building socialism with the clear objective of maintaining a close relationship with the Soviet Union and its other allies. It also marked the commencement of a rapid industrialization of Slovakia, which the Communists understood to be a vital part of the country's transition to socialism, calling it 'socialist industrialization'.

In 1948, the Two-year Plan ended. Its main objective to reinstate the pre-war economic standard had mostly been accomplished, although in some branches of industry (agriculture and construction) the pre-war figures were not met. Slovakia, however, enjoyed a period of strikingly dynamic industrial development. While in late 1948 Czechoslovak figures for industrial production exceeded the pre-war level by 10 per cent, in Slovakia the industrial output nearly doubled the figures from 1938 and was 20 per cent greater than the maximum production of the war years. Slovakia's industrial output represented 13.2 per cent and the agricultural output 30.7 per cent of the national production. In 1948, the Slovak contribution to the total national income was 19.2 per cent while the proportion actually used in Slovakia exceeded the income generated by 8.8 per cent.[10]

The Two-year Plan and its objectives for rapid industrialization of Slovakia as its integral part (unheard of in the pre-war Czechoslovakia), marked the beginning of speedy industrial development of Slovakia, thereby equalizing the economic levels of the new, post-war Czechoslovakia.

3.2 The centrally planned economy in the 1950s and 1960s

The turn of the 1940s and 1950s marked the beginning of deteriorated relations between the East and West known as the Cold War. For Czechoslovakia, these years represented a period of reorientating its international economic relations, so far linked to the Western Europe and the United States, to the Soviet Union and its allies. The advocates of this transformation stressed the restructuring of domestic production, giving preference to some branches of heavy industry (metallurgy, machine and chemical industries) over the production of consumer goods and services.

The restructuring efforts were intense. In 1951, in the middle of the Five-year Plan devised for 1949-53, the original objectives were further intensified. With the clear intention to prepare for a war, the Communists pressed for further exploitation of domestic resources (regardless of its effectiveness) and accelerated the process of restructuring the economy.[11] The ongoing industrialization of Slovakia became an integral part of this process.

Although the attempt to expand the new targets of the Five-year Plan were not met, the speed of economic development during this period was considerable: the average annual national income growth exceeded 9 per cent; annual industrial output growth was over 14 per cent; and in Slovakia, industrial output grew 18 per cent annually. However, toward the end of the Five-year Plan and in the following years, some of the unrealistic objectives of the plan began to have a negative effect and a visible deceleration of economic growth ensued (the 10 per cent national income growth in 1952 decreased to 6 per cent in 1953 and 4 per cent in 1954).

In 1954-55, this negative development brought about a number of changes in economic planning, partly associated with the easing of international tensions, however, they were mainly caused by internal demands to remove the accumulated problems and distortions in the national economy. These changes did not affect the policy of accelerated Slovak industrialization and deliberate transfer of funds to Slovakia. In these two years, the annual growth of national income reached 7.1 per cent and the index of industrial production 7.8 per cent. The matching figures for Slovakia were 8.8 per cent and 9.8 per cent respectively.

Compared to the averages of 1954-55, the second Five-year Plan (for 1956-60) proposed a higher rate of economic growth, although it was slower compared to the figures initially planned for the first Five-year Plan. In Slovakia, the national income growth was again faster with 9.1 per cent compared to the Czechoslovak rate of 7.1 per cent; in personal consumption it was 8.1 per cent compared to 6.4 per cent; and in industrial production 13.7 per cent compared to 10.7 per cent.

Despite the above achievements, some Slovaks began to claim that the concept of Slovak industrialization did not give their agencies enough power to effectively promote Slovakia. In the 1960s, this growing Slovak opposition called for equality between Czechs and Slovaks and requested a federal system of government.

In the beginning of the 1960s, the Communists announced that socialism in Czechoslovakia had been accomplished and declared a 'Socialist Constitution', which instituted the leading role of Communist Party. The Republic was officially renamed the Czechoslovak Socialist Republic (CSSR).

At the end of the 1950s, the Communists announced the third Five-year Plan (for 1961-65). Nevertheless, the economic reality showed that the execution of this plan and its optimistic and overly ambitious objectives were incompatible and the Party and Government leaders later abandoned it. Since the command system, as designed for Czechoslovakia, could not exist without planning, the Government decided to produce a separate One-year Plan for 1963. The remaining two years of the collapsed third Five-year Plan were to become part of the Seven-year Plan for 1964-70. The One-year Plan for 1963 was not fulfilled, forcing the Communists to revoke the Seven-year Plan and, as of 1965, devise one-year plans only.

Even in these years marked by failure, Slovakia kept its dynamic lead in economic development. The average national income growth for the years of the failed third Five-year Plan (1961-65) was 2 per cent, in Slovakia it was 3.1 per cent; annual national industrial output growth was 5.3 per cent, the Slovak figure was almost one half higher at 7.5 per cent; the annual growth of construction in Slovakia was 5.3 per cent, while the annual figure for Czechoslovakia was merely half that at 2.6 per cent.

A similar picture was reached for the fourth Five-year Plan (1966-70). The annual national income growth was 6.9 per cent, in Slovakia it was 8.5 per cent; national industrial output growth was 6.7 per cent, the Slovak figure was 9.7 per cent; the annual growth of the construction industry in Slovakia was 8.1 per cent, while the national figure was 7.9 per cent.

Local voices, criticizing the existing command model of planned economy as well as its consequences for the economic development of the country, were first raised as early as in the middle of the 1950s. The Central Committee of the Communist Party, the leading political body in the country, reacted with resolutions on an 'economic policy focused on efficiency' (1957) and on 'changes in methods of managing the economy' (1959). These resolutions had no force however and therefore, in the 1960s, caused a reappearance of a wave of disapproval with the system of central planning together with reformed proposals for a new economic order.

The disapprovals resulted in the so called 'Prague Spring 1968', a major change in the political direction of the Communist Party, now identified as 'Socialism with a human face'. In August 1968, the Government of the Soviet Union, along with other countries of the Soviet bloc reacted to this development with military intervention. This resulted in displacing the main leaders associated with changes in the country as well as laying foundations for so called 'normalization process'. Normalization meant severe political and personal persecution of anyone involved in the Prague Spring, including the Communists.

The year 1968 saw the transformation of Czechoslovakia into a Federation of two Republics - the Czech Republic and the Slovak Republic. The Constitution Act on Federation strengthened the position of Slovakia by expanding the powers of its national agencies. The onset of normalization, however, brought about a major modification in the former ideas, emphasizing a higher centralization of political power. Therefore, by again subordinating political life to a Communist monopoly, history did not allow the Federal concept to be developed and tested.

3.3 The gradual decay of the planned economy in the 1970s and 1980s

Rigid centralism, having overridden 'revisionist' market socialism in Czechoslovakia, reintroduced the pro-Soviet form of government. Although the establishment of a Federation removed the asymmetry in the political and administrative structure of Czechoslovakia, economic relations between the Eastern and Western parts of the country did not change much.[12] On the contrary, the budgetary system (comprising the federal budget, national budgets of the two Republics and regional budgets of local authorities) permitted a continuing transfer of resources between the two parts of Czechoslovakia.

The economic development in the 1970s was affected by the problems inherited from preceding years. Quality of Czechoslovak products was falling behind the standards of more advanced economies. Employment conditions were characterized by overmaning and, as a result, low level of productivity and organization. The Czechoslovak economy did not adjust to the changes brought on by the oil crisis, which in the world context led to an introduction of improved methods of energy consumption. The close trading relations with the Soviet Union and the introduction of administrative pricing (including crude oil prices) resulted in almost complete insulation of domestic businesses from competitive markets. The employment policy led to a significant levelling off in the standard of living which, in turn, translated into stagnating economic growth. The political leadership of the country was intent on not allowing the deep-felt resentment toward the government to be intensified by a substantial shortage of basic commodities.

Communist Party documents, which were subsequently reflected in Government Resolutions, called for higher effectiveness, a decrease in energy and material consumption and a widespread intensification of the economic process, foreign trade, etc. However, due to the political system and its consequences for the economy management, neither the fifth Five-year Plan (1971-75) nor the sixth Five-year Plan (1976-80) managed to institutionalize the required qualitative changes. Table 1.3 indicates the increase in gross output which was accomplished at the expense of a growing employment of production factors while their efficiency was declining.[13]

Table 1.3
Average growth rates of selected production factors and their partial efficiencies in material production

Period	*Gross output*	*Production factors*			*Partial efficiency*			*Total efficiency*
		Labour	Capital	Material	Labour	Capital	Material	
1951-55	7.7	1.0	4.0	7.5	6.7	3.7	0.2	3.3
1956-60	7.9	-0.1	4.9	8.8	8.0	3.0	-0.9	2.9
1961-65	3.7	0.4	4.9	5.0	3.3	-1.2	-1.3	0.2
1966-70	6.7	1.2	4.5	6.6	5.6	2.2	0.1	2.0
1971-75	5.7	0.3	5.7	5.6	5.3	0.0	0.1	1.5
1976-80	3.7	0.4	6.0	3.5	3.2	-2.3	0.2	0.6

Source: Vintrova (1984)

In the 1970s, the indicators used to describe economic growth in Czechoslovakia were again higher in Slovakia. The national income figures were 4.7 to 5.2 per cent; for gross industrial output it was 5.7 to 7.6 per cent; and for construction 6.5 to 7.3 per cent. The higher growth rates reached in Slovakia were mostly due to a greater exploitation of resources, mainly material and capital consumption.

The beginning of the 1980s were years of stagnation of the Czechoslovak economy as a result of the delayed reaction to the world raw material crisis of the 1970s. Drafting the seventh Five-year Plan and the overall planning for the 1980s were fully under the influence of the Communist ideology the main objective of which was, despite the deteriorating internal and international situation, to keep the population placated by maintaining the current standard of living.

The deteriorating external conditions can be briefly characterized by the deepening problems of the CMEA partners and their inability to pay for Czechoslovak goods which were hard to sell on western markets for their low quality. Internally, the country suffered from persistent and deepening problems, generated by the command methods of controlling the economy and by the distorted economic structure. The continued emphasis on allocating resources into the material sphere kept limiting the growth of the service sector. All branches of industry expanded, and the growing demand for materials and energy drained domestic and imported resources of commodities causing extensive damage to the environment. Inefficient management caused a stockpile of idle inventory as well as a significant volume of unfinished investments to such an extent that the government had to take additional administrative measures to regulate the situation.

The socialist industrialization of Slovakia remained an integral part of the existing economic policy. Until the very end of the central planning era, the economic growth in Slovakia continued to exceed that of the country as a whole. From 1981-89, the growth of national income was 1.8 per cent for Czechoslovakia and 2.6 per cent for Slovakia; for industrial production it was 2.4 to 2.9 per cent; for the construction industry it was 0.0 to 0.4 per cent.

4 The process of catching-up of Slovakia with the Czech Lands and its social consequences

Based on the documented acceleration of the Slovak economic growth compared with that of the Czech Lands, we can observe a gradual economic convergence of both parts of Czechoslovakia. As Table 1.4 indicates, in some areas Slovakia not only caught up but outstripped the Czech Lands. Table 1.5 demonstrates the rapid development of Slovakia in 1960-90 using growth indexes.

Table 1.4
Selected indicators of the Czech and Slovak economy

Indicator	1948	1960	1970	1980	1989
National income generated (per capita, current prices)	0.61	0.74	0.79	0.85	0.88
National income used (per capita, current prices)	0.71	0.83	0.91	0.94	0.87
Personal consumption (per capita, current prices)	0.81	0.82	0.86	0.91	0.92
Household revenues (per capita)	0.71[a)]	0.75	0.81	0.90	0.91
Medical practitioners (per 1000 inhabitants)	0.57	0.83	0.91	1.01	0.93
Secondary school graduates (per 1000 inhabitants)	0.60[b)]	0.88	1.02	1.11	1.14
University graduates (per 1000 inhabitants)	0.58[b)]	0.84	0.96	1.10	1.16
Capital-labour ratio	0.58	0.79	0.85	0.93	0.95

Note: Czech Lands = 100; a) in 1953; b) in 1950
Source: *Czechoslovak Statistical Yearbooks*, various volumes

The Slovak economy structure also changed and became more similar to that of the rest of the country. In 1948, the share of industry in the Slovak economy (as measured by gross material product) was 43 per cent, while in

1989 it was 68 per cent. The share of agriculture, at the same time, dropped from 37 to 13 per cent.

There were also important changes taking place in industry. Industrialization introduced new branches to the Slovak economy and Slovakia became an important supplier of a number of new products. In some cases (refrigerators, freezers, colour TVs, heaters, chemical products, etc.) Slovakia had a total corner on the market. Slovakia's strategic proximity to the Soviet Union was an equally important factor in encouraging the development of heavy industry, metallurgy and armaments.

Table 1.5

Selected development indexes of the Czech and Slovak economy

Index		1960	1970	1980	1989
National income generated	CR	225.5	329.7	464.4	530.6
(per capita, constant prices)	SR	268.6	407.9	613.2	531.7
National income used	CR	210.1	320.1	443.9	500.6
(per capita, constant prices)	SR	250.7	345.1	500.3	536.7
Personal consumption	CR	179.9	256.1	324.4	374.2
(per capita, constant prices)	SR	187.9	280.0	376.1	437.9
Net investment [a)]	CR	630.8	1,236.8	1,878.5	1,747.9
(per capita, constant prices)	SR	922.9	1,604.5	2,527.3	1,644.4
Fixed assets	CR	124.5	157.7	246.1	338.4
(per employee, constant prices)	SR	169.8	232.1	383.1	538.0

Note: a) 1951 = 100, values of gross investment for 1948-50 are negative
Source: *Czechoslovak Statistical Yearbooks*, various volumes

The rapid growth of employment was also an important component in the economic development of Slovakia. From 1948-89, employment in Slovakia grew by 68 per cent, while in the Czech Lands only by 35 per cent. The industrialization process generated many job opportunities, mainly in industry and infrastructure. The structure of employment also changed. The number of jobs in agriculture declined from 60.6 to 12.2 per cent, while in industry it rose from 14.9 to 33.5 per cent. Professional education parallelled these changes. Official figures show that in this area Slovakia even overtook the Czech Lands. By 1989 in Slovakia, 36.1 workers out of 100 had completed a secondary or University education compared to 31.7 out of 100 in the Czech Lands.

The question of what were the sources of the rapid development of the Slovak economy directs us to the politically sensitive topic of the transferring of resources from the Czech part of the country to Slovakia.

A common starting point when attempting to explain the extent of these transfers are statistical figures for the national income used in Slovakia compared to that generated there. Based on the statistical figures, we can estimate the transfers in the 1970s and the first half of the 1980s to be approximately CSK 10 billion a year; and in the second half of the 1980s to be approximately CSK 5 billion annually (see Table 1.6).[14]

Table 1.6
Transfer of resources from the Czech Lands to Slovakia

Period	Absolute [a)]	Relative [b)]
1950-60	48.4	14.7
1961-70	80.4	14.1
1971-80	124.0	10.3
1981-88	86.1	6.8

Note: a) Current prices in billions CSK; b) share in the Slovak national income used

Source: J. Krovak and J. Zamrazilova (1990)

Nevertheless, it is necessary to note how elusive it is to unfold the correct data. To express numerically the real transfer of resources, one would have to simulate the balance of payments between the Czech Lands and Slovakia and demonstrate how the above difference in national incomes used and generated was financed. This would be the only feasible way to analyze to what extent Slovakia financed the deficit by repayable forms (loans from the western part of the country, direct and portfolio investments of Czech businesses in Slovakia) and which transfers had a form of a grant from the Czech Lands to Slovakia. Such a simulation is, however, bound to fail and doomed to run into intransparency of fiscal flows, distorted tax rates and price relations as well as hidden forms of financing (e.g. carried out by the State Bank of Czechoslovakia).

The objections we just outlined here can merely cast doubts on the numerical data on the total volume of transfers but cannot hamper the process as such. The transfers make it possible to explain why Slovakia, while effecting significantly greater amount of investments than the Czech Lands, still maintained a very high level of individual consumption at about 92 per cent of the Czech level. Looking at hypothetical balance of payments we will not succeed in finding an entry which would counter-balance decades-long difference between the used and generated national incomes.

The transfer of resources from the Czech Lands to Slovakia can be looked upon as a type of regional policy. One can say that the transfers enabled Slovakia to reach its level of economic development in half the time it would have taken otherwise. The process of the Slovak economy catching-up with the Czech Lands was a world unique phenomenon. Neither Italy with its regional policies to support the underdeveloped south, nor Britain attempting to promote its northern parts have managed to reach similar results.

Table 1.7
Share of gross investment in national income

	1951-55	1956-60	1961-65	1966-70	1971-75	1976-80	1981-89
Czech Republic	20.9	24.3	24.8	26.7	29.6	30.4	30.5
Slovak Republic	34.8	36.1	38.1	36.2	39.3	39.0	36.7

Source: Integration is Possible, *Hospodarske noviny*, no. 14, 1991

It is necessary to note, however, that the process of economic catching-up was under the full influence of the centrally planned economy which promoted material balance and political aspects over the market efficiency. Many cooperation relations on both domestic and CMEA levels were created artificially and were not logically suited for a market economy and competitive environment. It is understandable that some of the investments originating from the socialist industrialization became a burden to the Slovak economy immediately after the market-oriented reform started to renew the principle of healthy financial management.

5 Conclusion

The nearly seventy-year history of the Czech-Slovak economic relations encompassed not only a very heterogeneous period of structuring the Czechoslovak economy, but also the process of forming specific perspectives and attitudes of the public to the economic policy and administrative set-up of the country.

On one hand, there was a majority of the Czech public who were positive about the economic prosperity of the pre-war so called First Republic, a period when Czechoslovakia, thanks to the efficiency of its economy, counted itself as one of the most developed countries in Europe as well as one of its true democracies. On the other hand, there was the painful experience of the war-related economy during World War II and, especially, of the post-war years of socialism which were marked by a gradual economic devolution, the loss of its respectable position in Europe and a final descent into the group of underdeveloped Eastern European economies.

From the Slovak point of view, the events were much different. Despite some economic growth during the period of the First Republic, the difference in the economic levels of the two parts of the country persisted and Slovakia continued existing on the European economic periphery. World War II was not only an era of Slovak 'independence', but also a period of relatively successful economic development. Post-war industrialization in Slovakia and forty years of centrally planned economy symbolized a period of rapid economic growth, moving it closer to the economic potential of the Czech Republic. It took no more than one generation to change an underdeveloped agrarian country into an industrial economy with a relatively high standard of living. It is only a minor overstatement to say that Slovakia, despite all kinds of distortions, experienced an economic miracle in terms of Eastern European standards.

Understandingly, the common but differently perceived history the Czechs and Slovaks experienced in one state found its reflection in the attitudes of the Czech and Slovak public when it came to the discussion of economic reform. While in the Czech Republic the radical transformation to a market economy after forty years of economic stagnation under central planning acquired spontaneous support, in the Slovak Republic, disapproval with the policy of state intervention was less pronounced given that the centrally planned economy had played such a major role in achieving its economic progress.

Notes

1. The attitude of the German and Hungarian minorities to the new state was quite negative. In December 1918, Hungary backed unrest in Slovakia leading to a declaration of martial law. The situation stabilized in 1920, when international agreements guarantied the borders of the Czechoslovak state (the borders with Hungary, which never previously existed, were agreed upon by the Trianon Treaty on 4 June 1920). In the first years of the Republic, minorities had no participation in constitutional bodies.
2. The founding of the common state on 28 October 1918 is closely connected to the idea of 'Czechoslovakism', a concept of one nation comprising of two parts - Czech and Slovak. Proclamations about a united nation had major significance for both domestic and international politics by constituting a majority of the Czechs and Slovaks in their multinational state. Currently, some historians theorize that this was only fabricated to serve temporary tactical purposes. In the first year in the existence of Czechoslovakia, however, many people, including President T.G. Masaryk, perceived the idea as a long lasting concept analogous to that of the Swiss or American 'nations'. This concept was based on the idea of a political nation where similar languages were spoken. This attitude, however, ignored the cultural and historical differences which had developed over the centuries as well as the existence of minorities, who were not to be integrated into one 'nation' (as they were in Switzerland and the United States).
3. The last three secondary schools in Slovakia before the founding of Czechoslovakia were abolished in 1874.
4. During the crisis, unemployment grew rapidly. While in 1929, there were 42,000 people unemployed, in 1930 it was 105,000 and by 1933 the figure had reached 738,000 people, with 88,000 unemployed in Slovakia. In the Czech Lands, the unemployment rate in 1930 was roughly 11.7 per cent, in Slovakia it was about 7.7 per cent. Some Slovak sources claim that in Slovakia people without work did not register as being unemployed and therefore the rates displayed by the statistics were lower than in reality.

5. In the 1930s, calls for autonomy in Slovakia and the Sudetenland, a territory densely populated by Germans, became very strong. Political parties supporting autonomy (and supported from abroad) started exhibiting nondemocratic tendencies. The Sudeten-German Party, for example, became a direct arm of Nazi Germany in Czechoslovakia. Similarly, though not as violent, was Hlinka's Slovak National Party, especially its separatist faction which as early as 1921 presented a draft for a confederal makeup of so called Czecho-Slovakia.
6. According to this Act, central agencies were granted powers over the constitution, national defense, foreign affairs, monetary issues, common budget, state debt and a majority of state-owned businesses, while other matters were under the jurisdiction of the Slovak institutions. Further, the Slovak government was responsible only to the Slovak assembly, established in December 1938. Also, immediately after its enactment, other political parties ended their operations, fusing with the Slovak National Party.
7. The political doctrine of the Czechoslovak Government in exile (also called the London Exiled Government) was based on the idea of the legal continuity of the Czechoslovakia which legally never ceased to exist (and the Slovak State never became a subject of international law). For Czech-Slovak relations, this would mean, among other things, a re-establishment of the Czechoslovak Republic based upon 'Czechoslovakism', a basic principle of the Constitution of 1920. This principle was rejected by the Slovak National Council, the supreme body of the antifascist resistance in Slovakia. On 1 September 1944, immediately following the start of the Slovak National Uprising, the Slovak National Council announced a declaration proclaiming its authority over the making of laws and government and executive decisions, declaring itself the revolutionary representative of the Slovak nation and the representative of the Czechoslovak Republic in Slovakia. This meant the birth of a new power centre with demands for the equal treatment of Czechs and Slovaks with regards to the future state makeup.
8. From April 1939 to March 1945, the amount of money in circulation rose in Slovakia 9.5 times and in the Czech Lands about 7.5 times.
9. The political spectrum in Slovakia, where the Democratic party won a majority of 62 per cent, and the Communist party received 30.4 per cent of the vote, was different from the Czech Lands.
10. The figures are based on the so called national economy balance following the Soviet system of material products.
11. This period is characterized by an intensive mechanical adoption of Soviet methods and working styles into all branches of the economy, including statistics. In the atmosphere of widespread attempts to speed up growth, the new methodology increased the danger of biased macroeconomic indicators. All this should be taken into account when analyzing the noticeably high annual growth rates of the 1950s.

12. The asymmetrical model was preserved in the structure of the Communist parties and therefore there were only the Czechoslovak Communist Party and the Slovak Communist Party.
13. Given the Soviet based way of measuring macroeconomic development, gross output was quantified in material production sphere only.
14. Measuring the transfer of resources by the difference between the national incomes generated and used brings about a thorny problem. The official statistics failed to break-down the figures and apportion to the Republics the totals in that part of national income which was generated by the foreign trade sector. This failure led to an introduction of various rules of thumb (partly subjective).

Part Two
DECLINE OF THE CZECHOSLOVAK FEDERATION (1990-92)

1 The break-up of Czechoslovakia from the political point of view

The fall of the Communist regime in November 1989 gave birth to many ideas of how to solve the numerous problems which had accumulated under the old political system, one of the most complicated of which was the question of the constitutional arrangement of Czechoslovakia in the new political environment. At the beginning, political representatives of both the Czech and Slovak nations agreed on the benefits of cooperation of the Czechs and Slovaks in one state. The form of such cooperation, however, brought about numerous disputes. Controversies over the constitutional set-up grew into a major debate about the future of Czech-Slovak relations and finally resulted in the break-up of Czechoslovakia on 31 December 1992, at midnight. The Czechoslovak crisis (the second in the seventy years of its existence) revealed the existence of deeper Czech-Slovak conflicts. Controversies concerning the scope and speed of economic reform seem to have been of secondary importance although the public could have perceived them as the core problem. Simply, the Federation meant an introduction of a uniform concept of economic transformation throughout its entire territory, while a looser coexistence of the Czechs and Slovaks, e.g. in a confederation, would have allowed a more differentiated approach responding to the demands of both the Czech and Slovak representations.

The political development after November 1989 was shaped by various circumstances, the most important of which are the following:

1. Social, economic and cultural differences between the CR and the SR. Despite the fact that in the 1980s there were minimal differences left between the two Republics, the transformation process ensuing the fall of the Communist regime brought the dissimilarities back and even deepened them. These centrifugal tendencies were stronger than the language similarities, common history and mutual compassion of both nations;

2. Bilateral nature of the Federation which was founded in 1968 as a successor of the former administratively united state. Every federation consisting of two units is constantly under threat of a break-up caused by a decision of one party to leave the federal unit or by a consensus of both parties to terminate the federation. The tendency of the parties to the bilateral federation to negotiate problems directly without the mediation of the federal bodies weakens the federal framework of cooperation and sometimes even endangers its very existence, a predicament unheard of in multilateral federations.[1]

3. International political situation after the break-up of the bipolar system in Europe and world-wide. The new political climate stressed the right of every nation for self-determination including independence. The Slovak decision-makers also found inspiration in other federations based on the national principle.

1.1 Specifics of the Czechoslovak Federation

Although the Czechoslovak Federation was not founded as an arrangement between two independent entities, it was presented as a unit founded 'from the bottom up' by an agreement of the member states-to-be. The preamble of the constitutional Act establishing the Czechoslovak Federation specified the relationship between the parties as follows: 'We, the Czech and Slovak nations, based on our historical will to coexist in one state, declare...' and 'represented by our delegates in the Czech and Slovak National Councils, agreed to establish the Czechoslovak Federation'. Unlike the Slovak National Council, the Czech National Council had not existed before spring 1968 and was established, after the decision on the federalization of the state was reached, by vote of the then National Assembly and therefore without a direct vote.

A federation based on national principle was considered to be the only option. The Commission for Preparation of the Federation rejected the tri-polar model of federation promoted by representatives of Moravia and Silesia. Nevertheless, the ideas both of a federation based on the voluntary coexistence of national states with equal rights, and of so called 'Czechoslovakism' were equally fictitious, for such concepts clearly intermingled nationality and state citizenship.[2]

The Federation as a constitutional expression of a relationship of two nations necessarily involved the concept of an open exit. Although there were no explicit procedures prescribed for terminating the Federation, the Czechoslovak Constitution declared the right for self-determination of both the Czech and Slovak nations and its preamble proclaimed the vested right of both nations both for self-determination and terminating the Federation.[3]

The fact that the Federation was composed of only two member states later influenced the structure and activities of the law-making body of the Federation - the Federal Assembly. The Federal Assembly had two chambers - the People's Chamber and the Chamber of Nations. Both Chambers were constitutionally equal and the Federal Assembly could legislate only based on a consensus of both Chambers.

The People's Chamber had 200 members (in 1990 the number was reduced to 150), the Chamber of Nations had 150 members, with 75 members elected in the CR and 75 in the SR. The People's Chamber reached a quorum with an absolute majority present; the Chamber of Nations with absolute majority of the Czech and Slovak members present. To pass resolutions, an absolute majority in both Chambers was required. A 3/5 majority of all members of the People's Assembly, 3/5 majority of members of the Chamber of Nations elected in the Czech Republic, and 3/5 majority of members of the Chamber of Nations elected in the Slovak Republic was necessary to adopt the Federal Constitution, constitutional Acts of the Federal Assembly and their amendments, to elect a President of the Republic, and to declare war. To pass selected laws, adopt a Government Program and vote on Government confidence there was a ban on an absolute majority clause. In these cases, members of the People's Assembly elected in the CR and in the SR voted separately and a resolution was passed only if consented to by an absolute majority in both groups.

As a consequence of this approval system, a minority of members had the power to halt a number of resolutions in the Federal Assembly (e.g., for passing constitutional laws or electing a President of the Republic it was 31 to 269). A measure was introduced to maintain equality of the member states. Since the ratio of Czech and Slovak members in the People's assembly was 2 to 1 (reflecting the distribution of Czech and Slovak citizens in the Federation, which was 10 million to 5 million), it acted as a protection for Slovakia, the member with fewer inhabitants.

In case the Chambers could not reach a consensus, there was the possibility to agree on a settlement process. The settlement committee established for this purpose usually had 20 members (10 for each Chamber). It was a constitutional body, which was a logical completion of the absolute majority clause. It represented a confederal aspect in the functioning of the Czechoslovak Federation, by presuming a consensus of both parties on basic issues. Absence of a consensus would have brought the Federation into crisis, the Federal Assembly would have to be dissolved by the President and a date of new elections announced within sixty days (nothing like that ever happened). The settlement process was compulsory only for approving the Federal budget.[4]

The confederative concept was expressed in the following quote: 'The Czechoslovak economy represents an integration of two national economies - the Czech and Slovak ones'. The single Czechoslovak economy from before 1968 was therefore to be divided into two national economies and the new economic system was to be based on mutually beneficial cooperation of two national economies and mutual support of both nations. The Federation had an objective to help remove economic and social differences between the two nations and to create equal conditions for generating and using the national income.

The rights and responsibilities of the Federation and the Republics were divided into those exclusively Federal, those to be enjoyed by both the Federation and the Republics, and those falling exclusively under control of the Republics. Foreign policy, national defense, Federal currency reserves, Federal jurisdiction, Federal affairs, control of Federal bodies and of Federal constitutionality fell under the control of the Federation. Within the framework of rights and responsibilities common for the Federation and the Republics, the powers of the Federation were clearly specified and the remaining matters fell under the authority of the Republics' bodies. Matters not designated by constitutional law as Federal were exclusively under the jurisdiction of the Republics.

The invasion of the Soviet troops which marked the end of the Prague Spring and the beginning of the so called normalization process had brought about attempts to centralize the Federation. The Federal Assembly passed a constitutional Act which strengthened the powers of the Federation by allowing the Federal government to act as a coordinator in solving matters originally under the jurisdiction of the Republics, or to establish, based upon an agreement with the governments of the Republics, coordinating bodies. The Federal government was also given powers to delay adoption of measures introduced by either of the Republic governments or to discontinue such measures in case they contradicted with measures introduced by the Federal government within the framework of the Federal powers. The concept of two national economies was removed and the Czechoslovak economy became a single unit again.

Nevertheless, the leading role in the process of centralizing the Federation was not performed by legislation but by constitutional practice (based on Article 4 of the 1960 Constitution) which established the leading role of the Czechoslovak Communist Party. A number of articles of the constitutional Act on the establishment of the Czechoslovak Federation therefore existed on paper only. The Federal Assembly performance was smooth and the settlement process was never tested. The Federal Constitutional Court which was to be established to help solve, among other matters, potential discrepancies between the legislative process and the federal Constitution, as well as disagreements over jurisdictions, was never confirmed. All major decisions were made or supervised by the leaders of the Czechoslovak Communist Party, with the Federal Assembly playing a minor role in this one-party system.

During the normalization process the Republics adopted identical measures even in the case of matters falling under the jurisdiction of the Republics. Up to 1990, this quasi-federal framework was supported by an extensive bureaucratic system of three law-making institutions, three governments, and number of Federal and Republic bodies which passed identical laws, regulations and instructions for both Republics.

A part of the federalization process was the establishment of Czech government bodies to achieve a more symmetrical administration system within the framework of the Czechoslovak Federation. Nevertheless, until 1990, the Czech National Council, Government of the Czech Republic and other bodies remained subordinated to the Federal agencies. Both the Czech and Federal bodies were located in Prague, which was the capital of the Federation as well as of the Czech Republic. On the one hand, the geographic position of Slovakia and its capital Bratislava, relatively far from the centre of Federal power, as well as the autonomous status of the Slovak Communist Party contributed to the relative independence of Slovakia. On the other hand, the concentration of key powers in the hands of the Federal bodies (government and party bodies) in Prague served as a basis for the subsequent criticism of the centralized character of Czechoslovakia (so called Praguecentralism) by Slovak politicians after November 1989.

The Czechoslovak Federation was never vital. The fact that it remained more or less on paper for the entire twenty years of its existence, at a time when the change of the political regime revealed its true nature, surprised not only the inhabitants but also the political representatives of both Republics.

1.2 Constitutional dispute and the crisis of the Czechoslovak Federation

The discussions on the future constitutional set-up of Czechoslovakia which took place soon after November 1989 revealed the Czech and Slovak representatives' different approaches to the problem. As a rule, the Czech politicians tended to blend Czech and Czechoslovak matters together, while the Slovak representatives made their decisions in connection with the historical demands for equality of the two nations.[5]

Initially, the Slovak leaders adopted a two-sided policy of, on the one hand, promoting a Federal framework, and on the other hand encouraging the clearly confederal measures to achieve what they called 'authentic Federation'. This internal conflict often contributed to communication problems. The Slovak representatives kept presenting the meetings with new suggestions and ideas on the transformation of the constitutional set-up and, as the negotiations advanced, the Slovak concepts abandoned the Federal platform and became an expression of the Slovak demands for political and economic union of the two sovereign Republics.[6] The Slovak concept presumed a transfer of broad powers from the Federal level to the Republics and a subsequent formation of two independent entities of international law - the Czech Republic and the Slovak Republic.

Czech representatives, on the other hand, urged for a model of a 'workable Federation' based on an efficient division of powers between the Federation and the Republics to protect both the rights of the Republics as well as the well-being of the Federal unit. The Czech politicians viewed a confederal set-up as a temporary solution which was not responding to the Czech needs of establishing a politically stable society based on a standard market economy. Generally, the confederation concept was considered worse than the total break-up of Czechoslovakia.[7]

When, at the end of 1990, Vaclav Havel, the Czechoslovak President, proposed to eliminate the word 'Socialist' from the official name of the state (Czechoslovak Socialist Republic), the ensuing dispute over the name caused the first constitutional crisis. The Slovak political representation refused Havel's proposal. In March 1990, as a result of fierce negotiations and a turbulent settlement process, the Federal Assembly adopted a constitutional Act on the change of the name of the state to the Czechoslovak Federal Republic, with the Czech-Slovak Federal Republic as the Slovak version.

This Act, however, remained in effect for a very short period of time (29 March 1990 - 23 April 1990) because the dash in the Slovak name reminded many people of the tragic period of the so called Second Republic and subsequent break-up of the Czechoslovak state in 1939. A new constitutional Act changed the name of the state to the Czech and Slovak Federal Republic.

In 1990, following some partial amendments of the constitutional Act on the Establishment of the Czechoslovak Federation, the Federal Assembly passed the so called 'Competence Act'. This Act, which determined that all matters but those listed in the Act fall under the jurisdiction of the Republics, marked a substantial shift of responsibilities to the hands of the Republics. The Act again declared the Federal economy to be an integrated unit composed of the Czech and Slovak economies based on the existence of a single internal market, one currency and the free movement of labour, goods and capital.

Government property, excluding oil pipelines, transit gas pipeline and the energy distribution network, was divided between the Federation and its member states.[8]

In 1991 and 1992, the political leaders of both Republics met many times to work on drafts of the Federal Constitution and Constitutions of the Republics. In the first meeting in Prague (February 1992), the Chairman of the Slovak Christian Democratic Party, Jan Carnogursky, presented a proposal to first write the Constitutions of the Republics and then determine the constitutional relationship between the Czech and Slovak Republics by an agreement. The idea of inter-Republic agreement was first refused by the Czech delegation but later accepted, and the representatives of both member states continued negotiating the draft in numerous meetings. A draft agreement was completed on 8 February 1992.

Nevertheless, the Presidium of the Slovak National Council rejected the outcome of the series of stormy and tiring meetings. The Czech National Council, in answer to the rejection, decided to discontinue the negotiations, declaring that there was nothing left to discuss. For the Czech politicians, the Slovak idea of a loose Federation represented an extreme concession, while some influential Slovak political forces (the Movement for Democratic Slovakia and the Slovak National Party) felt it to be, given the current situation, unsuitable and constraining. This turbulent development coincided with the beginning of the election campaign for the June 1992 Parliamentary elections.[9]

The winner of the elections (about 30 per cent of the vote) in the Czech Republic was the Civic Democratic Party (hereafter ODS) led by Vaclav Klaus, the political program of which rejected the process of further weakening the Federation. The program of the Movement for Democratic Slovakia (hereafter HZDS), winner of the elections in Slovakia led by Vladimir Meciar (about 37 per cent of the vote), presented a proposal for a coexistence of the Czech and Slovak Republics in a political and economic union. The supporters of the Federation in Slovakia (with the exception of the Hungarian parties), did not win any seats in either of the Parliaments (neither the Federal nor either of the Republics).

On 8 June 1992, at the meeting of the representatives of the winning political parties (ODS and HZDS) in Brno, the Slovak leaders presented a project for the Czech-Slovak union. This plan proposed that both the CR and the SR enjoy international sovereignty and effect independent economic, monetary and tax policies. The plan further suggested an establishment of a customs union and several committees to coordinate the policies of both Republics. Defense policy, currency, basic legislature and the judiciary system were to be common for both Republics and the Presidents of both Republics were to take turns in presiding over the Union. This draft was rejected by the representatives of ODS.

The meeting in Brno was followed by gatherings in Prague on 11 and 17 July 1992, and in Bratislava on 19 July 1992. When no consensus was reached (ODS insisted on a workable Federation and HZDS upheld the concept of a confederation), the political representatives of both parties decided to break the Federation into two separate Republics as of the end of 1992. The separation process was to be managed by a ten-member Federal government with parity representation of both ODS and HZDS. Jan Strasky, an ODS representative, was named the Prime Minister of this government, and Vaclav Klaus and Vladimir Meciar, the heads of the leading parties, became the Prime Ministers of the Republic governments.

At the same time, the Slovak National Council adopted the Declaration on Slovak Sovereignty and on 1 September 1992, the Constitution of the Slovak Republic which came to effect in 1 October 1992. Although this constitution partially respected the existence of the Federation, it treated it as a temporary issue. For all intents and purposes, it was a constitution of a sovereign and independent state.[10]

The June 1992 elections and diverging views between political representatives of both Republics left Czechoslovakia with only two directions to take -- either both parties would agree on the break-up of the Federation, or the Czech politicians would block the process of constitutional changes and insist on maintaining the current political status.

Most of the politicians, including the strongly pro-Federation ones, understood that reaching an agreement on the break-up was the most preferred way of solving the constitutional crisis. If an agreement could not be reached, the Czech-Slovak polarization threatened to grow into an uncontrollable process and would lead the country into chaos. As maintaining the Czechoslovak Federation became an obviously lost case, Czech political leaders started to facilitate a rapid and cost-minimizing separation.[11]

In light of the new situation, the Federal Assembly adopted the constitutional Act on Division of Federal Property between the succeeding Republics and the constitutional Act on the Break-up of the Czech and Slovak Federal Republic to be effected on 31 December 1992.

1.3 The break-up of the Czechoslovak Federation

Czechoslovakia employed constitutional means to terminate its existence and declared its suspension as a subject of international law; the Czech and Slovak Republics were then defined as the successors to the Czechoslovak Federation.

A special constitutional Act settled the question of the legal continuity of the newly established Republics vis-a-vis the aborted Czech and Slovak Federal Republic. Based on the succession principle, the Czechsolovak legislation effective on the day of the break-up remained binding. In case of a discrepancy between the legal principles of the Czech Republic declared before the break-up and the binding legal principles of the Czech and Slovak Federal Republics, the above Act declared the legal principles of the Czech Republic as having priority.

The above priority principle was adopted in a handful of cases, notably in determining the use of state symbols of the Federation by the successor Republics and solving the question of transferring the members of the Federal Assembly to the law-making bodies of the successor Republics.

The constitutional Act on the Break-up of the Czech and Slovak Federal Republic prohibited the use of state symbols of the Federation by any of the succeeding Republics. Nevertheless, the Act on State Symbols adopted by the Czech National Council defined the flag of the Czech Republic as identical to the Czechoslovak flag. Slovakia was exasperated by the Czech Republic seizing so called 'Federal know-how' and, during the meetings to determine the division of the Federal property, demanded financial compensation.

The politically sensitive question of the future fate of the members of the Federal Assembly who were, together with the members of the law-making bodies of the Republics, elected to four-year terms, was solved in both succeeding Republics to the detriment of these MPs. The constitutional Act on the Dissolution of the Czech and Slovak Federal Republic transferred (as of 1 January 1993) the law-making powers in the Czech Republic to a law-making body composed of the MPs elected in 1992 in the Czech Republic to both the Federal Assembly and the Czech National Council. This concept was later refuted by the new Czech Constitution which declared the Czech National Council an Assembly of the newly established Czech Parliament (as of 1 January 1993). Following the promise made before the break-up of Czechoslovakia, a group of the members of the former Federal Assembly was to form the second chamber of Parliament - the Senate, establishment of which was presumed by the Constitution. The constitutional Act to establish the Senate was not, however, adopted.

In general, the political developments in Slovakia were very similar with just one difference -- a transfer of Federal MPs to the new Parliament was not even considered as it was not in compliance with the Slovak Constitution, which declared the National Council to be the only constitutional and law-making body in the Slovak Republic. In any case, the promise to transfer the members of the Federal bodies to the Parliaments of the succeeding Republics was one of the points which caused the MPs to vote for the constitutional Act on the break-up of the Federation.

The course of the break-up of Czechoslovakia was quiet and relatively smooth. In Autumn 1992, the Czech and Slovak Republics passed numerous agreements (e.g. on the monetary and customs union) to regulate their future relations. There were no substantial controversies concerning either the delimitation of borders (although at the end of 1994 the borders had not been 100 per cent defined) or status of the nationals of one Republic as a minority in the other one.

The citizenship of these 'foreigners' proved a difficult problem to solve.[12] In 1969, citizenship was based on the land principle (people born in the Czech Republic or Slovakia acquired either Czech or Slovak citizenship). The right of choice was adopted only rarely since both Czechs and Slovaks enjoyed equal legal status throughout the Federation; at the time of the break-up of Czechoslovakia there were roughly 370,000 people who had permanent residence in one Republic and citizenship in the other Republic (there were more Slovak citizens in the Czech Republic than vice versa).

The Czech Republic granted the Slovak citizens who had a permanent residency in its territory the right to opt for Czech citizenship within the period of 18 months after the break-up of the Federation (the deadline was 30 June 1994). The applicants had to meet the following three conditions:

a) At least a two-year uninterrupted residence in the Czech Republic prior to the break-up of the Federation;

b) A certificate of release from Slovak citizenship (or proof that a request for the release had been filed and the applicant had subsequently renounced Slovak citizenship);

c) Applicant had not been sentenced for premeditated crime five years prior to the date of filing the application.

There were some Slovak citizens, residents of the Czech Republic, who did not meet the third condition and therefore were not granted Czech citizenship. Some applicants, especially the elderly, did not find the rejection of their old citizenship as a condition for acquiring the new one very reasonable.[13] The Czech citizens permanently residing in Slovakia protested the legislation which deprived them of the Czech citizenship at the moment they acquired the Slovak one.

1.4 Conclusion

Both the foundation and the break-up of the Czechoslovak Federation were based on an agreement of the political representatives of both nations. In Slovakia, many people applauded the break-up of the Federation and the foundation of an independent Slovak Republic, while most Czechs accepted the news with indifference and apathy. A public opinion survey made two years after the break-up revealed that 62 per cent of Czech citizens felt positive about Czech independence. At the same time, respondents showed strong compassion for Slovakia and the Slovaks, with 86 per cent of them considering Slovakia their closest country.[14] Two-thirds of the respondents in Slovakia wished to have closer relationship with the Czech Republic in the form of a federation, confederation or union but did not expect it to happen in the foreseeable future.[15]

2 Economic transformation and a comparative analysis of the Republics' economies

In Autumn 1990, the Czechoslovak Government presented to Parliament an 'economic and social reform scenario' which contained the basic concept of the transformation of the Czechoslovak economy. The objective of the radical economic reform was a transition from command to a market economy. The concept was based on a sweeping departure from central planning and refused to make marginal improvements in the current status quo or reconsideration of preceding reform attempts which had been seeking a 'third way'. The reform objectives were to be implemented as fast as possible, for it was expected that the more radical and speedy the reforms, the lower the costs of the transformation. A gradual process of introducing changes, or a possible postponement of the reform, were perceived as risky because potential delays could strengthen the resistance of the old bureaucratic system, heighten social tensions, and even cause the loss of the reform credibility of the government.

The transformation process was often accused of insensitivity vis-a-vis the specific needs of Slovakia. According to an OECD report, the unfavourable social impact of the reform in Slovakia had its political consequences. Growing dissatisfaction with the transformation process resulted in calls for slower reform, increased transfers and the 'independence of Prague'. The trend in the Czech Republic was just opposite. The public mostly supported the adoption of political measures to further deepen the economic transition and demanded a decrease of transfers to Slovakia. Differences between the Czech and Slovak experience from 1991-92 strongly influenced the parliamentary elections of June 1992.[16]

This chapter will address the question of whether the economic reform as it was implemented was not one of the main reasons for the break-up of the Federation; whether an implementation of the social, regional or structural policies would have contributed to a more favourable approach of the Slovak public to the reform and, if so, why they did not become an addition to the macroeconomic core of the reform.

2.1 Macroeconomic development

The program of economic transformation was based on a set of measures, the most important of which were the liberalization of prices and imports, introduction of internal convertibility, privatisation, and a macroeconomic stabilization based on fiscal and budget restrictions. Deceleration of the inflation process was a higher priority than the economic growth and employment. The core of the reform therefore included a plan to create a social security network to help maintain the basic standard of living for people suffering from the transformation changes.

Compared to the other post-communist countries, the starting conditions of the Czechoslovak economy were relatively favourable, especially due to its low foreign debt, relatively high consumption in the household sector, and a balanced consumer market. The government budgets before the introduction of price liberalization were relatively sound; the total government debt did not exceed 1 per cent of the GDP and statistics show that the annual inflation rate did not exceed 1-2 per cent (hidden inflation was estimated at the level 5 per cent annually).

On the other hand, during the period of central planning the Czechoslovak economy had suffered deep structural deformations, and the long-term nonexistence of the private sector was reflected in the lack of entrepreneurial experience of the businesses. The transformation process in Czechoslovakia was also affected by unfavourable international events, such as the break-up of the CMEA market, the reunification of Germany, the war in the Persian Gulf and the armed conflict in the Balkans, all of which influenced the Central European transition economies.

International institutions evaluated the first two years of the transformation more or less positively; some aspects (inflation rate, government budgets, unemployment) were even classified as remarkably successful. The following pages will review the basic results of the macroeconomic stabilization policy in order to determine whether there were more common trends than dissimilarities between the two parts of the Czechoslovak Federation.[17]

Inflation rate

A low inflation rate as a result of tight monetary and fiscal policies and a credible regime of a fixed exchange rate contributed to the positive evaluations of the transformation of the Czechoslovak economy by international organizations.

On the one hand, the level of consumer prices in 1992 was, compared to 1989, almost twice as high and industrial prices also almost double (index 196.5). Nevertheless, taking into consideration a one-time price rise due to the currency devaluation and liberalization of prices at the beginning of 1991, the average monthly inflation rate between April 1991 and December 1992 (measured by consumer prices) was 0.9 per cent only (measured by industrial prices it was even 0.6 per cent). Prices of agricultural products marked the slowest rise (average annual growth about 6.8 per cent).

These figures show that although the price increase at the beginning of 1991 highly exceeded all expectations and caused 58 per cent annual inflation (measured by consumer prices), prices stabilized quite fast. In 1992, the annual growth of consumer prices fell to 11 per cent (average monthly inflation rate 0.9 per cent). Therefore, the Czech Republic was the best among the post-communist countries in fighting inflation.

Table 2.1
Indexes of consumer prices of goods and services

	1990	1991	1992
Czechoslovakia	110.0	157.9	110.8
Czech Republic	109.7	156.6	111.1
Slovak Republic	110.4	161.2	110.0
Hungary	128.9	135.0	123.0
Poland	685.8	170.3	143.0

Note: Preceding year = 100
Source: *Statistical Bulletin*, no. 1, 1992 and no. 4, 1994, Czech Statistical Office

As indicated in Tables 2.2 and 2.3, the consumer and industrial prices in 1990-92 in both Republics differed only slightly. These tables show that, with some minor exceptions, the consumer prices grew a little bit slower in the CR than in the SR. However, as a result of the relative deceleration of the price increases in Slovakia, the differences in the cumulative growth of consumer prices in both Republics until 1992 were minor. In 1992, the Czech Republic marked a cumulative increase of price levels as well as a faster annual average growth rate of industrial and construction prices which slightly deepened the differences between the Republics.

Table 2.2
Consumer price indexes and related monthly inflation rate

	Years	*Price level in December (January 1989 = 100)*			*Annual averages (last year = 100)*			*Average monthly inflation rate*		
		CSFR	CR	SR	CSFR	CR	SR	CSFR	CR	SR
Consumer prices	1990	111.9	119.1	119.9	110.0	109.7	110.4	0.80	0.77	0.83
	1991	184.2	181.2	189.9	157.9	156.6	161.2	3.88	3.81	4.11
	1992	205.4	204.2	207.2	110.8	111.1	110.1	0.86	0.88	0.81
Food products	1990	123.4	122.6	124.2	111.1	111.1	111.0	0.88	0.88	0.87
	1991	167.9	166.3	170.8	145.3	144.4	147.4	3.16	3.11	3.29
	1992	186.7	187.6	187.6	108.4	109.1	109.1	0.67	0.73	0.57
Non-food products	1990	120.1	119.0	117.6	110.5	109.9	111.4	0.84	0.79	0.90
	1991	201.4	195.3	170.6	172.0	169.7	178.0	4.62	3.81	4.92
	1992	220.7	216.9	191.8	109.4	109.0	110.0	0.75	0.72	0.80
Public catering	1990	119.0	119.9	117.6	108.5	108.5	108.1	0.68	0.68	0.65
	1991	174.1	176.0	170.6	157.0	158.8	155.0	3.83	3.93	3.72
	1992	199.5	203.8	191.8	109.4	108.4	106.8	0.63	0.67	0.55
Services	1990	113.1	111.9	114.4	107.4	106.9	108.5	0.60	0.56	0.68
	1991	172.2	171.4	173.6	139.5	139.1	141.4	2.81	2.79	2.93
	1992	200.3	202.1	197.7	123.6	125.6	120.5	1.78	1.92	1.57

Table 2.3
Producer price indexes and related monthly inflation rate

	Years	*Price level in December*			*Annual averages (last year = 100)*			*Average monthly inflation rate*		
		CSFR	CR	SR	CSFR	CR	SR	CSFR	CR	SR
Industrial prices [a)]	1990	117.1	115.9	119.9	103.3	102.5	105.2	0.27	0.21	0.42
	1991	181.3	181.5	180.6	169.9	170.4	168.9	4.52	4.54	4.46
	1992	196.5	198.4	191.7	108.6	109.9	105.3	0.69	0.79	0.43
Construction prices [b)]	1990	104.6	105.3	103.7	100.4	100.4	100.3	0.03	0.03	0.02
	1991	154.1	154.9	154.2	149.1	146.9	152.1	3.38	3.26	3.56
	1992	167.3	168.5	162.7	106.2	111.8	102.6	0.50	0.92	0.21
Agricultural prices [c)]	1990	.	.	.	.	.	.	x	x	x
	1991	111.2	109.8	115.8	103.8	103.3	104.8	x	x	x
	1992	121.9	120.8	125.3	107.3	107.7	106.5	x	x	x

Note: a) For industrial prices 1 January 1989 = 100; b) for construction prices 1 January 1990 = 100; c) for agricultural prices 1989 = 100

Source: Bulletins of the Federal Statistical Office and the Czech Statistical Office; Slovak Republic Statistical Year-book 1992 and 1993, Slovak Statistical Office

Decline of output

The decline in national output was surprisingly steep. Although there were no official figures published on the development of GDP in Czechoslovakia, the retrospective data gathered by the Statistical Offices of the CR and the SR show a faster decline than Poland and Hungary (see Table 2.4).[18]

Table 2.4
Comparison of GDP annual growth rate

	1990	1991	1992
Czech Republic	-1.2	-14.2	-6.4
Slovak Republic	-2.5	-14.5	-6.1
Hungary	-3.5	-11.9	-4.3
Poland	-11.6	-7.6	2.6

Source: *Statistical data, National Accounts,* no. 3, 1994, Czech Statistical Office, Prague, January 1995; *Short-term Indicators of Transition Economies,* no. 4, 1994, OECD, Paris

The differences between the GDP growth rates in the Czech and Slovak Republics were not significant. The Czech Statistical Office retrogressively displayed a GDP decline in the CR in 1990 of 1.2 per cent, in 1991 of 14.2 per cent, and in 1992 of 6.4 per cent; the Slovak figures were approximately 2.5, 14.5 and 2.2 per cent respectively. The data show a slightly deeper decline in the Slovak Republic in 1990 and 1991, while the situation in 1992 was reversed with a deeper decline of the Czech GDP. The differences between the national economies were less than one per cent and are therefore insignificant given possible errors in statistical data collection.

Economic decline was in most cases due to the structural deformations inherited from the years of central planning. The negative impact of this factor was visible especially after the break-up of the CMEA market which used to absorb most of the products of the overdeveloped heavy industry.

Nevertheless, the drop of internal demand was the most important factor of the economic decline. In connection with the privatisation process, managements of state-owned companies designed for privatisation lost interest in making long-term investments and therefore the demand for investments suffered the most. The decrease of real wages after the liberalization of prices caused a decrease of private consumption which played a major role in decreasing the demand on the domestic market. A more detailed analysis of the causes of the economic decline goes beyond the scope of this book. What remains of importance, however, is that it was not a standard economic recession but a unique depression of an economy in transition which affected both parts of Czechoslovakia with almost the same intensity (measured by decrease of GDP).

Table 2.5.
Gross domestic product in 1990-92

	Years	*Absolute* [a]			*Year-to-year changes* (%)		
		CR	SR	CSFR	CR	SR	CSFR
GDP	1990	503.7	215.4	719.1	-1.2	-2.5	-1.6
	1991	432.1	184.1	616.2	-14.2	-14.5	-14.3
	1992	404.5	180.0	584.5	-6.4	-2.2	-5.1
Net exports	1990	-1.8	-32.7	-34.5	x	x	x
	1991	30.2	-9.3	20.9	x	x	x
	1992	3.6	-1.2	2.4	-88.1	x	-88.5
Domestic demand	1990	505.5	248.1	753.6	4.6	5.7	4.9
	1991	401.9	193.4	595.3	-20.5	-22.0	-21.0
	1992	400.9	181.2	582.1	-0.2	-6.3	-2.2
Private consumption	1990	253.2	118.3	371.5	6.7	4.3	5.9
	1991	181.1	84.9	266.0	-28.5	-28.2	-28.4
	1992	206.6	82.6	289.2	14.1	-2.7	8.7
Public consumption	1990	103.4	51.1	154.5	0.9	1.0	0.9
	1991	94.1	42.0	136.1	-9.0	-17.8	-11.9
	1992	91.2	58.3	149.5	-3.1	38.8	9.8
Fixed capital formation	1990	136.8	73.5	210.3	-2.1	11.7	2.3
	1991	112.6	55.0	167.6	-17.7	-25.2	-20.3
	1992	122.6	46.6	69.2	8.9	-15.3	1.0
Change in inventories	1990	12.1	5.2	17.3	218.4	6.1	98.9
	1991	14.1	1.5	25.6	16.5	121.2	48.0
	1992	-19.5	-6.3	-25.8	x	x	x

Note: a) In constant prices 1994, in billion of CSK
Source: *Statistical data, National Accounts,* no. 1, 1994, Czech Statistical Office, Prague; *Short-term Indicators of Transition Economies,* no. 4, 1994, OECD, Paris; Institute of Economies of the Czech National Bank estimates

Unemployment rate

Unlike the preceding two macroeconomic variables (inflation rate and decline of output) the development of which was almost identical in both Republics, unemployment in the CR and the SR showed striking differences. While in 1990 the unemployment rate in Slovakia (number of registered unemployed) was about twice that of the Czech Republic, a year later it was three times more and at the end of 1992 even four times more (2.6 per cent in the CR and 10.4 per cent in the SR).

Beyond the average figures, we find considerable regional differences. The highest unemployment rate in the Slovak Republic (as of 31 December 1992) was observed in the regions of Eastern Slovakia (12.4 per cent) and Western Slovakia (11.4 per cent); Bratislava showed the lowest rate (3.8 per cent). The highest unemployment rate in the Czech Republic (as of 31 December 1992) was observed in the regions of Northern (4.0 per cent) and Southern (3.0 per cent) Moravia and in Northern Bohemia (2.9 per cent), the lowest in Prague (0.3 per cent).

Overall, unemployment was one of the relatively successful macro-economic characteristics of the Federation. It rose from 1.0 per cent in 1989 to 6.6 per cent at the end of 1991; in 1992 it decreased to 5.1 per cent. This decrease, which was unheard of in the transition economies of Central Europe (see Table 2.6), was marked both in the CR and the SR. In 1992, the Slovak unemployment rate still remained lower than in Hungary and Poland.

Table 2.6
Comparison of unemployment rates

	1990	1991	1992
Czechoslovakia	1.0	6.6	5.1
Czech Republic	0.8	4.1	2.6
Slovak Republic	1.5	11.8	10.4
Hungary	1.5	8.5	12.3
Poland	6.1	11.8	13.6

Note: End of the year
Source: *Statistical Bulletin,* no. 1, 1992 and no. 2, 1994, Prague; Focus: Eastern Europe, no.101, Deutsche Bank Research

The above comparisons reveal at least two paradoxical facts. First, the lowest inflation rate within the post-communist countries existed parallel to the lowest unemployment rate. Secondly, unemployment in both Republics decreased parallel to a output decline. These facts demonstrated the difficulties with collecting reliable statistical data on real production and unemployment, as well as signalled the non-market behaviour of some businesses which kept their facilities overstaffed.[19] Had these employees been laid off in 1992, the Czechoslovak unemployment rate would have risen by roughly four points and would have reached 9 per cent.

The different nature of the Czech and Slovak unemployment rates was not just a result of the generally lower adaptability of the Slovak producers. For example, in 1991, the decline of employment in companies with over 100 employees in Slovakia was -12.9 per cent while in the Czech Republic it was -11.6 per cent, just a little less. The negative development of the Slovak unemployment rates has to be understood on the basis of a number of factors, the most important of which will follow.

a) Demographic reasons. As a result of the population explosion of the middle of the 1970s, the number of Slovaks entering their first jobs at the beginning of the 1990s was very high and caused a rapid growth of unemployment in summer 1991. Since the average age of the economically active population in the CR (36.1) was higher than in the SR (33.4), the number of retiring Czech employees was relatively higher and therefore lowered the number of job applicants. On the other hand, Slovakia registered a larger group of inhabitants who traditionally experience more problems finding job opportunities (especially women on maternity leave and the Gypsies).

b) Social reasons. The Slovak nationals enjoyed, for a certain period of time, more generous social security benefits than the Czechs. The group of recipients of social benefits in the SR was larger than in the CR and included more people who were never employed or preferred receiving the social benefits to working (for details see below).

c) Geographic reasons. The fact that most of the Czech territory borders on developed economies (Germany, Austria), enabled tens of thousands of Czechs to commute to work in these countries and to relieve the Czech unemployment figures. In Slovakia, very few people commuted to work since the Slovak border with Austria, the only developed economy it borders on, is very short. The favourable geographic position of the Czech Republic also helped create a number of jobs in the tourist industry.

d) Structural reasons. The executors of the socialist industrialization of 1947-89 designed Slovakia to be a country of concentrated heavy industry, especially an armament industry focusing on the production of tanks and armed vehicles (unlike the Czech armament factories producing hand-guns, ammunition and radars). Therefore many employees of Slovak armament factories or their suppliers were laid off as a result of the armament industry conversion. Many Slovak businesses which were not able to face the loss of subsidies found the solution to their problems in laying their employees off. The development of small and medium-sized enterprises was also slower. At the end of 1991, there were 1.06 million private entrepreneurs registered in the CR (10.2 per cent of total population), while in the SR there were only 280,000 private entrepreneurs (5.3 per cent).

e) Other. In Slovakia, there were many towns and areas with just one company or factory which employed most of the inhabitants and there was no other facility to offer work to the redundant workers.

The higher unemployment rate in Slovakia was virtually the only field in which the impact of the economic transition on both Republics was remarkably different and, for the majority of the Slovak public, became one of the key reasons for refusing radical economic reform.

2.2 So called specifics of the Slovak economy

The nationally oriented groups, as well as all of the influential political forces in Slovakia, reacted to the first economic and social problems in Slovakia in late 1990 and at the beginning of 1991 by a wide-spread criticism of the economic reform and calls for higher independence. The Independent Association of Slovak Economists showed their attitude towards economic reform in the Declaration on Sovereignty of the Slovak Republic, publicized in March 1991.[20] The Association perceived the current rights and responsibilities of the Slovak government as insufficient and under the sway of the Federal concept of the reform; it demanded a declaration of economic sovereignty of Slovakia and a revision of the reform which would take into account the Slovak specifics. The Slovak Christian-Democratic Movement (KDH) adopted a similar approach in declaring that the Federal scenario of the radical economic reform does not sufficiently respect the specifics of the Slovak economy and therefore does not allow for a process of effective transformation.[21]

This was a clash of two philosophies. On the one hand, there were the promoters of radical economic reform with their belief in the uniformity of the basic transformation measures for the Czechoslovak economy based on similarly devised principles and implemented with a similar speed. Other approaches threatened to break the existing unified economic environment, and implementation of separate economic policies for the CR and the SR could cause conflicts and contribute to political tension, which would discourage foreign investments and decelerate the transformation process.

This philosophy provoked a negative response from many Slovak economists, who pointed at the different structure of the Czech and Slovak economies and maintained that the uniform implementation of the economic policy would have different impacts on individual regions.

The question therefore remains to be answered whether the Slovak specifics were an argument strong enough to vindicate a differentiated reform process in the CR and the SR. The list of the so called Slovak specifics usually included the following items: [22]

- higher concentration in Slovakia of production facilities manufacturing semi-finished goods or businesses oriented towards the supply of raw materials and semi-finished goods to the Czech Republic;
- higher dependency on imports, especially from the former CMEA members and the USSR;
- orientation of most exports to the former CMEA and the USSR;
- higher share of the armament industry;
- lower efficiency of the Slovak economy vis-a-vis the Czech one.

A more detailed analysis of the first argument (i.e. the less finished nature of the Slovak production) did not reveal any substantial differences between the CR and the SR at the turn of the 1980s and 1990s. In mid-1980s Slovak sources indicated that only 21 per cent of the Czech industrial output was semi-finished goods consumed in the SR, while in Slovakia the corresponding number was 56 per cent.[23] At the end of the 1980s, however, in 16 of the 30 Czech industrial branches, the Czech Republic displayed a higher production of semi-finished products intended for further industrial processing than Slovakia. It was also impossible to prove the claim about the higher share of exports of finished goods from the CR to the SR. The statistical data have shown that 64.1 per cent of the Czech exports to Slovakia were semi-finished goods, while from the SR to the CR it was only 52.4 per cent.

Data from a 1989 input/output table show higher demand of Slovak economy for raw materials, materials and semi-finished products and its dependency on import of these commodities from the USSR. The Czech imports from the socialist countries represented 66 per cent of total imports; for Slovakia it was 72 per cent. In the case of imports for industrial production it was 65.8 per cent in the CR and 73.5 per cent in the SR. Volumewise, the CR imported at least twice as much as the SR in almost all product categories. After the first two years of the transformation process, the Slovak dependence on imports from the USSR deepened. The trade figures from 1992 show that 36 per cent of all Slovak imports came from the USSR, while in the Czech Republic it was 18 per cent; for imports from the European transition economies it was 7 per cent in the SR and 6 per cent in the CR.[24]

Although the Slovak economists often stressed the dependence of the Slovak exports on the CMEA and especially the USSR markets, the data show no extreme differences between the CR and the SR. Following the 1987 input/output table, Slovak exports to the Soviet bloc represented 13 per cent of the exports of 30 selected branches of the economy; in the Czech Republic it was 11.8 per cent. In 1992, the figures for the European transition economies (excluding the former USSR) were not much different (13 per cent in the SR and 12 per cent in the the CR), for the former USSR, however, the figures were quite different (17 per cent in the SR and 9 per cent in the CR).[25]

Conversion of the armament industry was presented by the Slovak economists and politicians as one of the worst problems of the Slovak economy. In Czechoslovakia, the production of arms peaked in 1987 when it represented almost 3 per cent of the total industrial output and employed about 100,000 people. In 1992, the total volume of the armament industry in Czechoslovakia was only 15 per cent of the 1987 volume. Slovakia produced 60 per cent of the total Czechoslovak armament industry output and the decrease of production there was to be faster, reducing its share to 40 per cent and affecting about 50,000 employees. It is necessary to realize that the conversion equally affected the Czech armament industry (Southern Moravia produced 20 per cent and Prague and its vicinity 17 per cent of the total Czechoslovak armament industry output).

The Slovak leaders accused the policymakers in Prague of having caused this problem by making political gestures to show the democratic and humanitarian nature of the post-revolutionary development without considering its impact on the prosperous armament industry and the social and economic impact on Slovakia. The fact that the main recipients of the armament industry products were the Warsaw Pact countries, and that the demand and subsequently the production would have decreased anyway as a consequence of the break-up of this Pact, was not often taken into account. Exports to risky areas (as far as both political situations and solvency of clients were concerned) to balance the loss of the Warsaw Pact market could have caused significant political problems and subsequent economic difficulties.[26] The benefits of such a solution were therefore quite questionable. On the top of all this, many Slovak armament factories did not respond to the decision to limit armament production because there was no legal enforcement body to make them do so. They continued producing arms without selling them or exported them to the former USSR despite the insolvency of the clients there, and their financial situation deteriorated.[27]

2.3 Remarks on structural and regional policies and the social safety net

The preceding analyses show that apart from many common features there were also differences between the Czech and Slovak economies that deepened after the transformation process had been launched. This raises the question of whether the scenario of liberal reform had not been too one-sided in not paying enough attention to appropriate forms of structural, regional and social policies which caused important differences between the two Republics to grow bigger. After all, certain economic theories argue that the market mechanism itself deepens the gap between economically less developed regions and the more developed ones.[28] An answer to the question of how much the absence of such policies influenced the break-up of Czechoslovakia will be presented in this chapter.

Structural policy

The scenario of the economic reform originally included a structural policy as an integral part of economic reform in order to eliminate old distortions caused by central planning and to react to newly arising problems. This policy considered the introduction of separate programmes for selected branches of industry, as well as a horizontal policy to furnish support to promising business plans and activities. The Government Fund for Structural Changes which was to be established on the Federal level and supported from the government budget was to promote the following objectives:

- reduction of heavy industry and support of the traditional and prospective branches of light industry;
- reduction of energy and raw materials consumption and the introduction of environment-preserving technologies;
- development of the service sector, especially travel and public services, including modernization of banking and insurance systems;
- promoting economic growth and business activities;
- creation of information networks, development of telecommunication and transportation systems;
- cultural development and improvement of the environment.

The initial objective was to prepare, by the end of 1990, a set of programmes for the environmental, raw-material and transportation policies, for restructuring of fuel and energy systems, the metallurgy and mining industry, and construction of nuclear power plants as well as the basic principles of managing foreign investments. However, Memorandum on the Economic Policy drafted by the Federal government to present to the International Monetary Fund in December 1990 did not include a structural policy as an economic reform tool. The government activities were focused on liberalization of prices and foreign trade, rapid privatisation, and stabilization of the foreign exchange rate as well as restrictive fiscal and monetary policies, with the income policy of limited indexation of wages as its new supplement.

This absence of structural policies was explained by the argument that after forty years of allocating resources to the branches and regions based on distorted economic and political criteria, and given the conditions in which basic market institutions and mechanisms were created, any central authority would lack objective information about the real needs of the transition economy. Secondly, providing a wider space for structural policies within the environment of a tight budgetary policy would have necessitated a reduction of expenditures in other parts of the budget. Such a reduction would then cast doubt on whether the outcomes of the structural programmes sufficiently compensated for tensions caused by the budget cuts elsewhere.

Despite the negative attitude of the government towards the wider concept of a structural policy, some of its provisions were brought to life within the framework of the globally limited resources, mostly for the benefit of Slovakia. This claim can be illustrated by the data on drawing resources for the support of structural changes from the Federal budget. From the total sum of CSK 1,500 million released for conversion of the armament industry in 1991, CSK 1,188 million (79 per cent) were spent in the SR while in the CR it was CSK 312 million only (21 per cent). For 1992, it was CSK 593 million (74 per cent) in the SR and CSK 207 million (26 per cent) in the CR. The allocations of funds to effect the conversion were decided by a committee set up by the Federal Ministry of Economy on the basis of submitted projects.

The expenditure of the Federal Fund of Market Regulation in agriculture can be seen as another structural measure as well. From its resources, the Fund spent CSK 4.8 billion (69 per cent) in the Czech Republic and CSK 2,2 billion (31 per cent) in the Slovak Republic in 1992. The Council of the Fund was authorized to determine the allocation of funds to concrete projects.

Foundation of an export insurance company called EGAP at the end of 1992 cost the Federal budget about CSK 1.5 billion. The government supported exports by providing loan guarantees and interest subsidies to support competitiveness of the domestic exporters on foreign markets. Activities of the EGAP were identical in both Republics with the contracts with individual exporters concluded completely on commercial basis.

The disappearance of the structural policy from the vocabulary of the government economists did not mean that the Czechoslovak economy was not undergoing sweeping structural changes such as reorientation of exports to market economies, growth of services and particularly of the financial sector, substantial reduction of heavy industry without unemployment growth, and a substantial reshuffling of ownership during the process of privatisation.

Regional policy

The danger of undermining the economic integrity of Czechoslovakia (beside inflation and widespread unemployment) had already been discussed in the introduction to the economic reform scenario. The design of the economic reform, however, did not mention the possibility of using the regional policy tools to avoid those dangers. The absence of regional policies both in the draft and in the realization of the economic reform thus raised the question whether it was not one of the major causes of growing disharmony between the Czech and Slovak economies.[29]

Regional policy is based on a hierarchization of regions following certain criteria, such as the unemployment rate, economic growth, income per capita or migration of labour forces. At the beginning of the 1990s, based on these criteria, most of the depressed regions would be found in Slovakia. Except for the towns of Bratislava and Kosice, and several western regions, the Slovak unemployment rate was over 7 per cent. On the other hand, the number of districts in the Czech Republic exceeding the 7 per cent unemployment rate was rather low. Experimental studies conducted at the beginning of the 1990s revealed remarkable differences in the performance of regions in the Czech and Slovak Republics (business performance indicators, small-scale privatisation and development of the private sector). Therefore, the potential regional policy expenditure would have had a very differentiated implementation in both Republics.[30]

It is important to note, however, that a major obstacle was the absence of explicit programmes and the negative attitudes of Slovakia toward any process of coordinating and harmonizing regional policy on the Federal level. In Spring 1991, the Federal government openly declared that the system of executive powers prevented the flexible implementation of economic policy and limited the decision-making powers of Federal government in the economic sphere.[31] The regional policy was not within the powers of the Federal government anymore and was transferred to the national governments. The only regional body the Slovak politicians were willing to create on the Federal level was a fund to channel the Federal subsidies for Slovakia to balance the difference in the GDP per capita.

Regional policy in this environment was therefore not very viable, since on the Federal level it was unacceptable to the Slovak government, while on the Republic level sufficient resources were lacking to solve the increasing problems.

Social safety net

The economic reform scenario saw unemployment as socially oppressive but inevitable phenomenon of transformation and therefore envisaged the establishment of an effective social safety net comprised both of the active (requalification, creation of new job opportunities and public jobs) as well as passive (unemployment benefits) components of an employment policy.

Expenditures for both the Czech and Slovak employment policy were covered by the Federal budget. Federal subsidies to the Republic budgets were allocated based on the actual unemployment figures (for details see Table 2.7).

The so called Competence Acts of 1990 transferred social policy entirely to the governments of the Republics and therefore in fact removed the uniform Federal social security network. The unemployment benefits were distributed by the Republic Ministries of Labour without any coordination. In 1991, these individual rules probably contributed to launching a different unemployment growth in the Czech and Slovak Republics.[32] Although the rules for granting the unemployment benefits in Slovakia changed substantially in 1992 and therefore became more similar to the Czech ones, one could not speak about a uniform employment policy.

Table 2.7
Employment policy expenditures

	Year	CSFR	CR	SR
Total expenditures	1991	5,909.0	2,447.5	3,461.5
	1992	8,668.7	3,145.1	5,523.6
Active employment policy	1991	1,295.5	773.0	522.5
	1992	5,534.5	1,721.7	3,812.8
Passive employment policy	1991	4,613.5	1,674.5	2,939.0
	1992	3,134.2	1,423.4	1,710.8

Note: In million of CSK
Source: CR Government closing account, 1992; Czech Ministry of Finance data

The implementation of the active employment policy was slower in the SR than in the CR. A shift in this trend surfaced as late as December 1992, right before the break-up of the Federation, when almost 45 per cent of the annual sum to be allocated for the active policy was drawn in Slovakia.

The social safety net performance serves an example of what happens if a systematic element of transformation does not follow uniform principles. Nevertheless, even under these conditions, this element could have had similar results in both Republics. The similarity was, however, not a result of the institutional and law enforced coordination but a result of the process of learning by mistakes.

2.4 Conclusion

The introduction of this chapter proposed a rather ambitious task: to answer the question of whether the design of the economic reform contributed to the split of Czechoslovakia. The process of macroeconomic stabilization proves, however, that there were more similarities than diversities between the Czech and Slovak parts of the Federation. Heightened social problems contributed to the more critical attitude in Slovakia towards the economic transformation.

In reality, however, one usually looks for the 'second-best solution'. In other words, if an optimal solution lies outside the set of feasible options, then what is the second-best solution? This is also why it is so difficult to explain the attitudes of the Slovak politicians from the point of economic reasoning. Disagreements with the concept and progress of radical economic reform (and the Czechs political opposition was equally critical toward the 'cold-turkey theraphy') did not result in the enforcing of pressures for strengthening those economic mechanisms which contributed to the process of smoothing the asymmetrical impacts of the reform, but resulted in a centrifugal process of reinforcing the economically stronger Republic to the detriment of the weaker one and thus destabilizing the integrity of the entire country.

As the Czech Republic with its more developed economic power represented the driving force of the transformation, the economic reasoning rather called for ways to make effective use of this force instead of breaking away from it. For the driving force it looked more favourable, however, to uncouple the damaged carriage than to wait until it ran the whole train off the rails.

3 Two issues in the fields of currency and budgets

A constant change in opinions regarding the extent of the decentralization of the government executive powers brought about many possible solutions of these problems in practice. One can, however, ask the question when does the decentralization and suppression of uniformity result in a break-up endangering the capacity of the system itself. Two important topics discussed during the transformation process in Czechoslovakia deserve special attention.

3.1 Disputes over the character of central banking

In the long-lasting discussions on where the Czechoslovak state starts and ends, which kept the politicians busy during the negotiations on the constitutional set-up, the Czech politicians insisted on three attributes of a workable common state: a single army, a single subject of international law, and a single currency. Regarding the third condition it was clear that unprofessional and experimental interferences in the institutional structure of the monetary system would result in a loss of monetary stability and confidence of the public in the domestic currency, as well as in an outbreak of an uncontrolled inflation damaging the whole process of economic transformation. This scenario explains the Czech denial of all concepts which would, either openly or through vague formulations, result in a single currency controlled from more than one centre.

The Slovak party had never openly cast doubt on the idea of preserving the common currency and the anti-inflationary monetary policy. The problem, however, was that the practical ideas about the set-up of the monetary system seemed to contradict with the above objectives.

Reform of the banking system had been prepared before 1989 by the Communists within the concept of the so called 'new economic mechanism'. The Communist government passed an Act on the Czechoslovak State Bank, Act on Banks and Savings Banks, and an Act on Foreign Exchange, and thus created a legislative background for the separation of the central bank from the commercial banking sector.[33]

The new Acts were under the sway of Communist ideology in many aspects, especially in the relationship to economic planning, and therefore it was necessary to make changes in the legislation and adopt new basic laws which would respond to the needs of the economic transformation. The Czech and Slovak representations, however, had different opinions on how to effect the adjustment, especially vis-a-vis the Act on the Czechoslovak State Bank.

The main dispute arose over determining the future status of the central bank where the Czech and Slovak representatives were choosing between the US Federal Reserve system and the German Bundesbank administrative system. The Slovak party preferred the US Federal Reserve system based on an existence of a central coordinating body and of reserve banks which enjoy independent legal status. If applied in Czechoslovakia, it would have meant the establishment of a Czechoslovak central bank as well as two Republic reserve banks as independent legal entities.[34] The rights and responsibilities of these three reserve banks would have to be determined by law. The planned supreme body of the release system was the Board of Governors staffed by Governors and Vice Governors of the reserve banks (based on a parity of the Czech and Slovak representatives). Banknotes of the same denomination released by the Czech and Slovak reserve banks were to bear either Czech or Slovak inscriptions. Since the character and scope of these changes were very substantial, the simple amending of the banking laws would have been insufficient, especially in the case of the Act on the Czechoslovak State Bank, and new legislation would have been necessary.[35]

The Czechs, on the other hand, felt inspired by the German Bundesbank model, applied also in Austria and Switzerland. The German model of a central banking system is characterized by the existence of a single central bank which is internally structured based on the regional prerequisites. If applied in Czechoslovakia, it would have smoothly followed to the organizational structure of the Czechoslovak State Bank, which consisted of a Federal Centre and a Central Office for the Slovak Republic. An implementation of this decision required a withdrawal from the Act on the Czechoslovak State Bank of articles related to the old planning system as well as an introduction of new clauses in order to provide a base for the

Czechoslovak accession to the banking and monetary systems of the EU and to newly determine the rights and responsibilities of the national centres.

The concept promoted by the Slovak representation was criticized by the Czechs for combining two different types of central banking and limiting those aspects which guarantied Federal supremacy in monetary issues. The major source of apprehensions was the potential dualism of the Czechoslovak system following the US model. The Slovak concept proposed an establishment of a central coordinating body and two reserve banks (in the US it is twelve district banks), powers of which would be determined nationally (unlike the US system, where the district banks represent the interests of more than one state). There were concerns that the disputes between the Czech and Slovak politicians concerning responsibilities of both Republics as well as political lobbying would penetrate the Czechoslovak Board of Governors in which both parties were to be equally represented. On top of this, acceding to the Slovak proposal to ban the majority principle would have paralysed the Board of Governors in case of any dissenting opinion. All this threatened to weaken the central body and force it into subordination to the powerful Republic reserve banks.

For the successful performance of a monetary system, it was necessary to ensure federal support of the following key issues:

- issuing banknotes and coins;
- drafting monetary policies;
- monitoring the development of the balance of payment;
- widespread powers in the field of exchange rate policies;
- relations vis-a-vis central banks abroad and international financial and banking institutions;
- determining the rules of banking supervision;
- determining the rules of foreign exchange treatment;
- regulating a single interbank market.

In case of the existence of two national reserve banks, one could expect very strong Slovak attempts to transfer some of the above key issues from the central body to the Republic banks. Based on the experience with the Slovak policy makers, it was clear that the demands would include the transfer of powers vis-a-vis foreign financial institutions, providing avenues which would allow the national banks to diverge from the centrally determined rules, appointing the senior staff as well as autonomy in managing financial matters.

In this respect, a historical analysis of the American system proves to be very instructive. Its evolution from a formerly decentralized system is marked by numerous conflicts between the Federal centre and the reserve banks with the centre constantly limiting the district banks' powers, as well as by many negative cases of the district banks acting not in coordination with or even in conflict with the instructions of the Federal centre. Had such a scheme been implemented in Czechoslovakia (especially based on the understanding that the sovereign Republics pass selected rights and responsibilities on the central body), it would have gone through a very similar process of learning by mistakes.

The German Bundesbank model did not carry the above described shortcomings of the model based on the coexistence of three reserve banks. Its concept provided a lot of room for negotiations over the division of rights and responsibilities between the Federal and Republic centres; the character of such division is, however, predetermined. The Federal centre was delegated many decision-making powers on all basic issues of the monetary policy, and the Republic centres exercised some executive powers. It was the high credibility of the German Bundesbank which contributed to the decision in Autumn 1990 to follow the proposal of the Czech representation to give the central banking system the form of one central bank and provide its Republic branches with wide executive powers.[36]

Act on the Czechoslovak State Bank

Passing the Act on the Czechoslovak State Bank marked the foundation of a legislative framework for a modern central banking system in Czechoslovakia.[37] The Act determined the stability of the Czechoslovak currency as the leading objective of the Czechoslovak State Bank and, to reach this goal, equipped it with wide powers in the field of monetary policy, release of banknotes and coins and banking supervision.

The Czechoslovak State Bank was given relative independence from the government to insure that the monetary timetable would not depend on the office terms of the Federal and Republic governments. A representative of the Federal government was allowed to participate in the Bank Board meetings (without the right to vote). The Czechoslovak State Bank was also empowered to express its viewpoint on government proposals which could potentially influence the functioning of the banking system and, to execute this right, the Governor of the Czechoslovak State Bank was entitled to participate in the meetings of the Federal government. The formal independence and impartiality of the Czechoslovak State Bank was also guarantied by incompatibility of membership in the Bank Board with Parliament membership (unlike Ministers as members of the government) and membership in economic organizations. The Governor and other members of the Bank Council were named by the President of the Federation to six-year terms (as opposed to the four-year cycles of the parliamentary elections). A member of the Bank Board could not be suspended for reasons other than those determined by law. This rule made it therefore impossible to suspend a member in connection with changes in the government or a new President.

The Czechoslovak State Bank was equipped with wide powers also in the fields of monetary policy and banking supervision. The Bank had the authority to use administrative forms of regulation necessitated by the transition character of the Czechoslovak economy. Therefore, it was possible for the Bank to determine minimal interest rates for deposits and maximal rates for loans. The Act on the Czechoslovak State Bank also served as a legislative background for future bank operations in a market-oriented environment, such as interbank trading and other open market transactions.

The Bank also determined requirements for interest-free compulsory reserves. Reserves were limited to maximum 30 per cent of the bank's liabilities. The Czechoslovak State Bank was also authorized to determine the rules of prudent bank behaviour. In the field of foreign exchange, the Bank was to closely cooperate with the Federal Ministry of Finance.

The Czechoslovak State Bank was empowered do provide short-term loans to the government budgets to cover temporary deficits (by purchasing short-term government bonds maximally up to 5 per cent of the given budget revenues). This measure did not, however, prevent the budgets from acquiring necessary resources somewhere else.

The Czechoslovak State Bank set-up was based on the existence of a Federal central body and of two Republic centres. The Federal centre was licensed to trade with the Federal budget and foreign entities, manage currency reserves, execute payments to and from foreign countries, release central bank securities as well as determine methods of banking supervision. The Republic centres were empowered to trade with the Republic budget in which they were located as well as to effect interbank transactions with banks based in that Republic. The Republic centres were given more power which was reflected especially in the set-up of the Bank Board as the top Czechoslovak State Bank authority, the members of which were the Governor (the highest Bank representative), two Vice Governors (a Czech and a Slovak citizen), Vice Governor for the Czech Republic centre and his/her deputy and a Vice Governor for the Slovak Republic centre and his/her deputy. Therefore, four of the seven members of the Bank Board were representatives of the Republic centres and, depending on the Governor nationality, the ratio between both nations was 4 to 3. The Bank Board adopted decisions by simple majority.

The successful pace of macroeconomic stabilization serves as proof that the model of central banking was chosen correctly. As far as the main objective of the Czechoslovak State Bank was concerned (stabilization of the currency), Czechoslovakia reached, by all means, the best outcome among the post-communist countries. After having absorbed the initial shock from the liberalization of prices, the inflation rate stabilized on the level of less than 1 per cent of the monthly price level increase. The growing credibility of the Czechoslovak currency was mainly due to its internal stability; the regime of a stable exchange rate supported by the initial devaluation served as an anchor for the transformation changes.

The feasibility of the chosen concept of central banking was also proven by the relatively fast and frictionless transfer to the market instruments of monetary policy. As soon as in 1992, all credit and interest rate ceilings were removed in exchange for indirect tools such as minimal reserves requirements, refinancing and open market operations. The Czech banking sector saw a great boom, all this while the Czechoslovak State Bank was learning the instruments of efficient banking supervision 'on the move'.

A more detailed survey of the development of the banking sector would probably disclose a number of problems. Nevertheless, the truth remains that the chosen model of central banking substantially contributed to maintaining a uniform economic environment throughout the entire territory of the former Czechoslovakia as well as helped give the banking sector a uniform base.

The threat of weakening the monetary centre

At the very beginning of the discussions concerning the character of the central banking system, one could speculate that the Slovak representation was promoting the American model just for the sake of seizing some formal attributes of independence, and that these demands could have been easily met in the process of finding compromises acceptable to both parties without necessarily undermining the uniformity of the banking system. However, the 1992 elections showed that such thoughts were rather outdated.

The winning party in Slovakia clearly declared that its opinion about the contents and sequence of the reform process was different from that of the Czech government. It is true that the program of the Slovak government did not directly challenge the existing objectives of the transformation process (privatisation, liberalization of prices and foreign trade, maintaining internal convertibility, anti-inflatory policy), but it stressed 'a more flexible use of monetary instruments to support the economy', 'approaching the budget balance from a long-term perspective' and 'preparing a concept of privatisation which would simplify the legal rules and requirements of privatisation, promote management buy-outs and sales to employees and minimize cheap sales of property abroad'. The Slovak macroeconomic strategy became 'a development policy based on selective stimulation of demand and support of structural changes instead of an across-the-board restrictive policy'. [38]

The draft of the Slovak Constitution represented a major challenge, for it stipulated, in paragraph 66, that 'The state establishes a reserve bank. Details will be determined by law'. This step interferred with the current legal system and the Slovak representation put forward the formerly rejected concept of three reserve banks more or less as an ultimatum. While the Czech government maintained that the existence of one state meant one uniform currency as well as a uniform monetary policy (effected by one central bank) throughout its entire territory, the Slovak representation sent a clear message that the formation of Republic reserve banks and a common reserve centre with a parity representation was the condition for the further existence of the common currency.

It seemed impossible to reach a compromise. The Slovak demand for its own reserve bank was just a part of its attempts for wider autonomy in the economic decision-making. For the Czech representation, the Slovak proclamations about stimulating monetary and fiscal policies represented a signal of growing pressure to influence the banking sector and to inject inflationary money into the economy. It wasn't difficult to imagine that the deficit financing of the Slovak government spurred by the expansionary policy as well as by the newly adopted principle 'each republic for its own money' would be much more successful in negotiating financing with the Slovak reserve bank than with the Federal central authority. The existence of a Republic reserve bank with powers to exercise banking supervision would make it easier to force the Slovak commercial banks to buy the Slovak government debt. Covering the central bank's debt would have had a side effect of increased inflation, while financing the debt outside the central bank would induce the growth of interest rates.[39]

A part of the Slovak preparations to start running the Slovak national bank was a demand to decentralize the payment systems which had been effected centrally by the Prague clearing centre, to disengage the information system and last but not least to revise the Czechoslovak State Bank budget in order to finance the Slovak plans.

In the situation after the June 1992 elections, the proposal of a strong reserve bank backed by the powerful Federation was less and less feasible. On the other hand, there was a danger that possible concessions of the Czech political representation in the name of saving the Federation would have ended in giving up the concept of uniform anti-inflationary monetary policy. In other words, it would mean questioning one of the attributes presented by the Czech party as indispensable for the existence of the Federation. Such a settlement was impalatable and therefore the question of the day was how to ensure that 'In case of a collapse of the Federation, the Czech Republic could continue to exist as an independent state and proceed with its economic transformation and the process of integrating itself into the Western world'.[40]

3.2 Decline of fiscal federalism

The fiscal system inherited from the command economy was devised to meet the needs of the extensive and omnipresent public sector.[41] Nationalizing private property helped the state concentrate in its hands almost everything, including small businesses. The government budgets provided extensive transfers from profitable companies to those less efficient.[42] Large-scale redistributions and excessive tax burdens were necessary to subsidize free-of-charge medical care and education system, cheap housing and other generous social programs.

This extensive system of transfers was also characteristic of so called fiscal federalism.[43] The constitutional Act on the Czechoslovak Federation of 1968 gave both the Federal and Republic governments powers to determine their own budgets which were to be then formally approved by the Federal Assembly and the National Councils of the Republics, respectively. The centrally planned economy led to an outstanding increase of the Federal budget share on total incomes of all public budgets and to the dependency of the Republics on Federal subsidies. Since this budgetary system resembled more a unitary state system than a Federal one, one of the components of the reform of fiscal federalism was aimed at a complete change of relations among the public budgets to meet the demanding objectives of economic transformation.

Reform of fiscal federalism

Intensive discussions about the reform of fiscal federalism which started already in 1990 were characterized by two quite different approaches. One group promoted the idea that all revenues should be directed to the Federal budget and than allocated to the Republic budgets based on a predetermined rule. The second group favored the approach based on minimizing the Federal government competencies. According to this approach, the Federal budget was supposed to have only secondary resources and no primary ones. All taxes and other revenues were meant to be allocated directly in the Republic budgets which would then contribute a certain portion of their revenues to the Federal budget to cover Federal activities.[44]

It is necessary to understand that these two approaches were not necessarily answers to what was the degree of centralization or decentralization, but more or less expressions of the perception of the constitutional set-up. On the one hand, the Federal citizenship ascendancy over Republic would ask for direct tax payments to the Federation, a Republic citizenship ascendancy over Federal would call, on the other hand, for tax payments directly to the Republics.[45]

Practical operations of any concept of fiscal federalism always run into the problem of assigning resources. While some tax revenues (property tax, income taxes) can be relatively easily assigned to one of the Republics, the situation with other taxes (consumption tax, turnover tax, profit tax) is more complex since any assignment always requires some arbitrary conventions. A natural answer to these problems were compromises which facilitated a wide area for various interpretations and negotiations.

Debates about the new concept of fiscal federalism influenced the process of drafting the Act on the Czechoslovak Federation (the so called Competence Act) which was adopted in Autumn 1990. This Act, some articles of which were formulated extremely vaguely, defined the Czechoslovak economy as an integration of the Czech and Slovak economies based on a single internal market, single currency and free movement of good and production factors, and declared the types of ownership (Federation, CR, SR). The Federation was given authority in the field of foreign affairs, trade and defense, monetary policy and principles of economic policy, and law-making powers in selected fields (transportation, production and distribution of energy, gas and heat, post offices and telecommunications, environmental issues), in the administration of railroad transportation, management of the single telecommunication system and for announcing key price regulations.

In the fiscal area, the Act determined uniform rules of budgetary policies which were to be agreed upon among the Czechoslovak government and the governments of the CR and the SR. The Federal Assembly was delegated powers to control and amend the Czechoslovak tax system. Administration of all taxes fell under supervision of the Republics (except for import surcharges and customs tariffs).

Czechoslovak, Czech and Slovak budgets were declared as separate. In case a certain tax revenue was to be shared by all three budgets, the Federal Assembly was empowered to determine the Federal budget share and rules to be followed by the Republics to secure the part of the income pertinent to the Federal budget. This arrangement in fact accepted the concept of fiscal federalism according to which the Federal budget was to have no primary revenues. Almost all revenues were to be assigned to the Republic budgets (following the regional principle) which would subsequently contribute a portion of the revenues to the Federal budget to cover its expenditures.

In practice, the agreed rules of sharing the revenues of selected taxes never adopted the profile prescribed by the constitutional legislation. Instead of determining a proportion of the Republic budgets to be allocated in the Federal budget, the Czech and Slovak representatives agreed on definite shares of the three budgets on the tax revenues.

In Autumn 1990, both Republics effected a reform of local government structure. The three-tier concept of the National Committees was abolished and replaced by a two-tier system of local and county offices. In the SR, this development led to a higher degree of centralization. While in the CR the activities of the former Regional National Committees were passed mainly on to lower ranking bodies (counties, municipalities), in the SR the activities of the Regional National Committees as well as some procedures of the Local National Committees (almost all education and health care expenditures in the SR fell under the framework of the Republic budget), were transferred to the Republic level. These differences surfaced in the process of preparing the local budgets (in the CR there were 76 county budgets prepared and approved on the Republic level while in the SR there were several thousands of municipal budgets).

After the adoption of the new Act on the Czechoslovak State Bank in December 1991, the budget deficits (as of 1991) were not to be covered by a direct loan from the central bank. The provisions of the Czechoslovak State Bank for financing the running deficits were similarly constrained.[46]

Coexistence of three government budgets

The Act on the Czechoslovak Federation only partly determined the rules of coexistence of the Federal and two Republic budgets. The vague phrasing of the Act which gave the Federal budget authority in the 'basic' and 'general' affairs, and for many others determined 'shared responsibilities' of the Republics and the Federation, became a source of permanent conflicts over the division of responsibilities. The overall system of fiscal federalism was provisional and problems were often bridged by ad hoc compromises.

In compliance with the previously agreed-upon objective to decrease direct transfers from the Federal budget to the Republic ones, the subsidies fell from approximately CSK 131 billion in 1989 to CSK 61 billion (see Table 2.8). This subsidy was allocated to the Czech and Slovak budgets in a 1.42 ratio (1989) and a 1.58 ratio (1990). In 1990, a system of sharing the turnover tax revenues by all three budgets was introduced (the CR/SR ratio was 0.82, see again Table 2.8). In 1991, the CR/SR ratio of the Federal subsidies and shared turnover tax revenues therefore reached only 1.19.

At the beginning of 1991, most of the subsidies from the Federal budget to the Republic ones were abolished. The three budgets acquired relative independence by sharing revenues from two types of taxes - turnover tax (the same as in 1990) and profit tax (including the profit tax as a component of the agriculture tax, however, without a transfer of the Czechoslovak State Bank profit). The share on total revenues from these taxes of the Federal and the

Republic budgets were agreed (for 1991) to be 35 (Federal), 40 (Czech) and 25 per cent (Slovak). For 1992 it was 35, 41.5 and 23.5 per cent respectively.

Table 2.8
Revenues of the Federal and Republic budgets from Federal subsidies and shared taxes

	1989	*1990*		
	Subsidies	Subsidies	Turnover tax	Total
Federal budget	-	-	65.8 (18.5)	65.8
Czech budget	76.8	37.6	20.7 (22.5)	58.3
Slovak budget	53.9	23.8	25.1 (59.0)	48.9
Total	130.7	61.4	111.6	-
Ratio CR/SR	1.42	-	-	1.19

	1991			
	Turnover tax	Profit tax	Subsidies	Total
Federal budget	43.2 (35.0)	44.7 (35.0)	-	87.9
Czech budget	49.3 (40.0)	51.0 (40.0)	2.6	103.0
Slovak budget	30.8 (25.0)	31.9 (25.0)	1.9	64.7
Total	123.4	127.1	4.5	-
Ratio CR/SR	1.60	1.60	-	1.59

	1992			
	Turnover tax	Profit tax	Subsidies	Total
Federal budget	44.0 (35.0)	36.4 (35.0)	-	80.4
Czech budget	52.2 (41.5)	43.1 (41.5)	3.3	98.6
Slovak budget	29.6 (23.5)	24.4 (23.5)	1.7	55.7
Total	125.8	103.9	5.0	-
Ratio CR/SR	1.77	1.77	-	1.77

Note: In bilion of CSK, the parentheses contain the percentage of shared taxes
Source: Final government accounts from 1989-92

The agreed shares did not, however, represent a framework for the preparation of the Republic budgets. In 1991, for example, the procedure was as follows: first, the revenues and expenditures of the Federal budget and consequently its balance (for 1991 it was a surplus of 5.7 per cent of its revenues) were agreed upon, followed by a ratio of estimated total expenditures of both Republics and local budgets (the CR/SR ratio was 1.91) and then a ratio of surpluses of the Federal and two Republic budgets (based on balanced local budgets) on the total budget revenues (for the CR it was 46 per cent and for the SR 56 per cent). Proportions of the shared revenues were deducted so that they guarantied the projected balances of all three budgets. The ratio of total expenditures (respectively revenues) of the public budgets in both Republics therefore became the main subject of negotiations after the Federal budget had been agreed upon.

Table 2.8 figures which show the development of the CR/SR share of the budget revenues in the form of Federal subsidies and revenues from shared taxes have to be viewed from a wider context of all budget revenues and expenditures. The CR/SR ratio (in projected figures) closely followed the ratio of inhabitants of both Republics. In other words, the criterion of equal budget revenues and expenditures per capita in each of the Republics provided a practical modus vivendi between the Czech and Slovak political representatives. The ratio of projected revenues of the Czech and Slovak budgets as a result of negotiations of both partners was, in 1991 and 1992, roughly 1.9, i.e. a bit lower than the ratio of inhabitants in both Republics (see the bottom row of Table 2.9).

Table 2.9
Total revenues and expenditures of the Republic and local budgets

	1989		*1990*		*1991*		*1992*	
	Rev.	Exp.	Rev.	Exp.	Rev.	Exp.	Rev.	Exp.
CR [a]	221.7	219.1	237.9	231.4	251.0	263.5	280.6	289.9
SR [a]	119.3	122.5	127.7	126.2	126.1	133.8	128.4	147.3
Ratio CR/SR	1.86	1.79	1.86	1.83	1.99	1.97	2.19	1.97
Inhabitants CR/SR	1.96		1.96		1.951		1.947	

Note: a) In billion of CSK; Methodology IMF, data for 1992 verified according to the final government account.

Source: *Statistical Yearbook 1993*, Czech Statistical Office 1993

As indicated in Table 2.9, the real revenues and expenditures in both Republics could have differed substantially from the initial projections. Such a difference is common even in the consolidated market economies and is very likely to surface in transition economies.

If we analyze development trends of revenues and expenditures in both Republics we see that in 1989-92 the CR/SR ratio displayed an inclination to grow. While in 1989 and 1990 this ratio was a bit lower than the ratio of the inhabitants of both Republics, in 1991 it was already slightly higher and in 1992 much higher. In terms of growth figures for 1989-92, the revenues (expenditures) of the public budgets in the CR grew by 26.6 (32.3) per cent while in the SR it was only 7.6 (20.2) per cent. In 1991 compared to 1990, the revenues of the Slovak budget even displayed a slight absolute decrease.

For better understanding, it is necessary to realize that had the CR/SR ratio of the revenues of the public budgets reflected the ratio of inhabitants, the revenues of the Czech public budgets in 1989 and 1990 would have had to be (given the identical total revenues of the public budgets in the CR and the SR) about CSK 4 billion higher, in 1991 less than CSK 2 billion lower and in 1992 about CSK 10 billion lower (these sums are relatively low).

The Federal budget was fully integrated in this concept, the objective of which was to guarantee the same proportion per head in both Republics. The partial increase of the Czech budget on the revenue from the shared taxes (from 40 to 41.5 per cent) and the relative decrease of the Slovak budget (from 25 to 23.5 per cent compared to 1991) was, in the process of preparing the 1992 budget and with the intention to balance the estimated Republic budgets, offset by changes in the structure of Federal budget expenditures (higher transfers to institutions under the supervision of the Republics).

In 1992, CSK 51.1 billion out of CSK 131 billion of total Federal budget expenditures were used by institutions under the supervision of the Republics (except for 5 billion of Federal subsidy) and as transfers to inhabitants. It is estimated that CSK 28.6 billion were used in the CR and CSK 22.5 billion in the SR.[47] E.g. from the total sum (CSK 8.7 billion) to support the policy of active employment (creation of job opportunities, requalifications, etc.), only 36.6 per cent were used in the CR while 63.7 per cent in the SR. The relatively lower use of Federal programmes in the CR was, in 1992, 50 per cent compensated for by a higher public budget income per head in the CR.

Between 1989 and 1992, the role of the Federal budget substantially changed. Its revenues (measured in compliance with IMF standards for the so called budget area) decreased by more than 50 per cent (the real decrease, after taking inflation into account, was about 75 per cent).[48] While in 1989 the total revenues of the Federal budget (measured in compliance with IMF standards) represented about 55 per cent of all revenues of the public budgets in Czechoslovakia, in 1992 this share fell to 23 per cent. The share of the Federal budget expenditures (including subsidies to Republic budgets) in the total expenditures of the public budgets in Czechoslovakia in 1989 was 42 per cent, in 1992 it was only 22 per cent. Such a share is, compared to other Federally structured economies, exceptionally low.[49]

There can be two conclusions made based on these figures. First, budget share and transfers per capita in both Republics were in 1989-92 almost identical (the relative position of the Czech Republic was slightly improving).

In this respect, the CR adopted a very correct attitude to the SR since it is indisputable that the Czech fiscal capacity (derived implicitly from the economic capacity) was more than twice as high as the Slovak one.

The significant reduction of subsidies and transfers as one of the features of the transformation process had a much worse impact on the Slovak budget. It was partly due to the slight improvement the Czech Republic enjoyed in 1992. The question thus remains whether the principle of identical revenues and expenditures per capita in both Republics was, with regard to the Federation on the verge of a break-up, the best solution for this time period.

'Each Republic for its own money'

The principle of actual revenues and expenditures per capita in both Republics was probably the only acceptable compromise given the law-making vacuum caused by the extremely general and improperly considered formulations of the so called Competence Act. As explained in the preceding paragraphs, this compromise often served as a basis for finding acceptable answers to the questions concerning budget preparation.

As a matter of fact, the rule of actual revenues and expenditures per capita was not sufficient to remove the question of who pays for whom. From the Czech point of view, it was obvious that the higher performance of the Czech economy in combination with the per capita rule had to result in a transfer of resources from the Czech Republic to the Slovak Republic. The Czech representatives therefore often accused the Slovak leaders of financing a substantial part of the Slovak separation process from the Czech tax-payers' money. On the other hand, the Slovaks did not feel like listening to the repeated accusations of draining the Czechs and pointed at cases of transfers effected in the other direction -- from Slovakia to the Czech Republic.[50] The Czech representatives considered these attempts as unilateral, and with a clear intention to improve the Slovak fiscal position, to obfuscate the functionality and transparency of the fiscal system, and to ignore the fact that in other cases it would be the Czech Republic who would profit from a change of the current rule.

The Gordian knot of the endless debates about who was living off whom seemed to be solved by the rule 'each Republic for its own money'. Given the time which has passed, it is probably impossible to clearly determine its origins. Maybe it is not important to trace who came out with it first, but it remains true that this principle was supposed to serve as a basis for preparing the 1993 government budgets.

The basic problem of the 'each Republic for its own money' is its unavoidable negative impact on the viability of the fiscal system of any Federal unit. The break-up of Czechoslovakia did not allow to test it in practice and therefore we can only speculate what kind of problems the idea of 'each Republic for its own money' would have brought.

The first problem would have been the need for an intelligible and transparent delineation of the tax titles of both of the Republic's budgets. The only conceptual solution would have probably been the formation of a so called fiscal border within which the Republic would represent independent subjects of law endowed with powers to determine tax rates and bases and to collect taxes. Problems of competing titles for a certain tax base (e.g. business profits) would then have to be settled following the rules for the settlement of disputes among sovereign states (i.e. by various coordinating regulations such as preventing double taxation, defining residentship, etc.). One of the practical questions to solve would have been the viability of a fiscal border without real borders.

Without further speculating about the possible outcomes of the fiscal border concept it is clear that it would have been a highly unusual regime of fiscal federalism in case Czechoslovakia wanted to maintain its Federal framework. On the other hand, the contemplations about possible confederal set-up of Czechoslovakia (which the Czech representatives rejected as less acceptable than the break-up into two separate entities) make this concept sound more logical.

The 'each Republic for its own money' concept could not avoid the problem of Republics´ contributions to meet the financial needs of the Federation. It is quite realistic to assume that this issue would have had the capacity to become a source of instability, since the winners of the June 1992 Parliamentary elections had quite dissenting opinions about the elements to be covered on the Federal level.

The 'each Republic for its own money' rule would have probably attempted at also meeting other ends than just defining the fiscal position of both Republics. Its wording and the time in which it was discussed points at a possible attempt to discontinue the one-way transfers from the CR to the SR. The fact which speaks against this goal is that the fiscal transfer often remains the only flexible tool of regional policy when the uniform economic space prevents a less developed region from protecting itself by exchange rate policies. Would that mean, for example, that a less developed Republic would have to agree on lower unemployment benefits, lower retirement pensions, less money to spend on infrastructure, etc? Such issues will certainly undermine integrity of any state.

From a purely economic point of view, adoption of the 'each Republic for its own money' concept would be in contradiction with the formation of a workable system of fiscal federalism as a means of keeping Czechoslovakia together. On the other hand, speculations about a danger of this principle substantially accelerating the decision to dissolve Czechoslovakia would be a mistake, since it was more or less a passive resignation to the disruptive processes which considerably accelerated after the Parliamentary elections in June 1992.

4 Privatisation process

Privatisation of the business sector, represented by the transfer of thousands of state-owned enterprises to private owners had been devised as one of the fundamental pillars of radical economic reform. Basically, this process pursued four strategic objectives: encouraging inflow of foreign capital, alleviation of Communist injustice, the formation of the private sector and active involvement of the general public in the transformation process.

The drafting of the privatisation concept was accompanied by fierce discussions over the basic framework of the privatisation process. The question was whether to emphasize the speed of privatisation, which would minimize losses caused by the transformation of ownership rights and transfer the burden of restructuring to the new owners, or to stress greater involvement of the government in restructuring of the privatized units, giving preference to methods which guarantee an inflow of fresh capital into the business sphere. Finally, it was decided to effect a sweeping and rapid privatisation process without restructuring.

4.1 Institutional framework of privatisation

The privatisation process was drafted as a uniform Federal program which gave both Republics extensive potential for its creative implementation. Both Republics established new bodies -- Czech and Slovak Ministries of Privatisation and Funds of National Property, and a Federal Fund of National Property (hereafter NPF). The existing governmental agencies, particularly the Federal Ministry of Finance and selected ministries, also played a substantial role in the process of bringing privatisation into life.

The Czech and Slovak Ministries of Privatisation founded in August 1990 were given a number of tasks. They set up and managed activities of regional commissions designed to organize public auctions, approved lists of small business units to be auctioned, and monitored the course of the small-scale privatisation. Nevertheless, it was in the area of large-scale privatisation where the Ministries were charged with more complicated and substantial tasks, such as determining the contents of privatisations projects, selecting and approving submitted privatisation projects, and managing activities of the NPFs.

The Ministries of Privatisation of both Republics were responsible only for privatisation projects of those companies a founder of which (and thus the project submitter) was an administration agency of a respective Republic, i.e. a branch ministry or a municipality.[51] Preparation of projects of companies founded by Federal administration bodies became a responsibility of the Federal Ministry of Finance.[52] This Ministry (together with the Ministries of Finance of the Republics) played an important role in administering the demand side of the voucher privatisation.

The NPFs were established to exercise the rights of their governments and, in compliance with individual projects, concluded agreements and made other legal acts on behalf of their property. The Funds were entitled to set up joint stock companies, organize public auctions and tenders, determine the form of foreign participation, sell shares and to settle restitution claims. In case the NPF held any shares either on a long-term or temporary basis, it executed the rights of a shareholder.[53] The NPFs also administered the proceeds of auctions and sales of the government property stakes.

The powers of the Federal NPF were identical with those of the NPFs of the Republics, the property transferred to the NPF being the companies founded by Federal bodies. The NPF executed privatisation projects approved by the Federal Ministry of Finance and was directly subordinate to the Federal government.[54]

4.2 Restitution and small-scale privatisation

The restitution process was designed to make up for the injustice caused by expropriation of private property in the late 1940s and 1950s, with the intention of returning this property to the former owners. Its basic principles were determined by three Federal Acts, thus unifying its implementation in both Republics.

Based on the first of these Acts, the church and religious congregations were restituted a portion of their property. The second Act was designed to alleviate the effects of some cases of forced expropriation during the last wave of nationalization in 1955. About 30,000 former owners of small businesses, restaurants, workshops and apartment houses in the Czech Republic and 5,000 former owners in Slovakia filed claims for restitution of their property.

The third Act addressed the issue of nationalized property from a broader perspective. The key problems during the drafting of this Act were setting the date in the past from which restitution claims would become effective and determining the group of people who would be entitled to file their claims. It was decided to limit the restitution to 25 February 1948 (i.e., the date the Communist Party seized power). This date was questioned by supporters of an earlier deadline but finally became binding since any other solution would have brought up the politically very sensitive question of the restitution claims of the Sudeten Germans and the Hungarians who were forced to leave Czechoslovakia after WWII. This Act applied exclusively to Czechoslovak citizens and emigrants with permanent residence in Czechoslovakia.[55]

Those who submitted restitution claims either received the claimed property back or obtained shares of the claimed company. Former owners of destroyed or sold property received financial compensation from the Restitution Investment Fund, to which 3 per cent of shares of each privatized joint stock company were transferred to cover the cost. In cases when property had risen in value by extension or the purchase of technology, those claiming the property in restitution were obliged to make compensation for the difference between the original and contemporary value of the claimed property.

Restitution claims for farming land and forests were regulated by a separate Federal Act (the so called Land Act). This Act was designed to compensate the former owners for expropriation of their farming land and forests from 1948 to 1989 and to establish a legal framework for the development of private business activities in agriculture. The Act also outlined conditions for restitution of homes and out-buildings which were originally integral parts of farms as well as compensations for the live stock (including inventory) the owner transferred into a cooperative farm or was forced to give up. Privatisation of state-owned farms and transformation of cooperatives was contemplated for the same period of time. Since the individual restitution claims were to be settled first, the process of privatisation and transformation of agriculture was slower compared to that of other branches of the economy.

Transfer of the state-owned property to other corporate entities or physical persons began at the end of 1990 with the so called small privatisation of companies, retail outlets and services. The small privatisation authorized the sale or long-term lease of small businesses through public auctions, organized by regional privatisation committees. The first run of the auctions was for Czechoslovak citizens only, while the second one was open to foreigners.

Small-scale privatisation was, thanks to its swift introduction and rapid course, finished (with some exceptions) before the end of 1992. Statistics showed a relatively balanced development in both Republics. Before the end of 1993, there were 24,359 units worth CSK 31 billion sold in auctions in the Czech Republic. Small-scale privatisation in the Slovak Republic was completed in March 1993 with almost 9,700 business units sold for CSK 14.5 billion. Revenues from the small privatisation were transferred to the NPFs of the respective Republics.

4.3 Large-scale privatisation

Privatisation of larger state-owned businesses was understood to be an integral part of radical economic reform. The Federal Transformation Act provided a legal basis for a uniform concept in both Republics. Nevertheless, the privatisation strategy proposed by this Act represented a highly decentralized system based on transfer of most of the agenda onto the authorities of the Republics (Ministries of Privatisation and NPFs).

Financial restructuring of companies and banks

The concept of large-scale privatisation was based on the general idea that, in a turbulent period of transformation of a command economy to a market economy, the government is not able to make competent decisions on the restructuring of microeconomic units and therefore this role should be performed by the new private owners. Regardless of this somewhat passive role, the government introduced several measures aimed at the economic restructuring and financial recovery of companies and banks.

The involvement of both NPFs in the settlement of debts of the state-owned companies entering the privatisation process as well as in the capital reinforcement of the commercial banks was very important. To meet these objectives, the NPFs made available CSK 50 billion (approximately 8 per cent of total business credits) and at the end of 1991 issued five-year bonds (in total CSK 30 billion in the CR and CSK 20 billion in the SR). These bonds were used by the banks to partly write-off selected non-performing loans [56] and partly enforce their capital base to cover for future losses related to bankrupt debtors.[57]

The foundation of the Consolidation Bank in March 1991 represented another system measure designed to help the problem of debts and bad credits in bank portfolios. One of the first operations of this bank was a take-over of credits worth CSK 110 billion for the so called permanently revolving inventories (25 per cent of the total amount accounted for the Slovak companies).[58] A part of those credits was repaid after the Bank announced more favourable credit conditions for debtors while losses and the non-performing loans were covered from its reserve fund which was regularly replenished from revenues of the NPFs.[59]

General strategy of large-scale privatisation

The original schedule of large-scale privatisation proposed to divide the whole process into two privatisation waves. Based on the estimates of the Federal Ministry of Finance, large-scale privatisation was to involve approximately 4,400 Czech and 1,600 Slovak companies, 2,210 of which in the CR and 900 in the SR were selected for the first wave. It was planned to complete the first wave of large-scale privatisation by the end of 1992 and to start the second wave soon after.[60]

The large-scale privatisation scheme included mainly privatisation of large-scale and middle sized industrial, construction and service companies and also involved financial institutions and state-owned agricultural companies.

One or more privatisation projects were prepared for each company to be privatized. The initial concept charged the existing management of the state-owned companies or the founding Ministries with drafting the privatisation project. Under the pressure of the business community, the privatisation authorities allowed competing projects from the public to be submitted next to the basic projects.

The privatisation projects included a proposed privatisation method (or a combination of several methods), the book value of the property to be privatized using the proposed method, and the business plan. The finished projects were submitted for review and verification to the founder of the company who subsequently submitted it to the Ministry of Privatisation of the Republic (or the Federal Ministry of Privatisation). The Ministry of Privatisation selected the project to be effected considering the size of the company to be privatized, requirements for efficient technical cooperation and the necessity to demonopolize the given business sector. During the decision-making process, it was important to make sure that there was enough property offered in the voucher privatisation. In case there were doubts concerning consistency of the submitted projects or there were more competing projects submitted for one business, public tender or auction should be given priority. Sale of a company with more than 3,000 employees or its part was subjected to the approval of the governments of the Republics (or the Federal government) based on a recommendation of the Republic Ministry of Privatisation. After having gone through all the above described phases, the project was passed over to the respective NPF to bring it to life.

The submitted privatisation projects were permitted to propose the following methods of privatisation:

- public auction;
- tender or a direct sale of the property to domestic or foreign bidders;
- transfer of property for free to municipalities, health and retirement funds, banks and savings banks;
- foundation of a joint stock company with the following treatment of shares: i) sale of shares by a bank, in the stock exchange or by a brokerage company; ii) transfer of shares for free to municipalities and health and retirement funds; iii) distribution of shares in voucher privatisation; iv) transfer to restitution funds administered by the NPFs; v) temporary or permanent holding of the shares by the NPFs.

The above privatisation methods were equal subjects of law but in practice differed by the time requirements and costs needed for drafting the privatisation project, searching for business partners or making foreign contacts.

Voucher privatisation was an innovative method which permitted a rapid privatisation of large volume of assets despite the lack of domestic capital. Thanks to its popularity, the Czechoslovak government managed to secure wide public support for the process of economic reform.

Large-scale privatisation spurred more activity in the CR than in the SR. The number of privatisation projects submitted in the CR was higher -- 11,349 projects in total (basic and competing ones) for 2,404 companies to be privatized in the first wave (an average of 4-5 projects per one company). In the SR, where the bidders submitted 1,500 projects for 736 companies to be privatized in the first wave of privatisation, the ratio was approximately 2 projects per one company.

In addition, the first privatisation projects for the second wave of large-scale privatisation in the Czech Republic were submitted as early as the first half of 1992. At the end of the year, the number of submitted privatisation projects reached 16,609 projects for 3,638 companies.

The higher number of projects represented a big pressure on the approval process by the Ministry of Privatisation of the Czech Republic. By the end of 1992, however, the Ministry approved 3,858 projects for 2,200 formerly state-owned companies the total book value of which was CSK 469 billion. The end of 1992 thus marked the end of the process of approving projects for the first wave of large-scale privatisation and the beginning of the second wave.

Although the completion of the first wave of large-scale privatisation in the Slovak Republic was scheduled for the end of 1992, some projects remained unapproved as late as in Autumn 1993. By 31 December 1992, the Slovak

Ministry of Privatisation approved 874 projects the book value of which was CSK 165 billion.

Table 2.10
Structure of the approved privatisation projects

Method of privatisation	*Czech Republic* [a] Number of units	Property value in bn CSK	%	*Slovak Republic* [b] Number of units	Property value in bn SKK	%
Public auction	335	3,887	0.83	17	157	0.08
Public tender	301	10,121	2.16	57	5,968	3.14
Direct sale	973	26,497	5.65	247	11,002	5.79
Transformation into joint-stock companies, privatisation of the existing ones	1,215	418,702	89.30	563	171,926	90.48
of which:						
by vouchers [c]	1,167	237,237	50.59	537	146,581	77.15
by vouchers in the first wave	946	203,987	43.51	503	87,000	45.79
Transfers of property for free to municipalities, retirement funds and banks	1,034	9,659	2.06	106	953	0.50
Total	3,858	468,866	100.00	990	190,006	100.00

Note: a) Figures for the Czech Republic were calculated making use of the database of privatisation projects approved as of 31 December 1992 and also include part of the projects approved for the second wave; b) Slovak figures are based on: The Czech Republic, The Slovak Republic, *Economic Surveys*, OECD, Paris 1994 and reflect the situation as of 21 October 1993; c) Including the second wave of the voucher privatisation.

Table 2.10 shows the structure of approved privatisation projects. In both Republics the method of transformation into joint stock companies with a substantial number of their shares allotted for the voucher privatisation prevailed. In the SR, 77 per cent of property was privatized by the voucher method and often it was proposed to privatize the whole company this way (except for the 3 per cent reserved for restitution fund). In the CR, more shares were left for privatisation by standard methods (direct sale to a selected domestic or foreign buyer, sale through banks, stock-exchange, etc.) with 51 per cent of the property reserved for sale in voucher privatisation.

The first wave of the voucher privatisation

Voucher privatisation enabled citizens over eighteen years of age to purchase for a symbolic price of CSK 1,000 (i.e. 1/4 of an average monthly wage in 1991) the right to take part in a process in which individuals used their money tokens (so called investment points) either to directly purchase shares of privatized companies or to commission some of the privatisation investment funds (hereafter PIF) founded for this purpose to do so on their behalf.[61]

There were altogether five rounds of voucher privatisation. The individual investors were to receive their shares after the completion of the first wave (more precisely, it was just a transfer of ownership rights because the shares existed in the book-entry form only). The investors who invested their points in various PIFs became PIF shareholders.

There were 8.54 million individual bidders -5.95 million in the CR and 2.59 million in the SR (approximately 82 per cent inhabitants in the CR and 76 per cent in the SR over 18 years of age). In both Republics, the interest of the public in voucher privatisation exceeded all expectations, mostly due to the aggressive promotion campaign of some PIFs (their number finally reached 438).[62] In the pre-run, the individual investors in the CR entrusted 72 per cent of their investment points to the PIFs, in the SR it was 70 per cent.

The size of property offered for privatisation by vouchers matured in several iterations. Since in the CR there were more methods employed (which were time consuming), the problem was to mobilize a sufficient volume of property for the supply side of the voucher privatisation. In the SR, on the other hand, there was a tendency to limit the volume of property reserved for privatisation by vouchers in order to keep balance between the two Republics.[63] The final offer for the first wave of voucher privatisation (including the property of Federal NPF) was 212 million shares of 988 joint stock companies located in the Czech Republic and 87 million shares of 503 joint stock companies based in the Slovak Republic. The book value of the property offered per one registered investment voucher holder was about CSK 35,000, i.e. almost nine times the average monthly wage in Czechoslovakia in 1991.

Voucher privatisation was designed to become a Federal program with identical rules for both Republics. Thus the Czech IVHs were free to invest their points into the shares of Slovak companies or entrust their points into the Slovak PIFs while the Czech PIFs were allowed to bid for the shares of Slovak companies without any limits. Slovak IVHs and PIFs were in a similar situation concerning the Czech assets.

Some Czech politicians had expressed doubts about the desirability of the voucher privatisation as a Federal scheme even before the first round was launched in the middle of May 1992, i.e., when many of the sensitive points between the Czech and Slovak Republic started to emerge. Nevertheless, an argument prevailed that the Federal character of voucher privatisation which establishes property links between the Czech and Slovak citizens could act as a sustaining factor against the growing tendencies of disintegration.

Soon after the parliamentary elections in June 1992 it became clear that the voucher privatisation would result in major property transfers between the two Republics but would play no role in preventing the Federation from breaking up. At that moment it was impossible, however, to make any changes in the privatisation plans and therefore the government agencies started analyzing possible compensation for the potential asymmetrical transfer of property between the Republics.

Table 2.11
Transfers of shares between Republics

	Joint stock companies		
	in the CR	in the SR	Total
Total sold	198.00	79.72	277.72
IVHs directly	66.97	34.78	101.75
Czech IVHs	63.17	0.70	63.87
Slovak IVHs	3.80	34.08	37.88
IVHs through PIFs	131.03	44.94	175.97
Czech IVHs	108.55	5.71	114.26
Slovak IVHs	22.48	39.23	61.71
Total IVHs	198.00	79.72	277.72
Czech IVHs	171.72	6.41	178.13
Slovak IVHs	26.28	73.31	99.59
PIFs total	131.03	44.94	175.97
Czech PIFs	112.55	5.30	117.85
Slovak PIFs	18.48	39.64	58.12

Note: In billion of CSK
Source: Klvacova (1993)

As indicated in Table 2.11, the investors from the SR made successful bids for property in the CR of a total book value of CSK 20 billion more than the Czech investors in the Slovak Republic. Approximately 85 per cent of this difference was due to the Slovak and Czech investment funds bids. The Slovak IVHs entrusted 10 per cent of their investment points to the Czech

PIFs while the Czech IVHs were less interested in the Slovak PIFs entrusting in them only 1 per cent of investment points.

The final settlement of the first wave of voucher privatisation was effected right after the break-up of Czechoslovakia. There was also a period of discussion over unresolved property claims. The Czech government required compensation for the net balance of the inter-Republic transfers of property. It relied upon the 'gentlemen's agreement' between the representatives of the Czech and Slovak Ministries of Privatisation from July 1992. This agreement guarantied mutual compensation for the difference in case of the break-up of Czechoslovakia. The Slovak government, however, did not feel bound by such an oral agreement. The dispute reached its peak when the Czech Government decided to temporarily freeze the process of issuing shares to Slovak investors (according to the original schedule it was to take place by 29 March 1993). On the other hand, the shares of Slovak companies were handed over to their Czech and Slovak owners on time.

The Czech government decision proved to be counterproductive in several ways. Due to certain technical complications, the discontinuation of the process of issuing shares to the Slovak bidders was followed by a temporary break in the process of issuing shares to the shareholders in the Czech Republic as well. Thus the privatisation process in the Czech Republic was suspended for some time because the first shareholders' meetings could take place only after the shares were handed over to new owners. Particularly the Czech investment funds called for a prompt release of the shares to be able to execute their shareholders' rights. The Czech government was not able to stand up to the argument that such an approach would undermine the credibility of the privatisation process, since it seemed that the Czech Republic was planning on a kind of expropriation of Slovak citizens' property.

Such situation was unsustainable and therefore on 13 May 1993, the Czech Government decided to change its approach and announced that it would start distribution shares to the citizens of both Republics on 24 May 1993. The mutual compensation for the property transfer (from the first wave of voucher privatisation) between the Republics was postponed, to be solved within the larger-scale group of unsettled problems which resulted from the break-up of Czechoslovakia.

4.4 Conclusion

The privatisation process as it was effected in Czechoslovakia can be evaluated from many points of view. Logistically, it proved that it was possible to realize a uniform privatisation concept on a Federal level together with its discretionary implementation on the Republic levels. Thanks to its uniform nature, the process of privatisation in both Republics was very similar and was effected following the same time schedule. On the other hand, the individual responsibilities enjoyed by the national authorities in the field of choosing individual privatisation methods led to some competitiveness among the participating government bodies. The privatisation process results did not substantially reflect the differences in opinion of the political representations of the Republics. It was the break-up of the Federation which brought about a considerably different pace of privatisation in the two newly founded Republics.

Notes

1. This phenomenon explains the attempts of federal states to avoid duality (e.g. Belgium, where the capital enjoys an independent status and therefore acts as the third party).
2. The founders of the Federation must have recognized that as well, since a decision was made to pass, together with the Act on Federation, a constitutional Act on Nationalities.
3. The proclamatory character of this Act was removed as late as in 1991 when the National Assembly adopted a constitutional Act on Referendum. Article I of this act designated a referendum as the only possible way of deciding to terminate the Federation. The referendum was to be open to all citizens who had a right to vote for representatives of the National Councils. The referendum was to be announced by the President of the Federation within 15 days after receiving a proposal for it. It was to take place within 90 days after the day the President received the proposal. The Federation was to be terminated within one year after the announcement of the results of the referendum in case it was approved by an absolute majority of the voters. In case the majority was not acquired, the referendum could be repeated in 5 years at the earliest.
4. In 1990-92, the Peoples' Assembly and the Assembly of Nations votes often differed and the settlement process was applied. The activities of the National Assembly were, however, never discontinued.
5. The first official statements of separating Czech interests from Czechoslovak ones were formulated as late as mid-1992.
6. These proposals were necessitated by drafting of a new Federal Constitution and Constitutions of both Republics as was envisaged by the constitutional Act on the Czechoslovak Federation of 1968.
7. This position was typical especially for the representatives of the right-wing parties. The idea of a confederation, or a union, was acceptable to some social democrats and other politicians in the centre of the political spectrum.

8. By eliminating a sentence which did not allow the adoption of national constitutions without a Federal one, the lawmakers formally opened space for the constitutional initiatives of the Republics. The Slovak National Council used this opportunity to declare the Constitution of the Slovak Republic in 1992, which was at odds with Federal rules and regulations.
9. At the turn of 1991 and 1992, almost two million people signed a petition 'For a Common State'. However, it remained a mere gesture and, after the elections, many of its promoters left the pro-Federation camp and became open advocates of the idea of a break-up. The Slovak support of the petition was minimal.
10. Unlike the Slovak constitution, the Czech one was prepared from 1990-92 on the principle of preserving the Federation. A Commission to draft the Constitution of the Czech Republic as an independent state was established as late as in summer 1992 (it worked under considerable time-pressure and often using the old pro-Federal draft). The opinions of the government and the opposition on the articles of the constitution often differed. The resulting compromise was based on preserving the Bill of Fundamental Rights and Freedoms in its old Federal form as an amendment to the Constitution, and on accepting the concept of a two-chamber Parliament consisting of an Assembly and a Senate. Other disputes, such as the institution of the referendum and finalization of the administrative set-up, were postponed to be solved by passing future constitutional acts. The general determination of the MPs to start the existence of the Czech Republic with a new constitution finally contributed to its relatively smooth adoption.
11. The leading political representatives of both Republics agreed to effect the break-up without a referendum (a constitutional Act called for a referendum in the case of one subject terminating the Federation, not in the case of its break-up) although many people and the opposition argued that the final and legitimate decision should be made by a public vote. The pro-referendum forces, however, could not secure a referendum soon enough (e.g., it was realistic to expect a long-lasting debate concerning the question to be asked by the referendum, etc.) and were not able to guarantee that, in the case of the majority of the public voting against the break-up, the situation in the Federation would not become even more chaotic.
12. One of the consequences of establishing the Federation in 1968 was a double citizenship (i.e. of the Federation and of Republics). Every Czechoslovak citizen born after 1 January 1969 also became, upon his or her birth in one of the Republics, a citizen of that Republic. Babies born abroad became citizens of the Republic their parents were residents of. Citizens of both Republics were allowed to opt for citizenship in the other Republic, i.e., before 31 December 1969 to decide for citizenship in the other Republic than in which they were born. Dual Czech and Slovak citizenship was not allowed.
13. An amendment to the Act on Citizenship allowed Slovak citizens over 60 years of age residing in the Czech Republic to maintain their Slovak citizenship along with the Czech one they opted for.
14. IVVM survey of October/November 1994, *Rude Pravo,* 25 November 1994

15. Quotation from: The Founding of States; special issue of *Today's Problems of Slovakia after the Break-up of Czechoslovakia*, Brno 1994
16. The Czech and Slovak Republics, *Economic Surveys*, OECD, Paris, 1994, page 10-11
17. Although the economies of the CR and the SR were for many years statistically monitored as separate territories, until the end of 1992 they were just two regions of one country. Most of the macroeconomic figures therefore exist for the Czechoslovak economy only.
18. The process of replacing the old statistical system of macroeconomic indicators by a system based on national accounts had not been completed before the break-up of Czechoslovakia and, for 1992, there were no old-style figures for Czechoslovakia gathered and published. Collection of macroeconomic indicators based on the national accounts therefore fell into the hands of the Czech and Slovak Statistical Offices where the process of collecting the data was not uniform.
19. The Czechoslovak State Bank estimated that there were about 350,000 excess employees (data for 1992). The output decrease did not come hand in hand with a decrease in the employment base partly as a result of a 'wage solidarity', characterized by keeping wages low in order to secure more job opportunities, and partly as an attempt to keep good workers despite the depression. Given the low level of wages, this behaviour did not cost the businesses much.
20. The Independent Association of Slovak Economists on the Reform and Economic Independence of Slovakia, *Hospodarske Noviny*, 19 March 1991
21. Strategies for Further Development of the Economic Reform, *Hospodarske noviny*, 19 March 1991
22. See Čapek (1992)
23. Strategy of the Economic Development of Slovakia, Economic Institute of the Slovak Academy of Science 1990 (VP No. 81)
24. The Czech and Slovak Republics 1994, *Economic Surveys*,OECD
25. The Czech and Slovak Republics 1994, *Economic Surveys*, OECD
26. For example, in 1991 Czechoslovakia was criticized by the US and other western countries for exporting tanks to Syria.
27. Gabrielová, H.: Companies in the Second Year of the Transformation Process, *Economic Magazine*, no. 5, 1993
28. E.g., the so called 'backwash effects' (according to Myrdale) of the more developed and dynamic regions attracting capital or economic activities away from the weaker regions prevail over the so called 'spread effects' of the developing regions supporting the weaker ones by expanding markets and diffusing technology.
29. Regional policies are based on a regionally differentiated application of policy measures - of differentiated taxes or subsidies, or particular programmes to support depressed regions. Thus it can influence the performance of selected regions and the distribution of economic activities within particular areas.
30. The situation in 1992 when the total of CSK 3.3 billion from the Federal budget for the regional and national policy support was used only in Slovakia

can serve as an example (CSK 1.3 billion were spent on agriculture, CSK 2 billion for education and culture). The allocation of these resources followed the rules of the Ministry of Finance of the Slovak Republic only.

31. Report on the economic situation in Czechoslovakia and on the economic policy of the Federal government, *Hospodarske noviny*, 11 April 1991
32. The Slovak authorities allowed the compensation for a job loss to run parallel with unemployment benefits for a period of five months up to 160 per cent of the individual salaries. An income of up to CSK 800 (compared to CSK 400 in the CR) was permitted without losing unemployment benefits.
33. On 1 January 1990 the so called monobank system was replaced by a two-tier system which served as the basis for separation from the Czechoslovak State Bank of three successor commercial banks.
34. The proposal of the Slovak party revitalized a project from 1968 which considered a foundation of a network of three reserve banks (two Republic banks and one Federal bank) which was finally not realized, for the so called normalization process after 1968 did not support such an activity. The 1989 discussion therefore could not build on any experience from a coexistence of three reserve banks in the Czechoslovak environment.
35. See Approaches to the legislative amendments in the fields of currency and banking, Czechoslovak State Bank, main SR branch, June 1990.
36. The Slovak political representation revived the idea of three reserve banks again in Autumn 1991 when the Czech and Slovak governments negotiated the draft of the Act on the Czechoslovak State Bank. Had the Slovak proposal been accepted at that moment, the discussion would have gone back to that of a year before, when the so called Competence Act was negotiated. The main Slovak office of the Czechoslovak State Bank was the main initiator of these discussions. See Conclusions of the Committee of Economic Experts, October 1991.
37. This act, together with the Act on Banks were approved by the Federal Assembly on 20 December 1991 and took effect on 1 February 1992.
38. Slovak government program declaration adopted on 14 July 1992.
39. Development on the market of T-bills in the last months of 1992 served as an example of a disciplinary role of the financial market which can control the scope of deficit financing of one of the governments of a larger economic unit. While the emission of the Federal and Czech T-bills was smooth, there were problems with issuing the Slovak ones (despite the relatively higher interest of 15-16 per cent as compared with 9-10 per cent in the CR).
40. Czech government program declaration
41. The Czechoslovak budgetary system consisted, from the beginning of the 1970s on, of the Federal budget, two Republic budgets, a system of local budgets and of Republic government funds (in the Czechoslovak methodology these were extrabudgetary). The Federation and Republic budgets were considered government budgets. All three budget levels together represented the system of so called public budgets.

42. In 1990, the turnover tax rates were unified and the former 1,500 different rates were reduced to four (0, 12, 22 and 32 per cent).
43. The term fiscal federalism relates to the public sector with two or more decision-making levels (regardless of the constitutional set-up). It solves issues within the vertical structure of the public sector and solves problems arising in fiscal relations on different government levels or on the same levels.
44. This principle was adopted in 1969-70 when the Republic budgets transferred selected tax revenues to the Federal budget.
45. This attitude was reflected in the demands of the Slovak representation for concluding an agreement between the CR and the SR to delineate the extent of the Federal activities and therefore the volume of the Federal budget expenditures.
46. The total balance of the state budget accounts was not to be overdrafted and a short-term loan could adopt a form of purchase of short-term bills only. There was a limit of 5 per cent of the previous year's income of the given budget.
47. See Draft Federation final account for 1992 (for the Czech National Council)
48. The difference in 1989 and 1990 between the Federal budgets revenues in both domestic and IMF methodologies can be explained by the different monitoring of the turnover tax revenues (net in the former and gross in the latter).
49. E.g. in 1988 the given ratio reached (after adding the intergovernmental subsidies) 59.1 per cent in Germany, 70.5 per cent in Austria; in 1984 in Switzerland it was 43.7 per cent and in the USA in 1983 it was 60 per cent. See *Economic Surveys*, OECD (1991).
50. E.g. the Slovak proposal to divide the revenues from the transit pipeline according to the length of the line in the territories of the Republics. Slovak representation also demanded a change in gasoline taxes (instead of collecting based on the country of consumption to collect based on the country of production, for most of the gasoline produced in the SR was used in the CR).
51. The founder Ministries acted as intermediaries for the privatisation projects and took responsibility for the preparation and control of a given privatisation project, and for submitting it to the Ministry in due time. In some cases the Ministries not only supervised but also authored privatisation projects.
52. Since there were only a few such cases, it was not necessary to establish a Federal Ministry of Privatisation.
53. Nevertheless, the NPFs did not have enough staff to exercise corporate governance in an efficient way. The very concept of rapid privatisation already planned their early discontinuation.
54. This Fund terminated its activities after the break-up of the Federation. Its assets had been divided between the Republic NPFs following the 2:1 ratio.
55. The Constitutional Court of the Czech Republic ruling from 12 July 1994 abolished the permanent residence condition for it was in compliance with neither the Czech Constitution nor the Human Rights and Freedoms Charter.
56. Total value of the written-off credits was 22.2 billion in the Czech Republic and 11.2 billion in the Slovak Republic. The liabilities from the issued bonds

were honoured from the Funds' privatisation revenues and this part of the debt was redeemed before the original maturity of the bonds.

57. For this second purpose the banks of the Czech Republic kept CSK 7.8 billion and the banks of the Slovak Republic CSK 8.8 billion.

58. In the command economy, the permanently revolving inventory credits, representing approximately 1/5 of all company credits, were used to finance inventory and current business expenses. They were characterized by a long-term maturity and low interest rate (initially 3 per cent, since 1986 6 per cent). With the general interest rates increase these credits with a newly introduced 13 per cent interest rate became extremely risky for the creditor banks.

59. Later on, the Consolidation Bank extended their activities to purchases of risky company debts from the commercial banks for approximately 60-80 per cent of their nominal value.

60. Selection of companies for the two waves was rather pragmatic. To be selected for the first wave it was necessary to present the privatisation project on time, limit the number of problems concerning its implementation and show the attractiveness of the company for the bidders in voucher privatisation. Most of the more troublesome companies were left to be privatized in the second wave.

61. Voucher privatisation was organized in privatisation rounds. In the so called pre-round the Investment Vouchers Holders (hereafter IVH) could (but did not have to) invest all their points or just some of them in PIFs, which then acted as investors of the entrusted points. The pre-round was followed by regular privatisation rounds, each of them lasting approximately 4-5 weeks and consisting of four phases:

i) Announcement of the price of shares of individual joint-stock companies in terms of the number of investment points per one share. The first round started with one uniform price (3 shares per 100 points), for the following rounds the prices were adjusted in accordance with excess supply and demand. The prices were set by a price committee, nominated by the Federal Minister of Finance.

ii) Submitting of bids by the IVHs and the PIFs.

iii) Transfer of bids to the Centre of Voucher Privatisation (CVP). In case the demand was higher than supply and this problem could not be settled by truncating the number of PIF bids, all bids for the particular set of shares were scratched and investment points were returned to the investors to be used in the next round. In case the supply was higher than the demand, the bids were successful and the individual investors were informed about it by the CVP after the round had been completed.

iv) Announcing of the privatisation round results (i.e. release of the results to press and distribution of the individual investors' statements).

62. The strategies of the PIFs for recruiting individual IVHs were different, with some promising to pay out as much as tenfold of the original price of the voucher book to the investors one year after the shares were advanced to their fund, others organized voucher books lottery or provided loans guaranteed by the shares.

63. The national Ministries of Privatisation (or the Federal Ministry of Finance) were responsible for the supply side of the voucher privatisation. These institutions approved the property of companies reserved for voucher privatisation (on the basis of the privatisation projects submitted by the founders of the companies). Corresponding amount of shares was then transferred to the national Funds of National Property (or the Federal Fund) for future distribution to the new shareholders. The demand side of the voucher privatisation including the distribution of the shares was organized by the Federal Ministry of Finance or by its centre for Voucher Privatisation as an agency established just for this reason. These institutions were responsible for the logistics, i. e. printing of the voucher books, stamps, information leaflets, setting up the computer network, setting up the registration points, etc.

Part Three
FIELDS OF COOPERATION BETWEEN THE SUCCESSOR REPUBLICS OF CZECHOSLOVAKIA

1 The division of federal property between successor Republics

1.1 The delineation of common property

After a political agreement of the representatives of both Republics to split the country was reached, less than six months were left to clarify the conditions of a peaceful dissolution and to endorse the framework for such a dissolution. During the long-term coexistence of the Czechs and the Slovaks, the form of this coexistence changed significantly, including changes in the legal norms regulating the relationship between citizens and state power. The most significant changes were brought about by the far-reaching process of nationalisation and enforced collectivization under the communist regime, and by the expansion of communal forms of economic activity. These processes resulted in a transfer of the decisive majority of private property to the sector referred to as 'socialist'.

In the unitary state, which existed until 1968, this meant that the state became owner and administrator of the enormous volume of assets located in Czechoslovakia. The state exercised its ownership rights through state-owned enterprises and organisations. In 1968 a constitutional Act changed the unitary form of the state to a federation, and this was reflected in the increasing powers and ownership rights vested in the administrations of the two Republics. The strengthening of the powers of the Republics influenced the way the economy was managed and structured, and led to an increase in the number of enterprises managed from the Republic level. This process of changes in the organisational structure and management of the economy continued after the November revolution in 1989, particularly due to the pressure of the Slovak political representation, which aimed at a shift of legislative and executive powers further to the level of the national Republics.

Apart from changes in the powers of the state administration, another factor affecting the development of the organisational structure of the economy was the privatisation process. As a part of its preparation, the internal structure of state-owned enterprises became more transparent. These enterprises broke up into independent units, which were often converted into shareholding companies under the control of the Republic administrations. The problem of splitting the assets of the Federation was thus substantially simplified. Thus, although federally controlled enterprises still existed during the preparation of the split of the Federation, they were fewer in number. The problem was, however, that many of them had organisational units located in the other Republic.

In some industries, there were no federally controlled enterprises or organisations at all (e.g. education, health, culture, commerce, forestry and water management, consumer industries, chemical industry, etc.). In agriculture, the Federal Ministry of Agriculture existed until 1992, but in that period it was only responsible for the Czechoslovak Agricultural Academy, the research institutes, the state testing laboratories and the administrative apparatus of the ministry. In the same way, the powers of the former Federal Ministry of Communications (later merged into the Federal Ministry of Transport) decreased.

Federal and Republic powers were intertwined in the field of transport. A logically consistent, territorial organisational structure emerged in the industry as soon as in 1965, when the large state enterprise Czechoslovak Coach Transport, (CSAD - also providing freight transport services) was restructured along regional boundaries and subordinated to the Regional National Committees.

In air transport, the Czechoslovak Airlines (CSA) and Slov-air operated in parallel, and they were included in the Federal Ministry of Transport, together with air traffic control and the aviation inspection. In 1992, CSA changed into Czech Airlines and was transferred under the control of Republic bodies together with Slov-air. Air traffic control and aviation inspection remained under federal administration.

Railway transport services were provided by a complex state organisation controlled by the Federal Ministry of Transport, the Czechoslovak State Railways. The same ministry was responsible for the supervision of state organisations providing water transport services, and for all seafaring ships and other property in their respective home ports.

Another part of the property to be divided consisted in the tangible and intangible assets and liabilities of the federal administration itself, including the three federal state funds. In 1992, the number of federal bodies decreased significantly, so that the last federal government consisted only of 10 ministers, including the prime minister. Nevertheless, the assets and liabilities of the federal administration still remained large in the time of the division.

Extensive wealth was administered particularly by the Federal Ministry of Defence, while the Federal Ministry of the Interior only administered some of the special security departments (e.g. the Security Information Service). The policing of public law and order was carried out by the formations of the Republic Ministries of the Interior, financed through the Republic budgets. Other federal administrative bodies included the Federal Ministry of the Economy, the Federal Ministry of Foreign Affairs and the Federal Ministry of Foreign Trade (these ministries both managed a part of the federal assets abroad), the Federal Ministry for Supervision, the Federal Ministry of Labour and Social Affairs, the Federal Ministry of Finance (in charge of state financial assets and liabilities, both domestic and foreign) and the Federal Ministry of Transport and Communications.[1] Apart from these institutions, federal administration was extended to the Czechoslovak State Bank, the Federal Statistical Office, the Attorney General's Office, the Supreme Court, the Office of the President, the Office of the Federal Assembly, the Government Office of CSFR, and some other offices and public agencies.

It cannot be omitted that the powers of the federal administration extended to numerous research institutes, with some of these owning subsidiaries (of a federal nature) in cities of the other Republic. The Czechoslovak Academy of Sciences was also a federally administered body, and it was financed - analogously with the financing of the Slovak Academy of Sciences - by the state budget of the Czech Republic.

Another element of the property to divide consisted in real estate abroad (such as buildings and equipment used by the Federal Ministries of Foreign Affairs and Foreign Trade) and in the state financial assets and liabilities of the CSFR. Significant items among these resulted from:

- government loans borrowed abroad and lent abroad;
- ownership stakes of the CSFR in foreign monetary and financial institutions;
- international agreements about the participation of the CSFR in certain investment projects abroad, such as the Krivoj Rog combine in the Ukraine;
- the ownership share of CSFR in the property of the former CMEA.

The delineation of these assets and liabilities was made more difficult by the fact that some of them were expressed in convertible currencies and some in nonconvertible currencies.

This brief outline of the main items of the property of the Federation which was to be divided between the Czech and Slovak Republics does not aim to be an exhaustive list of all property subject to division: it merely illustrates the diversity of property forms, and the complexity of the problem. For this reason, the legislative norms addressing this issue could be drafted in general terms only. They were expected to be made more specific in subsequent agreements between the governments of the two Republics.

1.2 The legal framework regulating the division of property

The property subject to division

The constitutional act about the break-up of Czechoslovakia, passed by the Federal Assembly, provided the legislative framework for the dissolution of the Federation, and defined how federal powers would be transferred to the two successor Republics. Another constitutional act then dealt with the delineation of CSFR property, and its division between the CR and the SR. This Act stipulated that the following items were to be considered for the purposes of division:

- tangible and intangible objects in the ownership of the Federation;
- state financial assets and liabilities of the Federation;
- monetary assets, liabilities and reserves of the Federation;
- other ownership claims and obligations belonging to the Federation and federal state organisations.

With regard to the break-up of the CSFR as of 31 December 1992, an agreement was reached between the CR and the SR to adopt this Act into the legal systems of the successor Republics. This ensured the validity of the legislative treatment of the division of property even after the break-up of the Federation.

The method of division of property

Apart from the delineation and definition of common property, a suitable approach to its division also had to be found. In the short time left until the split, it was soon clear that if various proposals for complicated methods of division were to be accepted (such as criteria considering the contribution of the respective Republics to the property, asset quality, market price of the property, functional characteristics), the process of division would inevitably cause numerous disputes. Such quarrels would threaten the short deadline for the division of property, and could bring in emotional attitudes. The selection of the simplest possible method of division, utilizing the experience gathered during the separation of the property of the Republics from Federation property, was seen as the only feasible option.

On the other hand, simple rules cannot avoid cases of unfairness. Thus, both parties had to exercise a degree of benevolence when confronted with such cases, and they had to realise that only some of these injustices could be compensated financially or in kind.

On the basis of the above consensus, the Act stipulated the two basic principles of the division of federal property:

a) The territorial principle, which meant that property would be transferred to the successor state on whose territory it was located. The principle was to be applied to real estate situated on the territory of the Czech Republic and Slovak Republic, for tangible objects it was to be applied in cases where these objects were accessories of immovable assets, due to their designation, utilisation, or nature.

b) The principle of the ratio of the respective populations of the CR and the SR, which meant that property was transferred to the Czech and Slovak Republic in the ratio of two to one. This principle was also applied in all cases where the previously mentioned territorial principle could not be used.

In order to enable normal utilisation of the divided property, a particular agreement did not have to be governed by a strict application of the two basic principles, and the Act did not preclude reasonable adaptation of the principles to the nature of individual cases. Apparent cases of unfairness resulting from the division could be solved by compensation in kind or by financial settlement. The Act also stipulated the guidelines for the application of the said principles to the main types of property.

Individual agreements pertaining to the division of property were concluded between the governments of the two Republics and between their appointed ministers. Other agreements were signed by plenipotentiaries of the governments of the two Republics, by the appointees of their sectoral ministers, and by other statutory representatives of official institutions of the CR and the SR.

The Act provided other important rules applicable to the division of property, such as the duration of the transfer of the divided property to the Czech or Slovak Republics. The day of the transfer of property was deemed to be the day of signature of the agreement pertaining to the given asset, or, in case such agreement was not signed, the day of the break-up of the Federation. A special Commission for the Final Settlement was formed which consisted of an equal number of representatives of both Republics appointed by their respective governments. Its major task was to complete the process of dividing federal property. Eventual disputes arising from the division of the property were to be settled by arbitration, and the finding of the body responsible for arbitration was to be binding for both Republics.

1.3 Selected examples of the division of important types of property

The division of the army

The territorial stationing of the army of the CSFR corresponded to the military doctrine of the former Warsaw Pact, and was therefore uneven, displaying a significant excess of personnel and weaponry on the territory of the CR. The governments of the CR and the SR were aware of this fact and they agreed on the overall valuation of military property and on the general principles governing its division as soon as in 1992. These principles were based on the Constitutional Act mentioned above and also considered the obligations accepted in international agreements on the reduction of the levels of military personnel and conventional weapons.

The ceiling of the number of military personnel was laid down in the agreement concluded in Helsinki in June 1992, which had been signed by 30 states including the CSFR. The limit of the CSFR was divided between the CR and the SR in the ratio of 2:1. It was agreed that during 1992, relocation of military personnel of Slovak nationality from Czech territory and a similar transfer of military personnel of Czech nationality from Slovakia would be taking place. Military personnel had the option of choosing the Republic in which they wished to continue their military careers, on condition that they accept the citizenship of the country in which they would be active. The real development of the level of military personnel was to be determined later, by the strategic doctrines of the two new armies of the CR and the SR.

The upper limits of the main systems of conventional weapons had been laid down in the Agreement on Armed Forces in Europe, concluded in November 1990 in Paris and further specified by the subsequent Vienna protocols on the limitation of conventional weapons. The Agreement and the protocols were signed by 22 states from the military formations of NATO and the Warsaw Treaty including the CSFR. The conditions laid down in these documents were to be met in the period from June 1992 to July 1995, when the armies of the signatory states were supposed to fall within the limits on their weaponry as laid down in the said agreements.

The limits on the main weapons systems, defined for the CSFR, were redefined for the CR and the SR in accordance with the Constitutional Act in the ratio of two to one, and thus assumed the values in Table 3.1.

The movable and immovable assets in the ownership of the Federal Ministry of Defence were valued at CSK 400 billion and the agreement between the CR and the SR governments applied both principles laid down in the Act to their division. The appropriate share of the SR in the movable assets (one third) was reached during November and December 1992 by transports involving the use of approximately 10,000 vehicles.

The immovable assets, acquired during the existence of the common state, were divided according to the territorial principle. At the time of the division of the army, a larger number of airports, service installations, barracks and other military buildings was located on the territory of the CR, while the majority of military training centres were located in the SR. The agreement therefore laid down the possibility of temporary joint use of certain facilities, or a compensation by transferring a part of the facilities to the other Republic. Accordingly, soldiers of the Czech army could finish the school year in military training centres of the SR (and vice versa).

Table 3.1
The division of limits on personnel and conventional weaponry

	CSFR	CR	SR
Military personnel	140,000	94,000	46,000
Tanks	1,435	957	478
Combat vehicles	3,583	2,388	1,195
Guns (from 100 mm)	1,150	766	384
Fighter planes	345	230	115
Combat helicopters	75	50	25

Source: *Osterr. Milit. Zeitsschrift,* Heft 3, 1993

The CR and SR governments also agreed that they would independently prepare their own concepts of reorganisation of their respective new armies, honouring their obligations regarding the limits on levels of military personnel and conventional weapons, and that they would liquidate surplus weaponry (including large stocks of non-usable ammunition).[2]

The division of the CSFR army between the CR and the SR represented a very complex technical and economic problem. Its solution involved both the application of the general principles of the division of property, and adherence to the obligations of the CSFR laid down in international agreements (which were accepted by both successor governments). These agreements stipulated demanding parameters of the further development of the two independent armies, at the same time, however, simplifying the problem of division of conventional weapons, as the surplus levels of equipment (with the exeption of aircraft and helicopters) led both Republics to focus on the liquidation of these superfluous stocks of weaponry.

The settlement of the property of state enterprises and organisations

i) The settlement of the property of subsidiary units of state enterprises on the territory of the other Republic. As has already been discussed, state enterprises founded by the state administration of one of the Republics could have one or more organisational units located on the territory of the other

Republic. The division of such property was governed by the territorial principle.

In the intergovernmental agreement between the CR and the SR the signatories agreed on the following:

- the parties would exchange inventories of property located in the other Republic within one month after the signature of this Agreement. These inventories were subject to the endorsement of the signatory governments, and the governments also specified the part of the respective state administration which would receive the given asset;

- the founders of the relevant state enterprises would hand over the assets specified in the endorsed inventories, in less than two months after the inventories had been endorsed by the governments of the Czech Republic and Slovak Republic;

- they would not allow transfers of assets listed in the inventories to other persons;

- the relevant authorities would not make decisions about the winding up of an enterprise, or its liquidation, if the enterprise possessed rights of disposition with property listed in the inventories (unless the signatories agree differently).

A written record of the handover and acceptance of property resulting from this agreement was to be prepared, and was to be signed by the statutory representatives of the state administration of both Republics and of the enterprises which had rights of disposition pertaining to the given asset. An inventory of the property handed over was a part of the written record.

The brief outline of this agreement shows how the territorial principle was applied generally during the division of this type of property. This property, understandably, no longer included privatised property, property of commercial banks, and other non-state property.[3]

ii) The Czechoslovak State Railways. An agreement regarding the division of property of the state owned Czechoslovak State Railways was signed by the plenipotentiaries of the two governments in December, 1992. The annex to the agreement contained an inventory of property. The inventory was updated in an Appendix to the agreement, signed on 31 December 1992. The property was listed in the agreement under 16 subheadings, corresponding to 16 organisational units, which had been managing the given assets at the time of the division. The property was grouped thus: immovable assets, movable assets making up an indivisible entity with immovable assets, other movable assets, and ownership claims and obligations. For all the 16 organisational units, the property was grouped into one of these four categories, and for each of them, the principle of their division was determined (the territorial, or the two-to-one principle).

The agreement further specified the revenues received and outlays incurred in the given period, and provided a final settlement of membership contributions to international organisations and of the obligations resulting from investment projects up until 31 December 1992. A protocol pertaining to the division of property has been prepared and signed.

iii) Air Traffic Control. The representatives of the Ministries of Transport of the CR and the SR agreed that the territorial principle of division would pertain to immovable property, or movable property making up a functional entity with the immovable asset.[4] This principle also applied to the division of the claims and obligations of the institution, while financial assets, deposits and securities were divided according to the two-to-one principle. Compensation for property, which could not be divided due to its function, was to take place through the free provision of services, up to the value of the compensation. As the inventory of property was compiled as of the 31 October 1992, the agreement contained a clause stipulating that the protocol would be updated by the differences accruing in the period from 1 November to 31 December 1992.

The division of the property of the Federal administration

Agreements regarding the division of such property were negotiated by the appointed authorities of the Federal and Republic administrations. Immovable assets were divided according to the territorial principle, and movable assets which did not make up an undivisible entity with the immovable asset were divided in the ratio of two to one, after deductions were made for the assets of the subsidiaries of federal research institutes in the cities of the other Republic. In the cases of such research institutes, the division of movable assets was carried out by the physical transportation of certain assets, such as information technology, books, cars etc. The same method of final settlement was applied to the division of movable assets of the Federal administrative offices and authorities.

The final share of the SR in the movable assets of the former central authorities, as agreed upon by the Commission for the Final Settlement, was CSK 630.1 million. This amount did not include the property of the SR arising from the division of the three federal funds: first, the Federal Fund of National Property (the share of the SR, as endorsed, was CSK 3.53 billion, out of the total of CSK 10.59 billion); second, the Federal Fund of Market Regulation in Agriculture (valued at CSK 674.56 million as of 31 December 1992, and divided in the ratio of two to one); third, the Fund of State Material Reserves and the reserves for the case of mobilisation (value endorsed by the

Commission at the level of CSK 2.78 billion). The Commission also agreed that the claims of the SR arising from the division of the above first and third fund would be used to offset the claim of the Czech National Bank against the National Bank of Slovakia.

Other state funds had been administered by the Republics, and therefore were not subject to division. In the CR, such funds included the State Fund for the Environment, the State Fund for the Fertilization of Soil, and the State Fund for the Support and Development of Czech Cinematography. In the SR, these funds included the State Fund for the Environment, the State Fund for the Protection and Improvement of Arable Land, the State Fund for the Development of Forests, the State Water Management Fund, the State Fund for Culture, and the State Fund of Market Regulation.

The final settlement of issues arising from the participation of the CSFR in investment projects abroad

i) The transit system of gas pipelines. Claims and obligations resulting from the intergovernmental agreement on a joint gas exploitation project (the Gas Combine), concluded between the governments of the former CSFR and the former USSR on 16 December 1985, were settled by a separate agreement between the governments of the CR and the SR. This was followed up by an agreement between the Ministers of Finance of the CR and the SR, which specified the division of claims of the CSFR, arising from activities related to the Gas Combine project, and provided for the co-financing of the completion of the project after 1 January 1993.

The two documents reflect the complexity of the problem solved, and therefore they are only briefly summarised here:

- The Government of the CR agreed to transfer all assets of the state-owned Czech Gas Enterprise Praha, which were located on the territory of the SR, to the Slovak Gas Enterprise Bratislava. The property of this Czech enterprise, which was located in the Ukraine or in Russia, was to be divided in the ratio of one to one. The Czech government agreed to carry out all related transfers of rights, obligations and claims in a manner that would not interfere with the operations of the transit pipeline system.

- Both Gas Enterprises of the SR and the CR agreed to sign a contract specifying a system of accounting for all operations carried out, and the related costs and profits. The contract would also identify the respective contributions of the two enterprises to the state budgets of the Republics. The temporary regime of invoicing for natural gas transport services in freely convertible currencies was to remain in effect until the border crossing installation of the pipeline started to operate.

- Existing contracts would be divided after agreement with the foreign contracting parties.

- The revenues from gas transport services through the territory of both Republics would be divided according to the territorial principle, and a separate agreement between the two Finance ministries would pertain to the division of returns to investments undertaken after 1 January 1993.

- The two said enteprises of the CR and the SR were to ensure an interim regime of operations of the pipeline, utilising its main control centre. The governments of both Republics were to prepare the hardware aspect of the division of the Czech and Slovak parts of the pipeline, by building a metering installation on the border. The transitory regime of operations was to terminate by 30 June 1994. The agreement included commitments regarding the volumes of supply by the Slovak side to the CR, a timetable for the transfer of assets, claims and obligations, and procedures for the solution of disputes. The annexes to the Agreement determined the shares of both Republics in the repayment of funds provided from federal sources to finance the gas transfer project. The Agreement also summarised the division of revenues from the transfer of gas through the territory of the CR, and the level of transit revenues, charged for the transfer of gas through the territory of the SR to the CR.

ii) Participation in the construction of the Krivoj Rog mining and processing combine in the Ukraine. The agreement between the governments of the CR and the SR provided for the transfer of claims and obligations of the former CSFR, arising from multilateral and bilateral agreements associated with the construction of the Krivoj Rog Combine in the years 1983 to 1992. The succession of the Czechoslovak participation in the project was accepted by the SR, and the appointed authorities agreed upon the necessary changes in existing contracts with foreign partners. The liabilities of the Federation resulting from the project against the Investicni Banka were settled from the budgets of the two Republics in the ratio of 2 to 1.[5]

The settlement of state financial assets and liabilities of the CSFR

i) The transfer of stakes of the CSFR in international monetary and financial institutions. The governments of the CR and the SR signed an agreement on the division of the assets and liabilities of the CSFR against the International Monetary Fund (IMF), and against other international institutions, i.e. the International Bank for Reconstruction and Development (IBRD), the International Bank for Economic Cooperation (IBEC), the European Bank for Reconstruction and Development (EBRD), the European

Investment Bank (EIB), the International Finance Corporation (IFC), the International Development Association (IDA), and the Multilateral Agency for Investment Guarantees (MIGA). The Agreement specified the contributions and liabilities of these institutions (in convertible and national currencies), and provided for the division:

- of assets and liabilities with the IMF in the ratio of 2.29 to 1 (in accordance with the IMF proposal);
- of the membership shares in the IBRD in the ratio of 2 to 1;
- of deposits and liabilities vis-a-vis other institutions in the ratio of 2:1.

ii) The division of foreign loans accepted by the CSFR government to support the balance of payments.

Table 3.2
Loans received by the CSFR

	Foreign currency (thousand)	*Equivalent in thousand of CSK*	*Of that divided in the ratio of 2:1*	
			CR	SR
The EU	ECU 375,000	13,092,000	8,728,000	4,364,000
Japan	USD 200,000	5,982,541	3,988,361	1,994,180
Austria	ATS 500,000	1,272,000	848,000	424,000
Switzerland	USD 40,000	1,155,960	770,640	385,320
Sweden	USD 25,000	722,475	481,650	240,825
Norway	USD 16,000	462,384	308,256	154,128
Finland	USD 15,000	433,485	288,990	144,495
SAL [a)]	USD 330,711	9,414,512	6,276,341	3,138,171

Note: The sums quoted refer to the principal and exclude the interest and other charges. The conversion into CSK was based on the exchange rate as of 31 December 1992.

a) The balance of the third tranche of the SAL loan facility up to the value of USD 450 million will be received by the central banks of the CR and the SR in the ratio of 2:1.

Source: Intergovernmental agreement

The governments of the CR and the SR concluded an arrangement on the division of convertible currency liabilities arising from the loan agreements of the CSFR government. The liabilities consisted of the repayment of the principal, interest and other costs associated with the loans. It was agreed that the successor states would conclude new agreements with the creditors, which would solve the problem of their individual or joint credit guarantees. Should the liability to pay interest arise prior to the conclusion of such agreements, two thirds of the costs would be borne by the Czech National Bank, and one third by the National Bank of Slovakia.

Government loans received for the support of the balance of payments of the CSFR exceeded CSK 32 billion, and were divided in the ratio of 2:1, i.e. approximately CSK 21.6 billion to the CR and CSK 10.8 to the SR (see Table 3.2 for the details).

ii) *The division of receivables arising from loans extended abroad by the CSFR.* The governments of the CR and the SR agreed on the division of claims arising from international loan agreements. The procedure consisted in the division of the nominal value of the claims (separately for each territory) in the ratio of two to one, between the CR and the SR. The Agreement contained provisions for further procedures regarding debtors, collection of debts, the payment of expenses, losses from exchange rate changes, and other provisions. The following table presents a summary of government claims as of 31 December 1993, and their division between the CR and the SR.

Table 3.3
Summary of government claims of the CSFR

	CSFR	CR	SR
Nonmilitary claims in non-convertible currencies	71,645,324	47,763,550	23,881,774
Nonmilitary claims in convertible currencies	25,807,752	17,205,168	8,602,584
Military claims	48,249,166	31,166,111	16,083,055

Note: In thousand of CSK
Source: References in the intergovernmental agreement

iv) Transfer of claims and liabilities of the CSFR resulting from repayable financial grants and from guarantees for domestic bank loans. The agreement between the CR and the SR pertaining to this area was concluded on the level of ministries of finance. It stipulated that all claims of the Federation resulting from financial aid extended are assumed by the Republic in which the debtor is resident. The same principle was applied to claims arising from realised guarantees and to liabilities arising from guarantees extended by the CSFR government.

v) Guarantees of the CSFR government for loans extended by foreign creditors. The division of convertible currency liabilities arising from loan guarantee contracts, concluded with foreign lenders, was the subject of an agreement between the CR and the SR. This agreement settled the liabilities arising from guarantees, securing loans to the following companies: the Czech Energy Company (CEZ), the Czechoslovak Airlines (CSA); and from the guarantee extended to secure a loan to the Czechoslovak Trading Bank (CSOB) (to be further channelled to the Chemoceluloza Zilina, a Slovak cellulose manufacturing company). The liabilities consisted of the repayment of the principal, interest and further charges. The agreement stipulated, that liabilities resulting from guarantees, and securing loans to:

- the CEZ and CSA are transferred to the CR;
- the CSOB (to be channelled to the Chemoceluloza Zilina company) are transferred jointly to the CR and the SR, with the sub-guarantee of the SR.

vi) The Export Guarantee and Insurance Company (EGAP). The EGAP is a company providing insurance against risks associated with the export of goods and services. It was founded in 1992 as a state (federal) joint stock company. The founders were 3 Federal ministries (the Ministry of Finance, the Ministry of the Economy and the Ministry of Foreign Trade) and both Republic Ministries of Finance. These shareholders concluded an Agreement on the Transformation of Federal Property in the EGAP. This property consisted of the ownership stakes of the Federal ministries, resources contributed from the Federal budget to capitalise the insurance funds, and a special Reserve Fund. The allocations for subsidies to exporters, financed from the Federal budget in 1992, were all used up for their designated purpose. According to the annual report, a transformation fund was created to facilitiate the settlement of property rights with Slovakia. Since the beginning of 1993 the EGAP has been a Czech shareholding company.

The division of the balance sheet of the Czechoslovak State Bank

i) The method of the division of assets and liabilities. In accordance with the constitutional act on the division of the Federal property, the Governor of the Czechoslovak State Bank (hereafter SBCS) Josef Tosovsky created a committee for the division of assets and liabilities of the SBCS. The first task of this committee consisted in determining guidelines for the division of all groups of assets and liabilities in the balance sheet of the SBCS, in a manner which would ensure that the assets and liabilities of the closing balance of the SBCS for the year of 1992 are carried over exactly into the two opening balance sheets of the CR and the SR.

Balance sheet items were usually divided in accordance with the two-to-one principle, in some cases (see the next point) they were divided using the territorial principle, and in special cases (such as the liabilities and receivables against the IMF and the division of gold) by special agreement. The final separation of balance sheet items was endorsed in 19 protocols, signed by the representatives of the Czech National Bank (CNB) and the National Bank of Slovakia (NBS). These protocols documented the origin of the items that made up the final claim of the CNB against the NBS. On the basis of the individual protocols, we only discuss the division of some key items:

1. The total gold reserves of the SBCS deposited domestically and abroad represented CSK 6,406 million. Out of this amount, the intergovernmental agreement stipulated that 7,492 tons of gold, valued at CSK 468.6 million, would be allocated for the NBS, which would pay the CNB two thirds of the book value of the gold. The remaining part of the gold was divided in the ratio of 2:1, so that the share of the CNB totalled CSK 3,958 million, and the share of the NBS totalled CSK 2,447 million.

The method of division of gold described above represented a compromise between the standpoints of the two parties, which had disagreed initially. The Slovak side claimed 7.5 tons of gold from the times of the Slovak State, and the Czech side pointed out the vagueness of the newly introduced principle of the origin of the property. This principle, if applied to the total stock of gold, could arguably lead to further disputes which might be difficult to solve. The compromise was advantageous for the Slovak side, in that the payment for the two thirds of the gold allocated to the NBS was set at the very low book value, which made the division more a symbolic gesture than a real transfer.

2. The assets (receivables) and liabilities (obligations) vis a vis the IMF were divided in accordance with the decision of the IMF, in the ratio of 2.29 to 1, to the benefit of the CR. The CR received CSK 1,279 million more resources as would result from the application of the 2:1 principle. With regard to the unsettled relationship of the SR with the IMF and less experience of the NBS staff with administering the assets and liabilities vis a vis this institution, the liability of the NBS to the IMF was included in the item 'liabilities against international institutions' of the CNB, and compensatory measures were agreed in different items (the reduction of the CNB liabilities vis a vis domestic banks).

3. Credits extended to commercial banks were divided territorially, and credits to the Konsolidacni banka were divided, by agreement, in the ratio of CSK 38.7 to 16.7 billion. The actual utilisation of the credits was higher in the

SR by CSK 4.49 billion than in the CR, as compared with the 2:1 ratio, and was covered from the sources of Czech banks.

4. The deposits of commercial banks with the SBCS were divided territorially. The Czech banks had higher deposits with the SBCS than would follow from the ratio of 2:1 as of 31 December 1992, with the difference being CSK 8.3 billion.

5. The receivables of the SBCS arising from credits to the Federal budget were divided in the ratio of 2:1. Receivables arising from credits to the Republic budgets were divided territorially.

6. Immovable assets valued at CSK 376.7 billion were divided according to the territorial principle (277.7:99.0). The same applied to the corresponding sum of the reserve funds of the SBCS. Movable assets valued at CSK 732.9 million were divided according to the territorial principle (i.e. they were left physically at their original locations), but financial compensation was agreed and carried out.

These accounting operations resulted in a higher (when compared to the 2:1 ratio) use of financial sources to cover loans extended to commercial banks (CSK +4.5 billion) by the NBS, and higher receivables against the SR budget. At the same time, the NBS had relatively less (compared with the 2:1 division) financial sources in the item of the IMF (CSK -1.3 billion), and in the deposits of the Slovak banks on SBCS accounts. The final claim of the CNB against the NBS thus reached CSK 22,297 million. This claim was further increased by the balance of the clearing payment system reaching CSK 2,446 million.

The completion of the final accounts of the SBCS was made complicated by the fact that it took place simultaneously with the termination of the Federal budget, the cessation of existence of a whole range of central administrative bodies, and with the creation of new ones. At the same time, the necessary conditions (in terms of knowhow) of the setting up of two new central banks had to be ensured. All this extraordinary effort has been carried out so that the closing balance sheet of the SBCS and the opening balance sheet of the CNB and the NBS were prepared as of 29 January 1993. Until the final separation of assets and liabilities (April 1993) took place, the undivided tangible and intangible assets were administered in accordance with an agreement between the CNB and the NBS. As laid down in the Act on the SBCS, Price Waterhouse carried out an audit of the annual financial statements of the SBCS for the year 1992.

ii) Reasons for the failure to implement the division as agreed. At the end of January 1993 an audited closing balance of the former SBCS was available, together with 19 signed partial protocols on the division of the key balance sheet items between the CNB and the NBS. On the basis of these protocols, the CNB claimed the resulting receivable item valued at CSK 22.3 billion, and declared that the signature of a general protocol, including the acceptance of the above receivable item, was a precondition for the implementation of the partial protocols (which included a transfer of gold to Slovakia).

The general protocol on the division of assets and liabilities of the SBCS was prepared by both sides, and its scope did not extend beyond the agreements in the 19 partial protocols. It was not, however, signed. The delays in the signature of this document were justified by a politically motivated assessment of the total claim of the CNB against the NBS, which was interpreted as creating unfavourable initial conditions for the Slovak Republic. This sort of critism was published in the Slovak press. Critical comments rarely questioned the contents of the partial protocols, but rather introduced new aspects into the agenda, such as:

- the demand that only some of the provisions of the protocols be implemented with higher priority (such as the physical division of gold), without implementing other provisions of the general agreement;
- exogenous factors, used as arguments to support the offsetting reduction of the claim held by the CNB against the NBS. One of the arguments in this group is the demand for a deduction of the value of the flag of the former Federation (assumed by the CR), and other arguments, which went beyond the issue of the division of the property of the SBCS and the powers of the CNB and the NBS.

The obvious reason why the division of the property of the SBCS was not completed consists in the fact that the issue was not limited to mere accounting relations of the two central banks, but extented to the wider agenda of the division of all Federal property. The final solution, therefore, has to come from negotiations on a higher level and cannot be expected from negotiations between the banks themselves.

1.4 Conclusion

The technical details of the methods applied during the division of the former CSFR have been addressed here. Although the discussion did not cover the division of all property, it was satisfactory to demonstrate the complex nature of the emerging task, and the efforts of both sides to solve the problem on a high technical standard and in accordance with the legislative acts in force. The division of the property of the Federation was accomplished quickly and to mutual satisfaction. Thanks to the speed and success of the overall operation, economic activity was not disrupted, and the transitional processes in both Republics were not endangered.

The fulfilment of the agreements led to some problems, which were treated by the Commission for the Final Settlement. Although the true final settlement is yet to come, the scope of unresolved issues seems marginal in comparison with the property that has been divided.

2 Short duration of single currency

2.1 Monetary Agreement

One of the priorities of the economic policy of both the Czech and the Slovak governments was to prevent the split of the Federation from undermining monetary stability and confidence in domestic currency. The credibility the Czechoslovak currency had enjoyed since the beginning of the transformation was not to be automatically inherited by the succeeding currencies. Both Republics wished to gain more time and did not want to further exacerbate the split of the Federation by immediately effecting a currency separation. It was understood that a switch to payments in convertible currencies would speed up the breakdown of existing monetary relations and induce a shock which might result in a rapid decline in production.

It remained a controversial issue whether, in the long run, it was desirable and realistic to consider a more integrated monetary arrangement given the trend towards relaxing the deep interdependence of both economies. The obvious intention of Slovakia to create its own independent economic policy indicated that after a certain transition period the succeeding states were likely to introduce separate currencies.

This development influenced the process of searching for a workable monetary settlement. The first result of negotiations towards this goal was the Monetary Agreement, concluded in October 1992. Among the thirty or so agreements concluded by both the Czech and the Slovak governments before the split of the Federation, this Agreement was undoubtedly one of the most important ones. Nevertheless, it had one fundamental inconsistency -- it demanded a coordination of economic policies at a time when the development of both economies as well as differences in the political climate implied divergent tendencies.

In reality, the Monetary Agreement tried to address the first phase of the gradual transition to independent currencies -- the period of the temporary use of a single currency. Clearly, the Agreement was not intended to establish a monetary union, since neither its title nor the long-term intentions of the parties indicated a need to do so. The preamble of the Monetary Agreement declared this arrangement temporary and predicted the later introduction of two separate currencies.

The Agreement established a Monetary Committee composed of representatives of the central banks of both Republics for the period of the temporary use of a single currency. The Monetary Committee was given executive powers to decide on common monetary policy.

The special provisions (the so called Articles of Termination) which were included in the Agreement specified circumstances for potential withdrawal from it. Either contracting party was allowed to withdraw from the Agreement under any of the following conditions:

- In the case of failure of the Monetary Committee to agree on basic monetary issues;
- In the case of failure to keep the budget deficit of one of the parties below 10 per cent (in terms of budget revenues);
- In the case of failure to keep the external reserves of one of the parties above the monthly volume of imports (measured in convertible currencies);
- In the case of a speculative capital flight from one country to another higher than 5 per cent of total bank deposits.

Both parties to the Monetary Agreement also agreed to coordinate their economic and monetary policies to prevent the occurrence of any of the above listed conditions until at least 30 June 1993. However, as early as at the beginning of February 1993, the agreement had to be terminated and the currency separation was effected on 8 February 1994.

2.2 Articles of Termination

Looking back at the period of a single currency, it is difficult to distinguish the influence of some of the underlying factors associated with long-term economic trends (especially changes due to the split of the Federal economy) from the merely speculative behavior of businesses, banks and the public in expectation of the currency separation. Nevertheless, it is interesting to explore to which degree the individual Articles of Termination contributed to the early termination of the Monetary Agreement.

Coordination of monetary policy

In the long run, the idea of coordinating the Czech and Slovak monetary policies as well as other areas of economic interest was not very credible. It was clear that the Slovak economic situation would demand implementation of more expansive policies than was necessary for the Czech Republic. In Slovakia, where the requirement of a coordinated application of economic transformation was increasingly understood and interpreted as an enforced subordination of the Slovak economy to the Federal one, the benefits of a concerted economic policy were already being questioned in 1991 and 1992.

Given these circumstances, it was quite unrealistic to expect the Monetary Committee to be able to keep reaching consensus on common monetary policy. Similarly, the other articles of termination were phrased in such a way that their fulfillment was anticipated in half a year at the latest. Therefore, most economic agents started expecting the currency separation to take place soon. On top of this, the development of the Slovak economy indicated that currency separation would be followed by an immediate devaluation of the Slovak currency. These expectations influenced the behavior of businesses as well as the public and thus undermined the credibility of the Monetary Agreement.

Ten percent deficit of the government budget

The 10 per cent deficit of the government budget was set up at a less demanding level than was normally required by the International Monetary Fund from countries granted stand-by loans. However, the deficit of the Slovak government budget for 1993 of 10 per cent of the budgetary revenues would have represented less than CZK 16 billion, while the termination of budget transfers from the Czech Republic to Slovakia alone could, according to some estimates, lower the annual budget revenues of Slovakia by CZK 25 billion. The OECD estimated that in 1992 the Slovak government budget (including its share of Federal revenues and expenditures) closed with a 31 billion deficit, while the Czech budget, using the same method, closed with a 15 billion surplus.[6]

It is necessary to evaluate real development of the government budgets within the framework of the Monetary Agreement using a time span longer than one month. In the first month after the break-up of the Federation (January 1993) both Czech and Slovak government budgets displayed deficits above 10 per cent; in the Czech Republic the deficit was CZK 2.8 billion (12.8 per cent of budget revenues). It is important to note that starting February

1993, the Czech budget showed a surplus and closed the year with an annual surplus of CZK 1.1 billion. The surplus trend was preserved even in 1994.

On the other hand, development in the Slovak Republic proved that a 10 per cent deficit was not sustainable over a longer term. As shown in Table 3.4, the Slovak budget deficit was in January 21.4 per cent of its actual revenues. In January and February (cumulatively) it fell to 8.6 per cent; in March, however, it rose to 43.4 per cent and stayed above 10 per cent until the end of the year. On average, in the first quarter of 1993, the Slovak deficit reached SKK 11 billion and by the end of the year it was SKK 23 billion (15.3 per cent of the budget revenues).

Table 3.4
Balance of the Czech and Slovak government budgets
January - December 1993

Czech Republic	*1*	*1-3*	*1-6*	*1-9*	*1-12*
Government budget revenues	21.8	86.4	175.2	258.6	358.0
Government budget balance	-2.8	10.4	5.6	4.3	1.1
Surplus (+) or deficit (-) as a percentage of revenues	-12.8	12.0	3.2	1.7	0.3
Slovak Republic	*1*	*1-3*	*1-6*	*1-9*	*1-12*
Government budget revenues	7.0	25.3	65.2	105.4	150.3
Government budget balance	-1.5	-11.0	-14.8	-15.9	-23.0
Surplus (+) or deficit (-) as a percentage of revenues	-21.4	-43.5	-22.7	-15.1	-15.3

Note: Revenues and balance in billion of CZK, figures cumulated at the end of the period

Source: *Indicators of the Monetary and Economic Development*, no. 5, 1994 and 7, 1994, Czech National Bank

External reserves

The development of external reserves deserves detailed analysis since the events in this area contributed significantly to the decision to implement currency separation. Specialists, pointing to the low performance of Slovak exports vis-a-vis Czech ones, forecast that problems concerning foreign reserves would mostly affect Slovakia. It was expected that for some time after the break-up of the Federation, Slovakia would not be able to prevent its reserves from falling under its monthly import level. The foreign exchange reserves, however, continued decreasing on both sides and currency separation came as a result of an agreement of both parties.

Common foreign exchange reserves had decreased substantially under the influence of the upcoming break-up of the Federation (see Table 3.5). The expected major changes in the economy caused the commercial banks, businesses and the public to speculate regarding currency devaluation. In November and December 1992, sales of foreign currency by the Czechoslovak State Bank became so heavy that on 22 December 1992, the Bank suspended trading for a period of time. At the end of the year, the cumulative balance of purchases and sales was negative (sales outstripped purchases by 4 billion). While at the end of August 1992 the foreign exchange reserves of the Czech and Slovak banks totaled USD 5.6 billion, by the end of December 1992 they fell to USD 4.4 billion, out of which USD 1.2 billion were the reserves of the central bank. In the period between September 1992 and the end of 1992, both the current and the capital accounts of the balance of payments deteriorated.

Table 3.5
Trading on interbank foreign exchange market

	1992				*1993*					
Month	9	10	11	12	1	2	3	4	5	6
Balance	2.7	-2.8	3.6	8.8	17.1	-3.3	-6.8	-10.5	-13.5	-7.5

Note: The balance of central banks' sales (+) and purchases (-) on the interbank forex market (in billion of CSK/CZK)

Source: *Indicators of the Monetary and Economic Development*, no. 12, 1993, Czech National Bank

The Czech Republic therefore commenced its independent existence with a relatively low level of reserves; on 1 January 1993, the foreign exchange reserves of the Czech National Bank were USD 3.58 billion. When trading on the interbank forex market was resumed on 9 January 1993 the volume of sales remained high.[7] Czech commercial banks had enough free reserves for the purchase of foreign exchange, as in anticipation of the currency separation the volume of money in circulation decreased while deposits rose. The greater need of the Czech commercial banks for foreign exchange was also partly caused by Slovak businesses effecting their payments to and purchases from abroad through the Czech banking sector.

On January 1993, the total foreign exchange reserves of the Czech banks were still USD 3.5 billion, out of which only USD 0.5 billion were the reserves of the Czech National Bank (in January 1993 the CNB reserves fell by $297 billion). Between 1 January 1993 and 9 February 1993, the CNB's foreign exchange reserves fell by USD 386 billion to USD 462 billion. The fall of the foreign exchange reserves of the Czech National Bank at the beginning of 1993 was one of the factors influencing the decision to effect the currency separation.

In January 1993, the so called parallel exchange rate of the Czechoslovak currency abroad fell as a consequence of a loss of credibility (see Figure 3.1). Some foreign banks even terminated trades and ceased quoting bid-ask spread.[8]

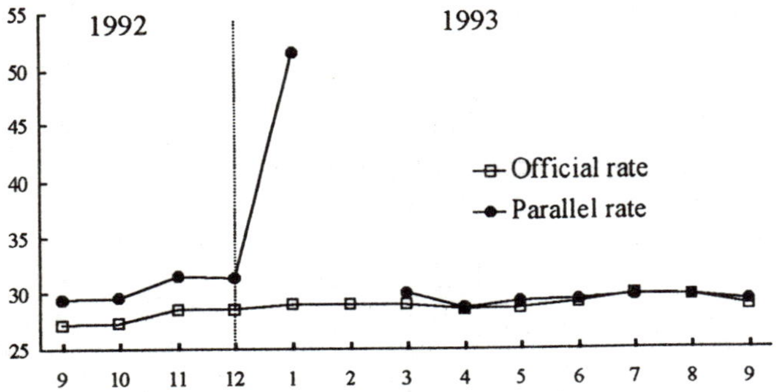

Figure 3.1 Official and parallel exchange rates CSK/USD and CZK/USD

Source: Financial Statistical Information, CNB; Monthly Statistics of the Czech Republic; *Main Economic Indicators*, OECD, Paris, January 1994

The Monetary Agreement did not specify in detail how to calculate a sufficient amount of reserves in terms of monthly imports, which would entail some method of averaging figures. Table 3.6. therefore displays only the initial volume of reserves and imports per month, indicating the feasibility of such criteria for the Czech Republic, thanks in part to currency separation. It is hard to estimate what the situation would have been without the separation.

The development of foreign exchange reserves in Slovakia was even more dramatic. After the split of the Federation, Slovakia's share of foreign exchange reserves was less than USD 1 billion, USD 350 million of which were reserves of the National Bank of Slovakia. While the turbulences over foreign exchange reserves in the Czech Republic mostly took the form of a transfer of foreign currency from the central bank to the commercial banks, Slovakia experienced a steady decrease of foreign exchange reserves due to an increased demand for foreign currency from the business sector, which financed higher purchases abroad, as well as from individuals.

Table 3.6
Czech and Slovak foreign exchange reserves and monthly imports

			1993		
	1	3	6	9	12
Czech Republic					
Foreign Exchange Reserves					
Banks total	3.50	4.00	4.90	5.90	6.20
CNB	0.50	1.20	2.30	3.20	3.80
Imports	0.43	1.15	1.19	1.14	1.42
Slovak Republic					
Foreign Exchange Reserves					
Banks total		0.80	0.87	1.32	1.42
NBS	0.14	0.19	0.25	0.57	0.48
Imports	0.26	0.53	0.60	0.52	0.74

Note: Foreign exchange reserves (in billion of USD) at the end of a month; imports (in billion of USD) without trade with the other Republic

Source: *Indicators of the Monetary and Economic Development*, no. 5, 1994 and 8, 1994, Czech National Bank ; *Bulletin of the Slovak Statistical Office*

It is estimated that in January 1993 the National Bank of Slovakia lost 60 per cent of its foreign exchange reserves. Problems persisted after the currency separation and the NBS was forced to introduce some regulatory measures constraining convertibility of the current account transactions in order to stop the foreign exchange reserves from further falling.[9] The situation improved after the devaluation of the Slovak currency in July 1993 and after the NBS obtained loans from abroad. The NBS reserves reached USD 500 million in September 1993; by the end of November 1993 they were about USD 490 million. For data on the development of the Slovak foreign exchange reserves compared to its monthly imports, see Table 3.6.

Speculative capital flows

The speculative capital flow from one Republic to the other over 5 per cent of total bank deposits represented the last potential reason for withdrawal from the Monetary Agreement. Before the currency separation, the banking systems of the Czech and Slovak Republics were not truly separated; the existence of a single currency gave both businesses and the public the alternative to use either Czech or Slovak banks. There were concerns that the expected currency separation and the subsequent devaluation of the Slovak currency would cause speculative transfer of deposits from Slovak to Czech banks. It is difficult to prove such transfers, since deposits rose in both Republics, with those in Slovakia rising noticeably slower. The sizes of deposits were influenced by the public depositing currency which would normally have been in circulation. While in January 1992 deposits into the Czech Savings Bank were about CZK 1.1 billion, in January 1993 they rose (along with the number of new clients) roughly 10 times higher (for deposits to Czech and Slovak banks before and immediately after the currency separation see Table 3.7).

Table 3.7
Deposits in the Czech and Slovak Republics at the beginning of 1993

Czech Republic	*Volume* billion of CSK	*Rise compared to Dec. 1992* billion of CSK	%
31.12.1992	515.8	-	-
29.01.1993	539.9	24.1	4.7
20.02.1993	546.9	31.1	6.0
4.02.1993	546.9	31.1	6.0
9.02.1993	555.0	39.2	7.6
11.02.1993	548.7	32.9	6.4
Slovak Republic	*Volume* billion of CSK	*Rise compared to Dec. 1992* billion of CSK	%
31.12.1992	175.3	-	-
29.01.1993	181.3	6.0	3.4
2.02.1993	181.3	6.0	3.4

Source: *Indicators of the Monetary and Economic Development*, February 1993, Czech National Bank,

Up until the time of the currency separation, deposits into Czech banks were used partly for the credit extension of Slovak banks (especially via the refinancing window of the central bank). Moreover, the overall increase of deposits led to excess free reserves in the banking system as a potential source of too-high credit expansion. Therefore, on 1 February 1993, the Czech National Bank introduced higher reserve requirements for four banks with deposits over CSK 25 billion. It also changed the conditions for access to central bank refinancing facilities (banks with large free reserves were not allowed to participate in auctions) and intensified open market operations. These measures neutralized the excess free reserves in the banking system but caused an increase of interest rates in money markets.

2.3 The purpose of the Monetary Agreement

Already the first month of the existence of the two separate Republics with single currency proved the instability of such a monetary arrangement. All economic subjects, such as entrepreneurs and households as well as commercial banks, kept undermining the feasibility of the Monetary Agreement by their behaviour. The clearly declared temporary nature of the monetary arrangement encouraged expectations of a currency separation in the near future.

The Czechoslovak State Bank anticipated the instability of a monetary arrangement based on a single currency even before the conclusion of the Monetary Agreement (and before dividing itself into two successor central banks). Steps necessary to effect a currency separation were introduced immediately when the split of the Federation seemed unavoidable, and in January 1993, the central banks of both Republics initialized the process of stamping; at the end of January, the Czech and Slovak Prime Ministers concluded an agreement on currency separation; and on 2 February currency separation legislation was passed by both Parliaments. On the same day, the Czech and Slovak governments announced the exact date of the currency separation for 8 February 1993. The monetary system based on a single currency therefore lasted only 38 days.

Despite its short duration, this system played at least one important role by providing a time lag between the split of the Federation and separation of the currency. Such a time period was necessary for reassuring the public, ensuring the technical and logistical background of the currency separation, and preparing a framework of payments for transactions after the separation. If these demanding problems had had to be solved in the period just prior to the break-up of the Federation, when a number of other issues were at hand, the cumulative pressures could have made it impossible to professionally resolve of all of the monetary questions arising in connection with such a deep intrusion into monetary conditions in the national economy.

3 Currency separation

February 1993, a month after the dissolution of Czechoslovakia, marked both an end to the single currency system and the birth of new national currencies for the succeeding Republics. For the economic transformation to continue successfully, this so called currency separation represented an extremely vital event. In contrast to how easily the currency separation was finally accomplished, both its preparation and implementation were very elaborate. In retrospect, it is clear that the successful implementation of the currency separation was one of the most significant contributions to the smooth performance of both the Czech and Slovak economies.[10]

3.1 Preparation of the currency separation

The preparatory phase in the Czech Republic, which commenced as early as July 1992 and reached its peak between November 1992 and January 1993, were not initially directed at implementing the currency separation as such. The initial considerations of the early summer of 1992 anticipated a speedy development in the political scene as a result of the July 1992 Parliamentary elections, and therefore the efforts were focused on establishing sufficient technical, logistical and legal underpinnings for the realization of the single currency separation in case it should become necessary.

The idea that further preparations would not be necessary after the legislative, technical and logistical base had been achieved in January 1993 proved to be wrong (see the previous part). On the contrary, the whole process needed to be accelerated.

The work done during the first stage helped to create a detailed currency separation scenario, which, however, never became a formal document. It existed more or less in the minds of the members of the Currency Separation

Central Management Committee and only later filtered down to the relevant legal norms: the constitutional Act on Currency Separation, the government decree to control the implementation of this Act, the Czech National Bank (hereafter CNB) instructions accompanying this Act, security measures and time schedules.

Currency outstanding and in reserves before the currency separation

In the second half of 1992, the value of currency in circulation in Czechoslovakia was about CSK 101 billion represented by roughly 350 million banknotes and 3.2 billion coins of various denominations.[11] The coins represented less than 3 per cent of the total value of the currency in circulation. The 10, 20 and 50 banknotes accounted for another 3 per cent of the total value but represented 45 per cent of the volume of banknotes. For this reason, these banknotes were not stamped.

While the volume of the issued currency was precisely noted down, the division of the money held between foreign countries and Czechoslovakia, as well as inside the country between the Czech and Slovak economies, populations, and businesses was unclear. The division of the Czechoslovak State Bank balance sheet used the ratio 2:1 for the division of common property. Such a ratio was truly hypothetical, 70-75 per cent to 30-35 per cent figure was considered more realistic. The estimation of the volume of currency in circulation in both Republics was based upon the number of inhabitants and institutions in both parts of the country, while also taking into account the Czech Republic's higher level of economic activity as well as its more rapidly growing private sector. The volume of Czechoslovak currency held by foreigners abroad was also undetermined. Figures varied from CSK 500 million to 15 billion, with the CNB inclining towards the lower figure.

Table 3.8, which lists the individual denominations, their gross weight in tons (gross weight depends upon packaging and storing and therefore is difficult to determine) and expected costs, demonstrates the complexity of the entire operation. Over a period of 12 to 18 months it was necessary to produce, transport, store, process and distribute into circulation more than 3,000 tons of new banknotes and coins while also having to withdraw from circulation, store, process and destroy approximately the same amount of the old currency.

Both the currency outstanding as well as that held in reserve needed to be taken into account. At the beginning of 1993, the reserves stored in the CNB and in the Komercni Banka totalled CSK 15 million in 1000 banknotes; CSK 69 million in 500 banknotes and CSK 54 million in 100 banknotes.

Table 3.8
Estimated volume and breakdown of denominations necessary to separate currencies

Denomination (CZK)	Volume (mil of banknotes/coins)	Expected expenses (mil CZK)	Gross weight (in tons)
5000 B	20	22.73	30
1000 B	40	87.05	50
500 B	50	52.59	55
200 B	40	9.15	43
100 B	60	60.12	60
50 B	40	39.15	38
20 B	60	58.00	55
10 B	75	72.00	65
50 C	35	120.00	331
20 C	55	99.00	491
10 C	70	119.00	588
5 C	70	91.00	406
2 C	80	88.00	420
1 C	100	70.00	420
0.50 C	70	24.50	66
0.20 C	80	16.00	67
0.10 C	100	20.00	69
Total	1,025	1,118.30	3,254
Banknotes	385	470.79	396
Coins	640	647.50	2,858

Note: B = banknote; C = coin
Source: Vokaty, F.: *Currency Separation - Report on the Preparatory Work*; Information for the Governor of the Czechoslovak State Bank, dated 6 October 1992

Reserves of banknotes always tended to equal or outnumber the volume of currency outstanding (reserves of 1000 denominations were extremely low at the end of 1992). Sufficient coin reserves were estimated at a 2-3 year supply of 1, 2, 5 and 10 denominations (measured by the volume of the annual release of coins into circulation) and at a 1-2 year supply of lower denominations. Coins withdrawn from circulation were to be immediately replaced by new ones. Analyses of similar coin exchanges in the 1950s - 1980s showed that such operations required amounts five to eight times higher than the average annual need.

Methods of differentiating the currency

There were several methods considered for differentiating Czech banknotes from Slovak ones. One plan proposed a circulation in the Czech Republic of banknotes with Czech themes and Czech text (20, 100, and 1000 denominations) and in Slovakia of those with Slovak themes and Slovak text (10, 50 and 500 denominations). There were other proposals such as the issue of temporary banknotes or the stamping of banknotes by special machines. The possibility of engraving stamps on banknotes was also considered but because of the insufficient capacity of the supplier this method was used only partially to distinguish the 1000 denominations.

Another option under consideration was the gluing of stamps on banknotes. Logistically, this method seemed to be the most laborious one. Also the number of people involved made it impossible to keep the stamping secret. Furthermore, the obligation to deposit currency above an agreed limit of exchange was expected to add pressure on the banks, first with deposits and subsequently with withdrawals. Regardless of these difficulties, stamping seemed to be the most reliable choice and thus became the most utilized method of differentiating the new currency.

Preparations for the currency separation coincided with the planned release of two new Czechoslovak banknotes (200 and 1000 denominations with Czech themes). This provoked some speculation about these denominations having been selected as the first to be withdrawn and replaced in order to make the separation easier for the Czech Republic. In fact, the idea to issue the 200 banknote arose in connection with the urgent need to withdraw the 100 banknote featuring K. Gottwald, an infamous Czech Communist leader. The old 1000 banknote had to be replaced for security reasons since, in 1991 and 1992, the number of its forgeries grew substantially.

Finally, it was decided to differentiate the new Czech currency by marking the three highest denominations (100, 500 and some 1000 notes) with adhesive stamps; by engraving stamps on a portion of the 1000 banknotes, and by issuing new 200 banknotes.[12]

Time horizons of the currency separation

The consideration of various timetables was an important issue during the preparatory stage of the currency separation. In case of an emergency, a scenario was drafted for the Governor of the Czechoslovak State Bank in which the authors speculated that the currency separation would take place as early as 15-30 September 1992.

In October 1992, the talks finally focused on two possible time horizons. The first, which assumed at least a six month coexistence of a single currency (in keeping with an Agreement concluded between the Czech and Slovak Republics) envisioned the currency separation in July or August 1993 at the soonest. The second alternative proposed an earlier currency split either as a response to significant disintegration tendencies in the monetary and economic policies of both countries, or if the monetary stability were threatened for other reasons. The Czech Republic was to be ready (vis-a-vis stamping and distribution of new banknotes) to adopt this alternative by 15 January 1993 at the latest.

During the preparatory stage, the government authorities started to seriously consider January or February 1993 (a particular date of 16 and 17 January was referred to) as the date of the separation. The days close to month's end were regarded as the best since the volume of currency in circulation tends to decrease significantly in the second half of the month. Finally, the Czech and Slovak representatives agreed to effect the separation on 4-7 February 1993 (thereby giving the Slovak party an extra week to arrange the prerequisites).

Stamping

There were 160 million stamps printed to differentiate the new Czech banknotes, adding up to a total value of CSK 72 billion.[13] Estimates showed that the necessary value of prestamped banknotes to accomplish exchanges was approximately CSK 50 billion. To insure that the exchanges began smoothly, it was necessary to immediately prestamp banknotes in the amount of roughly CSK 30 billion. The amount of stamped banknotes was also high enough to enable exchanges for entrepreneurs as well as withdrawals from bank accounts after the currency separation was over.

The government printing plant for securities supplied 25 thousand packs of new Czech (unstamped) 200 banknotes, the total value of which was CZK 5 billion. In the first part of February, the printing plant delivered the first half of the 20 thousand packs of new Czech (engraved with stamps) 1000 denominations, the total value of which was CZK 20 billion. The second part of the order was completed in April 1993.

Since it was possible that the demand for banknotes would be unreasonably high, Victoria Securities Printing (a private Czech company) quickly printed central bank receipts in CZK 2000 and 5000 denominations, the total value of which was CZK 42 billion. These receipts were counted upon as a possible solution for business exchanges in case of occasional cash shortages in banks.

Initially, stamps were to be printed in the Czech Republic but, for confidentiality, the order was placed with the British company Thomas De La Rue and the stamps were finally printed in Colombia. The order for stamp printing was placed confidentially by the Ministry of Finance following an agreement between Governor J. Tosovsky and Minister of Finance I. Kocarnik as early as 30 July 1992. In keeping with the agreement, 400 boxes with stamps arrived in Prague in September 1992. Surprisingly, their existence remained a secret. The reason for this prudent measure to print the stamps well before a definitive date of currency separation was to avoid any unwanted last minute improvisations and stressful situations.

Stamping federal banknotes was the most laborious and time-consuming part of the preparations. The most important role in this process was entrusted to Komercni banka, which had been assigned as the custodian over the Czech currency reserves (by the former Czechoslovak State Bank).

The stamping itself (of 100, 500 and 1000 banknotes) commenced at Komercni banka on 4 January 1993 and was performed by more than ten thousand employees. Before 31 January 1993 the bank was requested to stamp 20 per cent (of reserves as of 31 December 1992) of 1000 banknotes (2.9 million banknotes), 50 per cent of the 500 banknotes (34.7 million banknotes) and 20 per cent of the 100 banknotes (7.5 million banknotes). The stamping mostly took place during the weekends in January and February 1993. In total, Komercni banka stamped more than 152 thousand packages of Czechoslovak currency worth roughly CSK 65 billion. Other institutions performing stamping were the headquarters of the CNB and its branches (from January 1993 on) and other commercial banks (during the currency separation itself).

Establishing conditions of exchanges for the household sector

The maximum amount a person was allowed to change directly at bank counters became one of the most sensitive issue. The sum of CSK 1,000 per person under 15 years of age was applicable to both parents of the household since the elimination of duplicity seemed logistically too complicated.

From the range delineated by the 'worst case scenario' (CSK 1,000 per person above 15 and CSK 500 per person under 15 years of age) and the 'best case scenario' (CSK 4,000 per person over 15 years of age and CSK 1,000 per person under 15 years of age) the appointed government committee selected almost unanimously the 'best case scenario' as the technically and logistically manageable maximum. To dispense with currency over the CSK 4,000 limit, citizens were encouraged to use the banks' deposit instruments (savings accounts deposits, purchase of savings bonds, deposits of money into CDs, etc.) or to send money orders to their own address.

Determining the number of days in which exchanges could be executed turned out to be another problem. In the end, four days were established as the technically acceptable maximum.

It was also necessary to determine conditions when the parallel circulation of old Federal and new Czech banknotes during 'exchange' days could take place. Parallel circulation was opposed for two important reasons. First, the anticipated devaluation of the new Slovak currency threatened to provoke speculation.[14] Secondly, two types of valid banknotes in circulation might have created problems for business bookkeeping and the handling of banknotes in banks. These negative implications influenced the final decision not to circulate both currencies at the same time.

Three-tier management of the currency separation

Unofficial discussions amongst a narrow group of Czechoslovak State Bank top executives (Czech members of the Bank's Board of Directors and other invited experts) regarding strategies available for the currency separation had already began by September/October 1992. However, the key role was performed by the Currency Separation Central Management Committee (hereafter the Central Committee). The Central Committee was established and became operational in mid-November 1992, after representatives of both Governments agreed upon the future currency relationship between the Czech and Slovak Republics. The work of the Central Committee was discontinued on 15 February 1993 and further operations were carried out by regular Czech National Bank staff members following the Czech National Bank's rules and regulations.

Upon its establishment, the Central Committee had about twenty members, with its membership later growing to include fifty executives, mainly directors and executive directors of the CNB branches as well as representatives of institutions and state bodies chosen to take part in the currency separation process.[15]

During the exchanges, when members of the Central Committee managed the process in their institutions, the coordination was performed by a management team staffed by Czech National Bank employees, Police and Ministry of Internal Affairs personnel. It was divided into three divisions operating 24 hours a day for a total of eight days. During the exchanges, the team acted as a link among the leading organizers, provided logistical support, monitored major transports of banknotes and coins, and coordinated and supervised security measures.

On the local level, there were Regional Committees established in former district centers (eight Committees including one in Prague). Directors of the regional branches of the CNB were appointed as commanding directors. The Regional Committee setup copied the design of the Central Committee. It was, however, extended to include representatives of the local government. There were Local Committees established in 75 counties (mostly in the county seats) which were generally chaired by directors of local Komercni banka branches. Therefore, the management of the currency separation mainly had a three-tier setup.

Regional and Local Committees were assigned the task of establishing exchange points for the general public (about 4,000 points) as well as specialized exchange points in hospitals, prisons, retirement houses, garrisons, etc. They organized exchanges for the elderly and disabled and, when necessary, provided transportation to the exchange points for people from isolated villages.

The Central Committee concentrated on preparing the plan for the currency separation and designing its basic methods and principles, but was not involved in the exchange process itself. The strategies were communicated to the Regional Committees which then adopted individual strategies within the framework of the plan. The experience of the commanding officers of Regional and Local Committees helped provide guidance as to the preferences of the particular region.

The transport of money between the exchange points (post offices, Savings Bank branches) and places where the banknotes were stamped (Komercni banka, Czech National Bank) became the most challenging part of the exchanges. At the beginning of the exchanges nobody knew how many people would exchange their money and at which point. The distribution of money among the exchange points was based upon the estimated number of inhabitants in a given location. Old Federal banknotes were transported from the exchange points to the stamping points, where they were stamped and subsequently redistributed as needed.

A key role in the distribution process was played by a central team which handled the major transports, and local groups in charge of organizing transports of on the regional level. The Czech Police very often assisted transports of hundreds of millions in terms of currency value. In some regions, the bank vehicles were helped by Army reserve trucks.

About 40,000 people were involved in the organizational structure of the currency separation, a majority of them from ten major financial and governmental institutions (Czech National Bank, Komercni banka, Savings Bank, the Czech Postal Service, the Czech Police, the Ministry of Internal Affairs, the Ministry of Defense, special action squads, and local government bodies). All the institutions and people involved were well-managed, flexible and efficient. The noticeable success of the currency separation could be attributed to the concept of deliberate centralization during the preparatory stages followed by a substantial decentralization of the exchanges themselves.[16]

3.2 Realization of the currency separation and its complementary processes

Decision to effect the currency separation

By the middle of January 1993, the Czech Republic was about to complete the preparatory stage of the currency separation. The scenario was agreed upon and the necessary legal norms were about to be concluded. By then, Komercni banka and the Czech National Bank had stamped banknotes in the amount of roughly CSK 20 billion.

The alarming monetary developments of the end of 1992 combined with the negative trends at the beginning of 1993 removed the possibility of delaying the realization of the currency separation. Under these circumstances, the Czech Government appointed a Committee to rule on the most important issues concerning the currency separation. The members of the Committee were the Prime Minister; the three vice Prime Ministers; the Ministers of Economy, Industry and Internal Affairs; the Czech National Bank Governor and Vice Governor (Head of the Currency Separation Central Management Committee); and the head of the Czech National Bank Currency Department.

This Governmental Committee met only one time, on 19 January 1993. It reached the following conclusions:

- the decision to realize the currency separation should be made after an agreement with the Slovak government was reached (in keeping with the Monetary Agreement) and the actions of the Czech and Slovak representations should be coordinated;
- the exchanges for the general public should take place in a four day time period, and the maximum amount per head should be at the higher end of the suggested scale;
- cash flow across the border between the Czech and Slovak Republics should be immediately terminated following the official announcement of the currency separation date (in cooperation with the Slovak Republic);
- the decision was made to design a clearing payment system with Slovakia.

In Bratislava on 20 January 1993, following a request by the Slovak government, the Czech National Bank Vice Governor P. Kysilka, and the head of the Czech National Bank Currency Department L. Surga, met with the

Slovak Prime Minister V. Meciar, Slovak Minister of Finance J. Toth, Slovak National Bank Vice Governor M. Jusko and other Slovak representatives. The Czech delegates presented their Slovak partners with draft legislation for the realization of the currency separation. The two delegations discussed in detail the rules of exchange for different economic agents and agreed upon the dates of the exchanges. On the night of 27-28 January 1993, the Prime Ministers of both Republics met and confirmed the agreed dates.

On 2 February 1993, after the Parliaments of both Republics enacted the necessary legislation, the Czech and Slovak Prime Ministers officially announced to the media that the currency separation would commence on 8 February. Simultaneously, the general public learned about the plan and the details of the exchange procedure itself.

Measures taken to ensure a smooth currency separation process

Prior to the beginning of the currency separation, with the intention to avoid speculation and to keep the general public informed, the media started a wide information campaign introducing the main principles and technical background of the upcoming money exchanges. As of 3 February 1993, police introduced necessary security measures such as guarding exchange points and escorting money transports, and secured firmer customs control at the Czech-Slovak crossings.

To prevent speculation in the form of transferring money from Slovakia to the Czech Republic, both parties suspended payments across the border. Between 3 and 7 February all payments between the CR and the SR, either direct or via banks, were deferred. Simultaneously, it was necessary to adjust financial transactions between the Czech and Slovak banks, including the settlements of Slovak clients' claims, the termination of long-term payment orders and automatic transfers to accounts at Slovak banks.

The Czech National Bank and the National Bank of Slovakia also announced that as of 3 February 1993, in connection with the preparation of the currency separation, banks and other licensed exchange places would stop selling foreign currency for private trips abroad to Czech and Slovak nationals. Foreign currency sale was resumed in full on 8 February.

Exchanges of banknotes

Exchanges of currency for households (corporate entities) in the Czech Republic took place 4-7 February 1993 at exchange points set up by the Czech Savings Bank and the Czech Postal Service. The exchange points served only people registered in the Czech Republic or carrying a residential permit. Every person wishing to exchange money had to present an identification, or a substitute for an identification, such as a residence permit. The exchange was stamped in either of these documents. The percentage of new and stamped banknotes was determined by the individual exchange points. There was a limit of one exchange per person.

On 8 and 9 February 1993, selected bank branches and exchange points at border crossings exchanged money for foreign nationals (except for persons with permanent residence in Slovakia). To exchange old money for new or stamped ones, foreigners had to present an identification (usually a passport) and proof of official purchase of Czechoslovak currency (usually an exchange receipt). Foreigners were allowed to exchange as much money as was indicated on the receipt.

Legal entities with business locations in the Czech Republic and entrepreneurs with permanent residence in the Czech Republic exchanged their money on 7-9 February 1993, in the banks where they had their accounts. Upon presentation of an accounting book, the bank exchanged (within its limits) as much money as was indicated as the balance the day before the first day of the currency separation. The exchange was stamped into the accounting book.

The exchanges of unstamped banknotes for stamped ones were reported successful. According to Czech National Bank data, on 4-7 February 1993, the general public exchanged banknotes worth CSK 10 billion. This was less than 1/3 of the expected amount and resulted in less pressure on exchange points than previously expected.

The Czech Postal Service facilitated exchange in 2,857 branches (out of 3,500 branches) at a total of 4,090 exchanges counters. According to Czech Postal Service data, it exchanged money worth CSK 4 billion. The general public often used other means of exchange offered by the Czech Postal Service, such as savings accounts (there were 40,000 savings accounts opened just before or during the currency separation), or postal receipts which were delivered in new or stamped banknotes within 14 days. During the exchange days, the Czech Postal Service established about 350 special money transport lines. It concluded over 600 agreements with private security agencies and cooperated with the Czech Police to secure exchange and transport safety. There were no robberies of either post offices or transports during the exchange days.

The Czech Savings Bank facilitated exchanges in 833 selected branches where it provided 2,473 exchange counters. According to local need, it established special remote points in hospitals and retirement homes. Upon a request from the Members of Parliament, there was one exchange point open in the Parliament building. The Czech Savings Bank involved 12,000 of its employees (about 92 per cent of all employees). Its records show that it processed banknotes worth CSK 2.7 billion. For amounts above the CSK 4,000 limit, the Czech Savings Bank issued receipts, worth in total CSK 188.3 million; CSK 330 million of over-the-limit amounts were deposited by clients to accounts and other means of savings.[17]

Table 3.9
Timetable of currency separation in the Czech Republic

Termination of technical and logistical preparations	D-7	-Termination of preparatory work on the release of the Czech banknotes;
	D-7,6,5	-Distribution of banknotes to the institutions effecting the exchange and to the exchange points;
	D-6	-TV presentation of the Prime Minister and the Central Committee;
Culmination of information campaign and security measures		-Providing the media with a complex set of information;
		-Launching on TV of an instruction programme on the new banknotes and the rules of exchange;
		-Termination of direct transfers over the Czech-Slovak border;
	D-5	-Launching of the information campaign in the media and in the towns and municipalities;
Exchange days	D-4,3,2,1	-Exchanges for the public at the exchange points;
	D-1	-Termination of validity of the Czechoslovak banknotes on midnight of the Day-1;
	D	-Validity of new Czech banknotes at 00:00 Day D;
	D-1,D,D+1	-Exchange of banknotes for businesses;
	D,D+1	-Exchange of banknotes for foreigners at selected banks;
Ex post exchanges and new banknotes and coins release	D+180	-Deadline for exchanging currency over the established limit;
	September 1994	-Deadline for the release of the new (unstamped) Czech banknotes and coins.

Note: Day D = 8 February 1993
The official abbreviation for the old Federal currency (Czechoslovak Crown) was CSK. The successor currencies were CZK (Czech Crown in the Czech Republic) and SKK (Slovak Crown in the Slovak Republic).

Ex post exchanges of unstamped banknotes

For those who for serious reasons were not able to exchange money during the exchanges, the Act on Currency Separation allowed ex post exchange until

9 August 1993. The exchanges were performed by the CNB branches and, until the end of February 1993, also by selected Komercni banka branches (for amounts below CSK 2,000).

Although the Act on Currency Separation determined that the ex post exchange should be performed only for serious reasons, the public could not have been prevented from exchanging leftover unstamped banknotes for many reasons, primarily negligence. On the one hand, returning the unstamped banknotes to the public could have caused speculation, on the other hand, keeping the cash in banks and not returning it stamped would have caused severe public criticism. Therefore the most realistic option was to exchange small amounts of banknotes without delay while checking on larger amounts only.

Before the end of February, exchanges were made directly in the selected banks; from 1 March 1993 on, exchanges were performed only by mail. Processing the requests and checking the sums was a time consuming activity and therefore it was impossible to process all of the requests in a short period of time. The number of requests was estimated at approximately 150,000. In Prague and Central Bohemia only, the CNB processed requests to exchange banknotes worth CSK 60 million. The last requests were processed in the first half of 1994.

Completing the system of new Czech banknotes and coins

The currencies were formally separated on 8 February 1993. After this date, however, the authorities had to finish the whole operation by replacing the remaining Federal currency in circulation. Estimates show that it was necessary to distribute about 300 tons of banknotes and over 2,500 tons of new coins. As of 15 April 1995, there were more than 600 million banknotes (units) removed from circulation (including the stamped ones) which represented about 613 tons of paper, together with 1.17 billion coins (units), the total weight of which was 2,826 tons. At the same time, the CNB tried to minimize the time of co-circulation of the old and newly released banknotes and coins of the same denominations.

Despite the technical problems which accompanied the exchange of banknotes and coins (storing, transportation, overtime labour, etc.), the whole process basically followed the time schedule below (see Table 3.10.). As indicated in this table, between 8 February 1993 and September 1994, there were nine new Czech coins and eight new Czech banknotes to be released.[18]

The turning point between the old and new currencies appeared in July 1993, when the new banknotes in circulation outnumbered the old ones. In the first half of July many businesses paid wages in the new 100, 200 and 1000 banknotes; in the second half of the month they also paid with the 500 denomination. Therefore, the exchange of stamped banknotes for new ones partially materialized through wages, cash withdrawals from bank accounts and other cash payoffs.

Table 3.10
Time schedule for the replacement of the Czech currency

Denomination CZK	New currency issued into circulation	Termination of validity of the old currency	Last day of ex post exchange
Coins			
0.01	-	30.04.1993	31.08.1993
0.05	-	30.04.1993	31.08.1993
0.10	12.05.1993	31.07.1993	30.11.1993
0.20	12.05.1993	31.07.1993	30.11.1993
0.50	12.05.1993	31.07.1993	30.11.1993
1,-	9.06.1993	30.09.1993	31.01.1994
2,-	9.06.1993	30.11.1993	31.03.1994
5,-	9.06.1993	30.11.1993	31.03.1994
10,-	12.05.1993	31.07.1993	30.11.1993
20,-	12.05.1993	-	-
50,-	7.04.1993	-	-
Banknotes			
10	-	31.07.1993	30.11.1993
20	February 1994	31.07.1993	30.11.1993
50	22.09.1993	31.07.1993	30.11.1993
100	30.06.1993	31.08.1993 [a)]	31.05.1994 [a)]
200	8.02.1993	-	-
500	21.07.1993	31.08.1993 [a)]	31.05.1994 [a)]
1000	12.05.1993	31.08.1993 [a)]	31.05.1994 [a)]
2000	September 1994	-	-
5000	29.12.1993	-	-

Note: a) These dates are for stamped banknotes only. The validity of the unstamped banknotes was terminated on 7 February 1993; additional exchange was terminated on 9 August 1993

Source: Czech National Bank

On the other hand, despite the release of a large amount of new coins, there was hardly any change in the distribution of the old and new coins in circulation before July 1993. Since small denominations are used for paying wages only rarely, their introduction in circulation was possible only via some businesses and services which needed small denominations and obtained them from banks. It became obvious that in some regions, and especially in small villages, small denominations circulated in a vicious circle (pub - post office - shop). The need to terminate circulation of the old Federal unstamped banknotes and coins became urgent especially after the 10 per cent devaluation of Slovak currency in July 1993.

An important date in the money exchange timetable was 31 August 1993, the last day of validity of three stamped banknotes (100, 200 and 1000 denominations). The Czech Savings Bank and Komercni banka exchanged these denominations in advance and, together with the Czech Postal Service, also accepted stamped banknotes as deposits from businesses until 15 September 1993. From the second half of August 1993, the Czech Postal Service made all payments in new banknotes. This was mostly for retirement pensions and postal receipts. In this way, the Post Offices helped considerably to distribute the new banknotes in the necessary number. As of 1 September 1993, all banks providing services to the general public were obliged to perform exchange.

Despite occasional and temporary shortages of the smallest denominations (hellers) in some locations, the first half year of the exchanges was successful. There were some concerns about the possible currency crunch in summer when the volume of money in circulation at the beginning of the summer holidays usually increases substantially. The summer months of 1993, however, were not typical.

As of the middle of September 1993, the new 100, 200, 500 and 1000 banknotes and 10 coins and up circulated in sufficient quantity. The amount of currency in circulation as of 15 September 1993 rose due to the introduction of new banknotes and coins while the number of old stamped banknotes was decreasing. After 15 September however, the number of circulating new banknotes of all denominations and 10, 20 and 50 coins began to decrease. In the second half of September, the volume neared the normalized condition when the currency in circulation is backed 50 per cent by a stock of currencies in related denominations.

Financing the currency separation

All participating organizations in the Czech Republic were reimbursed for the costs of the currency separation (except for stamp delivery) by the Czech National Bank, which drew its resources from future profit based on lost or unexchanged Federal banknotes and coins. The costs were therefore not borne by taxpayers. The expenses directly linked to the currency separation, i.e., the costs of stamping the banknotes and exchange of the old Federal banknotes for stamped and new ones (including the ex post exchanges) reached CZK

400 million. Costs of production, maintenance and transportation of the new currency (and liquidation of old currency) were approximately four times higher. Since some plans for the future release of new banknotes and coins had existed even before the separation, the costs would have been incurred anyway.

Total costs of the first phase of the currency separation (stamping and exchanging banknotes during February 1993) reached CZK 344.4 million in the Czech Republic as follows:

- manufacturing stamps cost CZK 31.8 million and was fully covered by the Ministry of Finance of the Czech Republic;
- direct costs of the CNB branches reached CZK 7.9 million and included printing money receipts and overtime wages and bonuses to the employees involved;
- expenses of other institutions reimbursed by the CNB reached CZK 304.8 million and included reimbursement to the Czech Postal Services (CZK 103.4 million), Czech Savings Bank (CZK 60.2 million), Komercni banka (CZK 63.8 million), the Czech Police (CZK 74.5 million), Czech Army (CZK 2.1 million).[19]

Until 31 March 1994, the last day to exchange the remaining two Federal denominations (2 and 5), the CNB received for exchange Federal (unstamped) currency worth more than it should have been, based on the preliminary division of the Czechoslovak State Bank balance sheet between the Czech National Bank and the National Bank of Slovakia (2:1 ratio). Therefore, the exchange of the Federal currency represented a noticeable loss for the CNB showing a balance of CSK -1.6 billion. On the other hand, the NBS accumulated a positive balance of CSK 5.8 billion. The protocol on the distribution of currency decided to settle the total balance between the CNB and the NBS by using the 2:1 ratio.

3.3 Final observations

The currency separation avoided negative consequences for both the Czech and Slovak economies, was inflationary-neutral and, as soon as the end of the first quarter of 1993 arrived, proved that the potential risks had been successfully eliminated. It facilitated a base for independent monetary policies and created a positive environment for development of the Czech and Slovak banking sectors. It enabled the preservation of the policy of a stable exchange rate and increased confidence in the new monetary systems.

The currency separation was highly appreciated by both the domestic and international press and was carefully monitored by foreign observers. Its scenario and legislative background were studied in detail by International

Monetary Fund experts. In June 1993, the currency separation scenario was recommended by the IMF Mission for use in Moldava to support its withdrawal from the Rouble zone. It was also recommended by the IMF to assist the preparation and introduction of national currencies in Turkmenistan and Uzbekistan.

4 Clearing payment system

The foundation of the sovereign Czech and Slovak Republics at the beginning of 1993 brought about the necessity to newly define Czech-Slovak relations on almost all levels. As soon as in August 1992, representatives of both Republics-to-be were concerned with one of the key problems of their future co-existence: the establishment of a framework for payments between the Czech Republic and the Slovak Republic which would, after the break-up of Czechoslovakia, become international payments.

4.1 Expected benefits and shortcomings of the clearing arrangement

There were two conditions which influenced the decision on the character of the future payment system an integral part of which was the exchange rate regime. On the one hand, it was obvious that due to a long-term coexistence in one state, the economies of both Republics were highly integrated and interdependent, and therefore a concerted action would definitely contribute to mitigating the post-separation shock. On the other hand, the different positions of both economies and their dissimilar attitudes to the transformation process showed that the future would bring about some differences in the economic policies. The question central to the process of outlining the future payment system, therefore, was whether to stress a more coordinated or more autonomous approach.

The ultimate plan of the Czech government was to introduce a standard payment system in convertible currencies without any special regime for trade with Slovakia, and without an obligation to coordinate the process of effecting the full convertibility of the Czech currency with the Slovaks. Nevertheless, this plan could not be implemented immediately. The negative experience from the collapse of CMEA trade among the former Soviet bloc members, which contributed substantially to the deepening of the transformation depression in Czechoslovakia, raised concerns about the potential negative impact on both the CR and the SR of such a change and delayed the immediate introduction of a new payment system.

The first step towards the new payment system was represented by the Monetary Agreement between the Czech and the Slovak Governments (see Section 2), the concept of which reflected the necessity of paying attention to the economic interdependence of both Republics immediately after the split of the Federation. While considering possible scenarios for the period ensuing the currency separation, the policy makers had to take into account other factors, such as the fixed exchange rate.[20] A fixed exchange rate tends to create a stable environment for business transactions, for it removes risks connected with frequent realignments of the national currencies. Given the high level of economic integration of the western and eastern parts of the formerly unified state, preservation of the exchange rate stability represented an important step in preventing a radical decline in Czech-Slovak trade.

Conversion of the backlog of assets and liabilities denominated in the Federal currency, both between businesses and on the governmental level, became another important matter to be solved. Setting the relative rate of both currencies in a 1 to 1 ratio would eliminate the question of which currency to quote the old debts in and, respectively, which entity should bear the exchange rate related losses, thereby lowering the risk of irrecoverable debts.[21]

The insufficient level of the external reserves also had to be taken into account. The reserves were not high enough to meet the growing needs of businesses upon the introduction of payments in convertible currencies. Such an act could endanger the internal convertibility of the Czech and Slovak currencies, increase the number of irrecoverable debts and contribute to an overall decline in trading between the two Republics. Why would a Czech (or a Slovak) importer buy from a Slovak (or Czech) supplier when, with payments made in convertible currencies anyway, he or she could import from almost everywhere?

Representatives of the central banks and the Ministries of Finance agreed on the clearing payment system as the best strategy to meet the above requirements.[22] The reasons behind this decision were the following:

i) The clearing system, which allows participants in international trade to make payments in their domestic currencies, reduces requirements for hard currency reserves, which are used only to settle payment imbalances and are not used for trading as such. The clearing arrangement thus reduces the risk of shortage of the hard currency as means of payment.

ii) Since the Czechoslovak State Bank in its Prague and Bratislava branches had already administered payments among the Czech and Slovak banks, the clearing arrangement as such did not require a new infrastructure.

The only new thing to be introduced were new accounts to register all payments from the CR to the SR and vice versa.

iii) The exchange rate system within the clearing system could in itself combine advantages of both a fixed and floating exchange rate. The system of relating the exchange rate between the Czech and Slovak currencies crosswise, following the exchange rate of both national currencies vis-a-vis convertible currencies, allowed the maintenance of a stable relationship between the CZK and SKK to the extent to which both successor Republics maintained external purchasing power of their currencies. In this respect, the exchange rate between the Czech and Slovak currencies was also flexible, since it reflected the changes of both the national currencies vis-a-vis convertible currencies. It removed the need to create supranational intervention mechanisms (such as common reserves or a supranational fiscal system) in case both Republics were interested in the long-term stability of the exchange rate between the Czech and Slovak currencies.[23]

iv) Unlike a payment system using national currencies (probably based on some kind of flexible regime), the clearing payment system was able to eliminate potential unwillingness of commercial banks to take risks by keeping the national currency of the other party of the clearing agreement in their portfolios. Similarly, it did not seem useful to create a special intervention mechanism to limit volatility of the market-determined exchange rate between the Czech and Slovak currencies while all other payments with third countries were made under a fixed exchange rate regime.

v) In case of need, clearing could act as means of monitoring financial flows between the Republics (this function was used especially in the period after the split of currencies) and also facilitate a gradual process of transfer to direct payments by possibly modifying the rules of the system.

There were some shortcomings, too. If a country with low external reserves permanently showed trade deficits, it would lead to the repeated occurrence of hard currency draining and call into question the functioning of the entire system. Long-term payment imbalances could also bring about administrative restrictions which would, by their objective to reduce tensions in payment balance, act against the principles of free trade.

The clearing system also carries the risk of foreign exchange speculation, a danger to every system characterized by multiple exchange rates. The scheme which distinguished transactions before and after the currency separation, envisaged clearing realignments *sui generis*, and introduced a special regime for non-trade transactions, in fact, established a system of four exchange rates between the Czech and Slovak currencies.[24]

Re-exports (import from third countries via the other party in the clearing payment system) called for special attention.[25] If, for example, the decrease in external reserves of one country made its importers use the clearing for effecting their transactions, it would reflect in increased imports of the other member and draining of its external reserves. Excess re-exports could thus destabilize reserves of both parties to the clearing system.

When estimating benefits and costs of the clearing payment system, the prevailing feeling was that while the costs of introducing such a system could be compensated for in the future and possibly reduced by modifying its rules, the benefits could be seen immediately.

4.2 Description of the clearing payment system

The introduction of the clearing payment system was marked by four agreements and protocols (so called Payment Agreement) concluded on 4 February 1993 by the representatives of the Czech and Slovak Republics. These documents created a framework for all Czech-Slovak financial transactions, the majority of which fell under the clearing payment regime. In compliance with the agreements, all payments of the corporate entities were to be made within the clearing. In other words, such a system should be used for making not only all trade-related payments as usual for standard clearing arrangements, but also payments associated with capital account transactions. The payment agreement established the Czech and Slovak Governments (respectively Ministries of Finance) as administrators of the clearing system, with central banks acting as providers of technical support. To exercise their responsibilities, both central banks opened mutual accounts without commissions and charges. For the mechanics of a clearing transaction see Figure 3.2.

The clearing was divided into two blocks. The so called old block was used to settle claims and obligations from before the currency separation. The accounting unit of the old block was the so called clearing Crown signed XCS. Conversion of payments in national currencies was made at the fixed exchange rate XCS 1 = CZK 1 = SKK 1. The agreement settled on a 3 per cent annual interest rate charge for the outstanding balance. Initially, the balance was to be settled every three months by a payment in a convertible currency or by a transfer to the new block. From September 1993 on, the balance was automatically transferred to the new block at the end of each calendar month at a fixed exchange rate valid on the day of the currency separation.

The so called new clearing block was used to settle claims and obligations which originated after the currency separation. Conversion of payments in national currencies to the accounting unit (clearing ECU signed XCU) was made in compliance with the momentary exchange rates of both national currencies vis-a-vis ECU as quoted on a daily basis by the Czech or Slovak central banks. In case of a more permanent imbalance, both central banks could independently adjust the clearing rate of their currency vis-a-vis the clearing XCU within the band of 5 per cent in both directions from central parity. The outstanding balance was subjected to 5 per cent annual interest. Realignments of the national currencies vis-a-vis convertible currencies were not impaired by the agreement.

Slovak importer

Assets	Liabilities
(a) SKK -110 bank deposit	

Slovak commercial bank

Assets	Liabilities
(b) SKK -110 deposit at NBS	SKK -110 (a) business account

National Bank of Slovakia

Assets	Liabilities
	SKK -110 (b) bank account
	SKK +110 (c) government deposit

Slovak government budget

Revenues	Expenditures
(c) SKK +110 budget revenue	

Czech exporter

Assets	Liabilities
(f) CZK +100 bank deposit	

Czech commercial bank

Assets	Liabilities
(d) CZK +100 deposit at CNB	CZK + 100 (f) business account

Czech National Bank

Assets	Liabilities
(e) CZK +100 credit to government	CZK +100 (d) bank account

Czech government budget

Revenues	Expenditures
	CZK +100 (e) budget expenditure

Figure 3.2 Clearing transaction

Note: In this case, a Slovak importer is paying for Czech goods worth CZK 100. The exchange rate used for the transaction is 1.1:1 SKK/CZK. The transaction unfolds as follows: (a) the Slovak importer instructs his commercial bank to make a payment for imported goods; (b) the Slovak commercial bank makes a payment to the NBS clearing center by debiting its account held at NBS in the amount of SKK 110; (c) NBS registers this payment as budgetary revenue of the Slovak government; (d) the CNB clearing center makes a payment to the Czech exporter's commercial bank, and (e) registers it as a budgetary expenditure of the Czech government; (f) the Czech exporter's bank credits the client's account.

Czech exporter

Assets	Liabilities
(f) CZK +100 bank deposit	
(g) CZK -100 bank deposit	

Czech commercial bank

Assets	Liabilities
(d) CZK +100 deposit at CNB	CZK +100 (f) business account
(h) CZK -100 deposit at CNB	CZK -100 (g) business account

Czech National Bank

Assets	Liabilities
(e) CZK +100 credit to government	CZK +100 (d) bank account
	CZK -100 (h) bank account
	CZK +100 (i) government deposit

Czech government budget

Revenues	Expenditures
(i) CZK +100 budget income	CZK +100 (e) budget expenditure

Slovak importer

Assets	Liabilities
(a) SKK -100 bank deposit	
(l) SKK +110 bank deposit	

Slovak commercial bank

Assets	Liabilities
(b) SKK -100 deposit at NBS	SKK -100 (a) business account
(j) SKK +110 deposit at NBS	SKK +110 (l) business account

National Bank of Slovakia

Assets	Liabilities
(k) SKK +110 credit to government	SKK -100 (b) deposit at NBS
	SKK +100 (c) government deposit
	SKK +110 (j) bank account

Slovak government budget

Revenues	Expenditures
(c) SKK +100 government budget	SKK +110 (k) budget expenditure

Figure 3.3 Clearing speculation

Note: In this case, a Slovak importer makes a payment of SKK 100 via the old block (SKK/CSK exchange rate 1:1) which is (e.g., for incorrect invoicing) returned by the Czech exporter via the new block (1.1:1 SKK/CSK rate): (a) the debtor instructs his bank to make payment; (b) the payment is transferred to the NBS clearing center; (c) the transaction is marked to the Slovak government budget; (d) the CNB makes a payment to the creditor's bank; (e) the transaction is marked to the Czech government budget; (f) the Czech bank credits the client's bank account; (g) the Czech exporter instructs his bank to return payment; (h) - (l) are a reversed sequence of steps (b) - (f). Analyzing the account balances, we can see that the Slovak importer benefits from this speculation to the detriment of the Slovak budget and can divide the profits with his Czech counterpart.

The payment agreement also determined the so called marginal credit at XCU 130 million (i.e approximately CZK 4.5 billion). If the net balance on the clearing account did not exceed this limit, the government of the surplus party was debited (see Figure 3.2). In case the marginal credit was exceeded (after merging closing balances of both the new and old blocks), the debtor was obliged to settle it in convertible currencies before the 15th of the following month at the 1XCU=1ECU rate. Exceeding the marginal credit was subjected to 10 per cent annual interest. In case the installments were not made on time, the interest penalty rose to 15 per cent per annum.

Since the clearing payment system was planned as a temporary one, the Payment Agreement determined neither a monitoring mechanism to control the compliance with the Agreement when effecting transactions, nor penalties for breaking the Agreement. For example, the Czech National Bank received from commercial banks (as a part of the payment order) only the number of the creditor's and debtor's bank accounts and the payment code. There was no direct check whether payments corresponded with the nature of the reported transactions or contacting the holders of the bank accounts directly to acquire and verify information.[7] The nonexistence of a monitoring mechanism in a system where there were more exchange rates in use opened up a wide area for speculation. For example, at the end of 1993, there were speculations attempting at a misuse of the interest spread between the old and new blocks (see Figure 3.3).

There were two types of transactions which, in compliance with the agreements, were not to be effected via clearing. The first were the already mentioned re-exports, which were to be paid for by both parties to the agreement in convertible currencies. The non-existence of a monitoring mechanism and the vague definition of re-exports made the execution of this rule very tenuous.

The second exception was tourist and business travel. For example, a Czech citizen travelling to Slovakia was allowed to enter the country with a certain sum of CZK and change in Slovak banks as much of it as needed to SKK at the so called tourist rate.[27] This exchange rate was market-determined since banks enjoyed both the right to fix it based on local demand and supply conditions and to trade both currencies among themselves. To support this scheme, the central banks agreed to swap national currencies which could be subsequently sold to the central bank of the other member to the agreement within three months from the day of purchase (at the initial exchange rate).

4.3 Performance of the clearing payment system

Clearing proved to be a very important factor in supporting Czech-Slovak trade after the currency separation. It was very soon adopted by the business sphere and functioned without any major frictions. The volume of payments effected via clearing indicated that an immediate shift to a standard payment system would significantly restrict Czech-Slovak trade due to insufficient external reserves. To illustrate this point, the ratio of the monthly volume of clearing payments to the CNB external reserves was, in February 1993, 38 per cent (in May 1993 it was only 15 per cent). For Slovakia the respective figure was 59 per cent in February 1993 and 264 per cent in May 1993.

Figure 3.4 displays the development of payments effected via the new block of the clearing account. Between February and June 1993, the volume of both Czech and Slovak payments increased (payments from the CR to the SR rising faster than in the opposite direction). This development was influenced by several factors, e.g., by lower solvency of Slovak businesses as well as speculative delays of payments in reaction to the expected devaluation of the Slovak currency. Czech businesses, whose Slovak counterparts suddenly became foreigners, started choosing their partners more selectively and became more disciplined in making their payments. Many Slovak firms had representatives in the Czech Republic and opened bank accounts in Czech banks. Payments for imports made from these accounts were not reflected in the clearing figures.

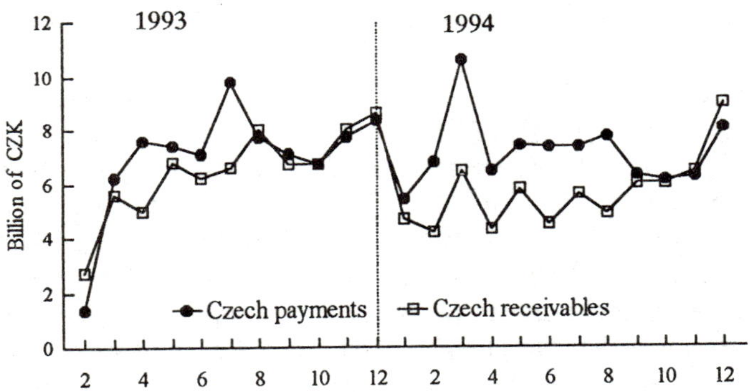

Figure 3.4 Financial flows in the new block (not cumulated)

Source: *Indicators of Monetary and Economic Development*, no. 1-8, 1994, CNB, Prague

Compulsory transfers of money balances of individuals and corporate entities to the country of the owner's residence also contributed to an unequal flow growth of payments in the new block.[28] This flow was bigger from the CR to the SR, partly as a consequence of speculative transfers before the currency separation.

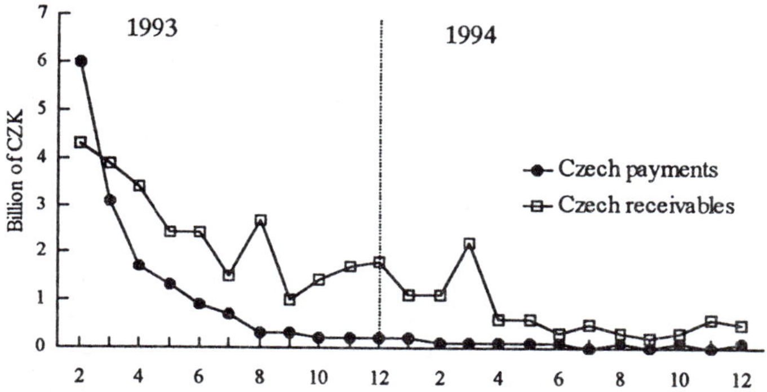

Figure 3.5 Financial flows in the old block (not cumulative)

Source: *Indicators of Monetary and Economic Development*, no. 1-8, 1994, CNB, Prague

Initially, the development in the old block was just opposite. The volume of both Czech and Slovak payments gradually decreased, this process was much slower with payments from the SR to the CR (see Figure 3.5). This trend responded to the initial forecasts that the role of the old block would gradually diminish with the step-by-step liquidation of receivables from before the currency separation.[29]

Both central banks reacted to the payment imbalance with modifications of the clearing rate, the NBS by devaluation and the CNB by revaluation vis-a-vis the central rate. The Czech currency thus strengthened vis-a-vis the Slovak one by 8 per cent (out of an allowed 10 per cent). This difference was diminished in May and June as a reaction to the improving Slovak deficit (see Figure 3.6).

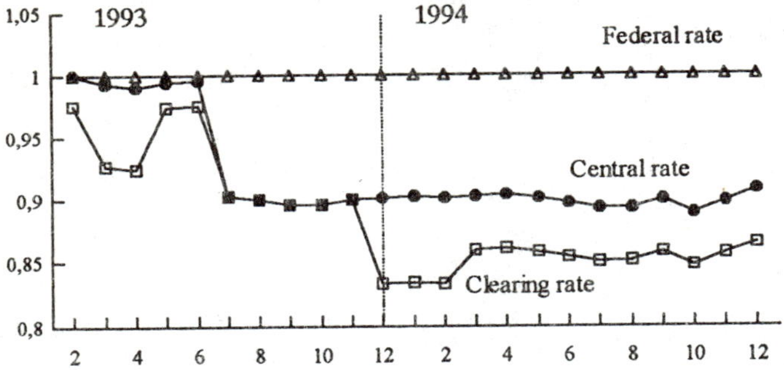

Figure 3.6 Development of clearing rate (CZK/SKK)

Note: *Central rate* is the price of SKK in CZK expressed crosswise based on the exchange rates of both currencies vis-a-vis ECU:

Central rate = (CZK/ECU)/(SKK/ECU).

The clearing rate (new block rate) is the central rate modified by the CNB and NBS in accordance with the articles of the Payment Agreement:

Clearing rate = Central rate $\cdot(1 + d)$,

where d can take a value up to 10 per cent since each party can devalue/revalue by 5 per cent.

Federal rate (old block rate) is 1 SKK =1 CZK.

In July 1993, the Slovak government devalued the Slovak currency vis-a-vis the convertible currencies by 10 per cent, and to the same extent changed the central parity of the clearing rate. As a result of this, the clearing revaluation of the Czech currency within the new block was canceled out in an attempt to moderate the negative outcome of the Slovak devaluation on the Czech exports. These realignments, however, caused a significant gap between the old and the new block exchange rates. The difference in rates further widened in December 1993, when the growing payment imbalance necessitated a clearing devaluation of the Slovak currency.

The devaluation of the Slovak currency in July 1993 brought to the new block a partial stability (volume of payments from the CR to the SR and vice versa was more or less even). Czech payments within the old block kept decreasing constantly and by August 1993 had almost completely stopped. Payments from Slovakia, on the other hand, marked an increase caused partly by exchange rate speculations and the situation resulted in increasing the Slovak deficit (see Figure 3.7).

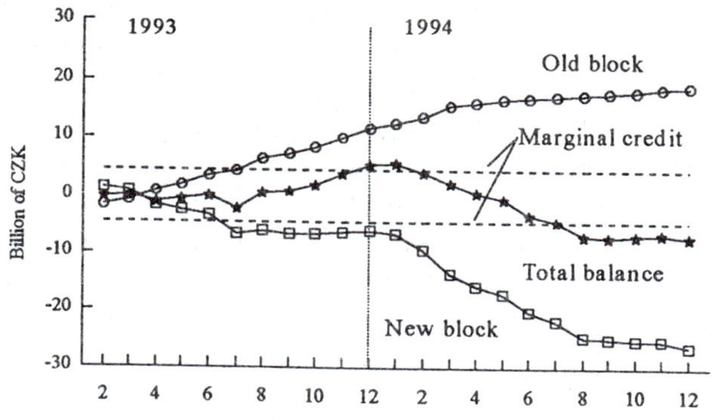

Figure 3.7 Slovak clearing deficits/surpluses (cumulated)

Source: *Indicators of Monetary and Economic Development*, no. 1-8, 1994, CNB, Prague

The payment imbalance peaked at the end of 1993, when the Slovak Republic overdrafted the marginal credit and twice had to settle the overdraft in convertible currencies. In January 1994, the December 1993 deficit of ECU 39 million (USD 43.5 million) was settled, and in February 1994, the January 1994 deficit of ECU 46 million (USD 51.6 million) was requited. In both cases, the Payment Agreement was honoured and the exceeded limit was settled by the SR in due time, although it caused a substantial decrease in the Slovak external reserves.

In February 1994, the Slovak government started introducing administrative measures to prevent further deterioration of the balance of payments and to support foreign exchange reserves which stagnated after the devaluation of the Slovak currency. An implementation of quality tests for food products imported to Slovakia was followed by a 10 per cent import surcharge (March 1994) for consumer goods and food products. The Czech Republic decided to offset the surcharge by a 3 per cent clearing devaluation.

Measures introduced by the Slovak government (devaluation of the Slovak currency vis-a-vis convertible currencies and the clearing ECU, introduction of import surcharge and quality tests requirements) brought about a completely reversed trend when the Czech government became a debtor of the

Slovak budget. A profound control of transactions within the old block, effected in Slovakia in order to eliminate speculative payments, also contributed to slowing down the growth of the Slovak deficit. In July 1994, the Czech Republic first exceeded the marginal credit by ECU 64,200. From August on, the CR exceeded the limit continually (for August it was ECU 68.8 million). The highest settlement of ECU 79 million was paid for September 1994. From October on, the CR had to liquidate claims of ECU 73 million for October, ECU 53 million for November, and ECU 16.7 million for December. Thanks to the growing foreign exchange reserves the settlements did not represent any serious problem for the CR.

The development of a payment imbalance on the clearing account in 1994 was, apart from trade-related transactions, also influenced by capital account transactions originating from the existence of different interest rates and unequal access to financial sources in both Republics. For the Slovak companies, the Czech financial market, with its lower interest rates, strong inflow of foreign capital and stable exchange rate represented a chance to acquire cheaper loans than those offered by the Slovak financial institutions.

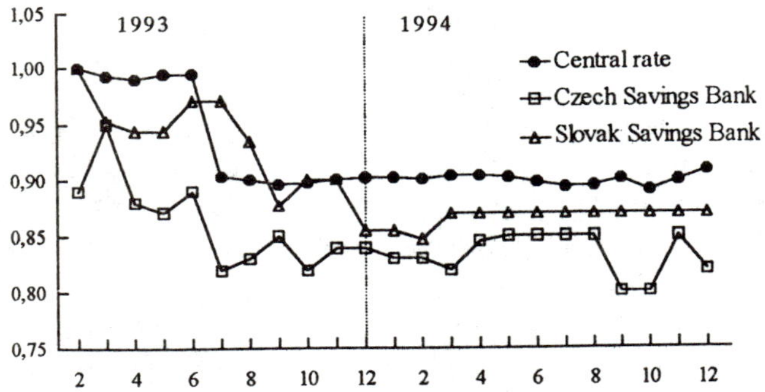

Figure 3.8 Development of tourist exchange rates (CZK/SKK)

Source: *Hospodarske noviny,* various issues

To give a more detailed picture, it is necessary to mention the development of the tourist exchange rate determined by banks following the supply-demand conditions. Based on the rates quoted by the Czech and Slovak Savings Banks we can document that tourist rates closely matched the official purchasing power of both national currencies.

The demand for Czech currency in Slovakia was often higher than the supply and the same was true for Slovak currency in the Czech Republic (demand higher than currency offered for sale). This development reflected the unwillingness, especially of the Czech banks, to substantially enlarge their portfolios to include Slovak currency and maintain an equilibrium exchange rate with the help of inter-bank transactions. The main source of the other Republic's currency was local purchases from tourists. Reserves of national currencies which the central banks exchanged after the currency separation to support this scheme remained mostly unused. The inflexibility of the financial institutions indicated the frictions the payment system might have faced given the mutual convertibility of both national currencies.

It is also interesting to analyze the role of the national budgets. An imbalance of the clearing account was disadvantageous for the budget of the surplus country which provided its debtor with long-term credit based on very good terms and at the same time bore the default risk up to the total of the provided credit. For example, the Czech budget credited the clearing system at the end of 1993 with ECU 169 million (see Table 3.11).

Table 3.11
Influence of the clearing balance on the government budgets

Government budgets (in billion of CZK)	Revenues	Expenditures	Balance	Position of budgets in the case of liquidating the clearing deficit as of December 1993
CR	358.0	356.9	1.1	6.6
SR	150.0	173.0	-23.0	- 28.5

Source: Czech National Bank, Slovak Statistical Office

The clearing mechanism therefore helped to moderate the impact of the dissolution of the Federal fiscal system by transferring a part of the Czech budget surplus to Slovakia. It acted in a way as a Czech government pro-export measure. Similarly, the Slovak government anti-import measures (which in the second half of 1994 contributed to the Slovak surplus on the clearing account) acted as an extra burden for the already strained Slovak government budget.

4.4 Termination of Czech-Slovak clearing

During the functioning of the clearing payment system, there were several suggestions made to modify the Payment Agreement. The first one was the Slovak proposal to increase the marginal credit up to ECU 150-160 million (resulting from fears of the unfavourable development of the Slovak foreign exchange reserves). This proposal was not acceptable for the Czech government, the budget of which was burdened by the marginal credit. It was also not clear if the Slovak deficit was going to grow further or not.

Another proposed measure to manage the payment imbalance was based on widening the range of the permitted clearing realignments, e.g., from 5 to 10 per cent. Such discretion might, however, cause significant price distortions in the system, creating different price levels which would paradoxically disadvantage one party to the agreement vis-a-vis economic agents from third countries. In addition, during a period of liberalization of capital flows, infrequent clearing realignments lose their importance in regulating the trade balance. The reason is simple, since the transactions on the capital account are driven by different forces (exchange rate differential, relative yields of securities, portfolio diversifications, exchange rate speculation, etc.).

The possible discontinuation of the old block became the most discussed measure. On the one hand, this payment block kept losing its importance in terms of payment volumes. On the other hand, it widened the exchange rate scissors within the clearing system and thus opened up space for speculative behaviour. Some economists, however, pointed to the potential for increased difficulties in claiming old receivables after possible discontinuation of the old block for the Slovak companies, as well as the government, were more willing to settle their debts based on the 1 to 1 CZK/SKK exchange rate.

Besides these partial modifications, the Czech government was considering the more radical solution of discontinuing the clearing payment system and switching to payments in convertible currencies. One of the reasons was a certain resentment of the Slovak administrative barriers causing distortions in trade relations between the business partners, as well their stubbornness in refusing to remove the clearing devaluation that impaired the Czech exporters vis-a-vis the third countries.[30]

The different speed of the Czech and Slovak programmes towards the full convertibility of their currencies also represented an important factor in considering the future of the clearing payment system. The Czech Republic announced a plan of a relatively fast move to full convertibility, while the Slovak government decided to implement mostly administrative measures to reach external balance. From this perspective, clearing thus could have become a mechanism to encourage destabilizing transactions between the convertible Czech and the unconvertible Slovak currency. The IMF argument that the Czech-Slovak clearing created unequal conditions among the subjects of international trade which would prevent the Czech currency (in compliance with Article VIII of the IMF Agreement) from acquiring the status of convertible currency was also very important in this respect.[31]

The shortage of foreign exchange reserves, another reason for the clearing arrangement, also kept losing its importance for the growing reserves of both the Czech and Slovak Republics in the second half of 1994.

These considerations resulted in meetings between Czech and Slovak representatives. In January 1995, it was agreed that it would be beneficial for both parties to maintain the clearing system then in operation at least until the end of 1995 and to consider some modifications of the existing rules (discontinuation of the old block, reduction of the marginal credit limit, restriction of the permitted divergences of the clearing rate). The Czech government, however, declared one condition -- to remove the exchange rate discrimination against Czech exporters to Slovakia in the form of a 5 per cent clearing devaluation. This request came at the time of a growing imbalance of clearing payments; in the first four months of 1995, the CR transferred to the SR a sum of ECU 374 million as a consequence of exceeding the marginal credit. At the same time, Slovakia prolonged the validity of the import surcharge, originally introduced as a transitory measure, for the whole of 1995.

At the beginning of May 1995, as a reaction to the unwillingness of the Slovak government to make compromises, the Czech government assigned the Ministry of Finance the task of drafting a proposal to terminate the Payment Agreement with Slovakia. At the same time, Czech representatives invited the Slovaks to start negotiations to insure a smooth transfer to the standard regime of payments in convertible currencies. However, the time period which the Czech government announced as a waiting period for the Slovak answer was understood by the Slovak party as an ultimatum which, subsequently, gave birth to numerous declarations of Slovak politicians doubting the benefits of the Customs Union. Although the Slovaks preferred modification of the clearing payment system to its termination (to prove this, it declared a 4 per cent clearing revaluation), the decision of the Czech government on the termination of the clearing payment system was irreversible.

Due to the impossibility of reaching a consensus, the Czech government decided to withdraw from the Payment Agreement. The decision was passed by the Czech Parliament in July 1995 and set the date of termination for 30 September 1995, the date when the new Foreign Exchange Act broadening the convertibility of the Czech currency was expected to take effect.

However dramatic the termination of the clearing payment system might seem, it is without a doubt that its existence contributed substantially to a smooth separation of the homogeneous Czechoslovak economy which had been characterized by numerous internal economic interrelations. Thanks to the clearing payment system, the process of dividing the single economic system into two separate economic entities each with its own monetary, fiscal and exchange rate policies was effected without major friction and provided the time necessary for adjustment.

5 Czech-Slovak Customs Union

Customs Union between the Czech and Slovak Republics has existed as an everyday reality for several years. It was created with certain skeptical anticipations caused by the unusual situation in which it was formed, that is, in a country in the process of splitting up. The Customs Union functioned with some friction which, however, were not disturbing enough to substantially discredit its performance. It will be useful to examine in detail the incentives and interests which gave birth to the Customs Union and kept it operational. The authors will also focus on the effectiveness of the Customs Union in fulfilling its central mission to prevent Czech-Slovak trade from collapsing.

5.1 Incentives to establish the Customs Union

The establishment of the Customs Union was a result of both internal attempts to find a framework for inter-Republic trade, and efforts to strengthen the Republics' international position by passing the EC Association Agreements as soon as possible and with a minimum of difficulty.

The pending break-up of Czechoslovakia increased the concerns that the separation of two such strongly interconnected economies would cause an instant decrease in mutual trade and the destruction of the cooperative links. At the same time, the disturbing issue of passing the EC Association Agreements threatened two potential complications. Resumed negotiations first meant a further delay in the association process, and, secondly, produced a risk of losing the previously agreed favorable conditions (customs duties, quotas), agreed upon in the light of the 'velvet revolution'. The only two solutions to at least partially alleviate the anticipated negative consequences of the break-up and, at the same time, not contradict international agreements ware to establish either a customs union or a free trade area.

By definition, a customs union is a form of international macroeconomic integration and usually features the following:

i) gradual decrease or even removal of customs duties and quotas in mutual trade with the intention to accomplish the free movement of goods and services between the parties to the agreement;

ii) creation of common customs tariffs vis-a-vis the third countries;

iii) common trade policy vis-a-vis the third countries.

On the other hand, a free trade area can exist based on the first condition only, i.e., abolishing tariffs and quotas between the parties.

There were many arguments made against establishing any kind of serious institutional framework for mutual Czech-Slovak trade beyond standard contacts between any two independent states and especially against a customs union. In the middle of 1991, the Czech government drafted a so called 'emergency scenario' to analyze the economic aspects of the potential break-up of the Federation, which questioned the viability of a customs union and claimed a workable customs union unfeasible unless it involved two economically equal partners. At the same time, failure to act was going to cause problems with the EC Association Agreements and a likely decline in Czech exports to Slovakia. The June 1992 elections and subsequent political development gave rise to a new wave of skepticism and minimized the chances of keeping the Federation together. The skeptics mainly pointed to the lower productivity of the Slovak economy in comparison with the Czech Republic, the lower performance of Slovak exports, the lack of foreign capital, inadequate savings, unfavourable industrial structure and poor competitiveness of Slovak agriculture. Potential problems with value-added tax payments by exporters and the unfeasibility of maintaining fixed exchange rates between the national currencies within the customs union also caused concerns.

The customs union advocates defended its existence with two main arguments -- it had the potential to mitigate the decline in mutual trade as a reaction to the disintegration of the economy, and to facilitate the smooth transfer of the EC Association Agreements to the successor states.

Despite the lack of reliable data, the deep interdependency of both economies was obvious. Various estimates showed Czech exports to the SR at 12-15 per cent of its industrial production and Slovak exports to the CR at 26-32 per cent of its production.[32] The cooperation and production networks of suppliers and buyers were extensive and had considerable longevity, and their instant termination could have caused severe damage. A 25 per cent fall of mutual trade as a consequence of the separation could directly affect 3-4 per cent of Czech production and 7-8 per cent of total Slovak production (the total indirect impact would be comparably larger). A break in commodity flows (e.g. in 1991 of raw materials and intermediate products shipped from the CR to the SR totaled about CSK 39 billion; supplies shipped from the SR to the CR totaled approximately CSK 36 billion could have also had critical consequences). Provided the decline was 25 per cent, a purchase of these commodities from third countries would have cost over USD 300 billion, a remarkable load especially for the Slovak economy.

The interdependency of the two economies was not a sufficient condition for the two Republics to establish a customs union. Had the interdependency been the only reason, a free trade area would have been a satisfactory option suitable for countries of different economic levels since it is less demanding for the coordination of economic, trade and tariff policies than a customs union.[33] At the same time, Poland, Hungary and Czechoslovakia were about to complete the Central European Free Trade Area (hereafter CEFTA) negotiations, within the framework of which the Czech and Slovak Republics had an option to conclude a separate arrangement for a customs-free zone prior to the establishment of CEFTA.[34]

The concern about having to re-enter the association talks with the EC thus seemed the main incentive for the establishment of a customs union. The representatives not only feared loss of time and related increase in expenses but also worsening conditions for approving quotas for sensitive commodities. Before the break-up of Czechoslovakia, the EC clearly communicated that the Association Agreements were not to be simply passed onto the succeeding state.[35] The successors to Czechoslovakia were potentially risking termination of the interim trade agreement with the EC and falling to the very end of the line of the Eastern European countries awaiting association.

The European Association Agreement between the former Czechoslovakia and the EC had already been signed on 16 December 1991. At the same time, the remaining members of the so called Visegrad Three (Hungary and Poland) signed their Association Agreements. Ratification by the European Parliament was expected to take place in the Autumn of 1992. The temporary trade agreement, however, had already taken effect on 1 March 1992, and it included the trade-related sections of the Association Agreement. It limited or removed a number of tariffs and quantity restrictions in trading between the Czechoslovakia and the EC. Based on the principle of asymmetrical advantages, the agreement favored exports from Czechoslovakia to the EC. For Czechoslovakia, the annual gains of this agreement, in terms of tariff relief only, were estimated at USD 100 to 300 billion.[36]

A customs union as a well-identified subject with common tariffs and trade policy seemed to be the only formation which would justify to the EC the preservation of the formerly agreed-upon trade concessions. Also, the import quotas agreed upon with the former Czechoslovakia could be divided simply following an internal agreement between the Czech and Slovak Republics. In the given situation it was the fastest way of passing the Association

Agreements onto the succeeding states. On the other hand, a free trade area which permits the states to impose different customs tariffs on third countries could provoke a negative reaction from the EC, which would argue that the preferential treatment of Czechoslovak exports was based on a certain level and structure of tariffs and therefore was not transferrable to the new states.

The new Association Agreement between the CR and the EC was renegotiated relatively quickly, and signed on 4 October 1993, and ratified by the European Parliament in an unprecedentedly short time period on 27 October 1993. The negotiations between the EC and the SR took place simultaneously.

The new agreements differed in three aspects, mostly of a political nature, which did not display a new attitude towards or mistrust of the CR or the SR but were merely a reflection of the new legislative approach of the EC vis-a-vis all applicants. First, the preamble was extended by adding a plea for human and minority rights and, secondly, there were two articles added to the main text in order to promote democratic principles, human rights, market economy principles and a so called 'suspension clause' to facilitate the possibility of discontinuing the Agreements in case of emergency. The political articles of the Agreement underscore the interest of both parties in an ongoing close communication and overall integration with the clear intention to integrate the CR and the SR into the EC.

The trade-related articles included trade concessions which both parties were to grant to each other with the intention of gradually removing all tariff and other barriers to mutual trade. Based on the principle of asymmetry, the Czech party benefitted from numerous advantages in the process of entering the EC market. Preferential quota, tariff and quantity restrictions in the Agreement were determined in keeping with the internal division between the CR and the SR. The succeeding states adopted in full the rights and responsibilities of the interim trade agreement which, among others, intended to establish a free trade area between the Czech Republic and the EC within ten years and guaranteed the validity of all concessions included in the Association Agreement upon its signature regardless of the length of the ratification process.

In keeping with the Association Agreement, the EC liberalized access to its market for about 60 per cent of Czech exports; the EC exports, on the other hand, were 20-25 per cent liberalized. For the remaining 40 per cent of Czech exports (mainly commodities such as steel, agricultural products and textiles) the Agreement designed a timetable of gradual tariff and quota withdrawal over a 5-6 year period (for imports of comparably sensitive commodities to the Czech markets it was 5-9 years). After the June 1993 EC Summit in Copenhagen, the Czech goods were given further advantages on the EC market, and the time for gradual withdrawal of restrictions shortened, depending on the nature of the commodity, by 1-2 years.

5.2 Institutional framework of the Czech-Slovak Customs Union

The Agreement to establish the Customs Union between the Czech and Slovak Republics was concluded on 29 October 1992 and took effect on 3 May 1993 (it was, however, in temporary effect as of 1 January 1993).

If the Czech-Slovak Customs Union had not been preceded by the disintegration of a unified economy (a process completely in opposition to that which a customs union tends to play in economic integration), it could have been formally labelled a standard arrangement. It meets the usual conditions, such as removal of tariffs and quantity restrictions in mutual trade, creation of a common customs tariff and introduction of common trade policy vis-a-vis third countries.

Objectives and principles of the Customs Union

The Customs Union Agreement is in line with the General Agreement on Tariffs and Trade (GATT) and reflects the interests of both countries in coordinating strategies to support the free movement of goods and services. The Agreement emphasizes the objective to actively participate in the process of European economic integration and to facilitate a smooth Czech and Slovak accession to the EC.

The main objectives of the Customs Union are:

- free movement of goods and services;
- integration of economic policies;
- creation of favorable conditions for trade with third countries;
- common trade and customs policy vis-a-vis third countries;
- common customs tariffs vis-a-vis third countries;
- removal of tariffs and quantitative restrictions between the two countries;
- identical rules on the origin of goods vis-a-vis third countries;
- identical customs legislation (rules for charging and paying duties);
- coordination of customs statistics by using identical documents, etc.

Mutual obligations of the contracting parties

The contracting parties agreed not to introduce any export or import charges, or any fees with a similar impact in order to guarantee the free movement of goods. Export and import quantity restrictions and all measures with similar effects were prohibited. The Agreement, however, gave relatively much room for exceptions in the so called public interest. Such bans and restrictions were not to be misused for discrimination or concealed trade restrictions and were to be communicated to the other party prior to their introduction. The contracting parties also agreed to refrain from introducing internal fiscal measures or procedures to discriminate against imported products of the other party vis-a-vis domestic goods.

The Agreement emphasized the importance of economic competition. The contracting parties agreed to prevent abuse of monopoly in the Customs Union territory, to protect intellectual property and to guarantee nondiscriminatory admission to public tenders. The parties distanced themselves from any kind of state support for the promotion of selected companies or industries in case it should threaten mutual trade.

The effectiveness of the Customs Union was to be guaranteed by the harmonization of legal norms, especially customs tariffs, customs administration and statistics, export/import licenses, intellectual property protection and anti-dumping measures. The Agreement also presumed a coordinated process of implementing and upholding of legal norms in trade and foreign exchange policies, economic competition, government support and public tenders.

The Agreement stressed the importance of the same trade policy vis-a-vis third countries, especially tariff policies, non-tariff measures, and export/import liberalization procedures as well as trade and domestic market protection, dumping and subsidies. The contracting parties agreed to unify the conditions for subsidizing export to third countries in order not to interfere with economic competition within the Customs Union.

The agreement contained special measures for agriculture. The contracting parties agreed to coordinate their agricultural policies, especially the export subsidies, taxes and other instruments of market regulation. The ban on government subsidies and export support which may limit domestic competition did not apply to agriculture.

Customs Union authorities

The Agreement appointed three Customs Union authorities - a Council, a Permanent Secretariat and an Arbitration Board.

The Customs Union Council was designed to coordinate international trade and customs policies, to represent the Union in international relations in all fields outlined in the Agreement, and to announce common trade tariffs. The Council consisted of the same number of members of the governments of both parties. The Czech Republic was represented in the Council by the Minister of Industry and Trade, the Minister of Finance, the Minister of Foreign Affairs and the Minister of Agriculture; the Slovak Republic was represented by their Slovak counterparts.

The Permanent Secretariat was the executive body of the Customs Union and is located in Bratislava, the capital of Slovakia. The Agreement defined its tasks as follows:

- monitoring the trade and customs policies of the Customs Union;
- monitoring the harmonization of export subsidies in order to protect economic competition on the domestic markets;
- coordination of customs statistics;
- monitoring the development of customs legislation in the member states and third countries;
- presenting proposals and recommendations related to the operation of the Council and managing its activities.

The Arbitration Board was designed to solve problems between the member states as they pertained to the Agreement. The Board was to be appointed ad hoc for each dispute. There should be three arbiters -- one appointed by the Czech government, one by the Slovak government, and the Head of the Board to be agreed upon by both parties (this person could be a national of a third country).

The contracting parties agreed to refrain from any measures which would breach its objectives and to act with minimal interference in the performance of the Customs Union Agreement. It was agreed to communicate without delay all measures to be taken to the Council and, upon request, consult them prior to their effect.

In case the Agreement was revoked, it remained legally binding for twelve months after the date on which the termination had been communicated to the second party.

Bottlenecks of the Agreement

An analysis of the text of the Agreement reveals several critical points and intricate phrasings which can (and already have) potentially interfere with the everyday operation of the Customs Union. One of the troubles is clearly the exclusive position of agriculture and agricultural products which have been excluded from prohibition of government subsidies interfering with economic competition and mutual trade, and no requirement to unify the export subsidies to the third countries.

The exceptions to the ban on quantity restrictions justified by protection of public morals, public interest or security, protection of human health or life, animal health or life, vegetation or environment are broadly and vaguely formulated. The articles on protection of national treasures of artistic, historical or archeological values and protection of intellectual property are equally ambiguous. The exceptions also extend to the rules regulating the control of gold, silver or the preservation of exhaustible natural resources, in case measures are taken in connection with discouraging development of domestic production or consumption. An exception to the nondiscriminatory rule in case of 'difficulties arising from increased imports as a consequence of operation of the Agreement which damage or threaten to damage the markets of the contracting parties' appears to be problematic as well.

Contrary to other customs unions, the Agreement gives relatively restricted powers to the Union authorities. A body to coordinate legislation in both member states and to represent the union vis-a-vis third parties is de facto missing. The Permanent Secretariat is not well structured to perform this role for it tends to act ex-post or suggest corrections. The idea of the Arbitration Board solving potential controversies between the member states is also doubtful, since it requires the consensus of both parties on the Head of Board and the decision-making rules. Here, the feasibility of ever constituting such a Board can be questioned.

5.3 The Performance of the Customs Union

Leafing through the newspaper coverage of the Customs Union performance, the mutual trade relations seem to be an assortment of problems and even failures. This is primarily because controversies are always given more publicity.

In reality, the objectives formulated in the Customs Union Agreement were more or less successfully fulfilled. The establishment of the Customs Union largely supported more active participation in the European economic integration and created an environment very supportive of the accession to the EU. The member states introduced an identical customs policy and, to a large extent, also a trade policy vis-a-vis the third countries and coordinated them through the Customs Union Council. They established common tariff rates, common rules for declaring the origins of goods, more or less identical customs legislation and rules for imposing and reimbursing duties, identical customs forms, and coordination of their customs statistics. There were neither duties nor quantity restrictions between the members and the free movement of goods and services was formally guaranteed.

Undoubtedly, the creation of a common customs area mitigated the possible negative consequences for mutual trade, cooperation, and, for member states economies in general, imposed fewer administrative hindrances than a standard foreign trade arrangement would have. Customs Union Council meetings adopted numerous measures and recommendations to ease mutual trade. The negotiations led to the adoption of an agreement on temporary administrative procedures for imports, exports and transit of goods within the Customs Union. The Council also formulated the Protocol defining the term 'original product' and outlining methods of administrative cooperation as well as an agreement to streamline customs procedures in railway and road transportation, and adopted a rule under which all customs, veterinary and vegetation quarantine measures regulating customs procedures on border crossings and influencing the movement of goods and services were to be communicated to the second party and Customs Union Permanent Secretariat at least 24 hours prior to their introduction.

The Council also considered an amendment to the Federal Decree which exempts selected intermediate products from import tariffs. The alteration took place in both countries and, despite initial controversies, a consensus was finally reached. This Decree had a clearly pro-export character.

The Council also considered amending the licensing procedures vis-a-vis third countries and the measures to prevent potential customs and tax evasion. It recommended an amendment to the Consumption Tax Act on alcoholic beverages, tobacco products and hydrocarbon fuels and lubricants. Simultaneously, all cigarettes produced in or imported to both the Czech and Slovak Republics were to be labelled with a stamp, and combustible fuels were to be dyed and labelled in a consistent way in both member states. The Council also established a procedure for reconsidering new duties on some agricultural and industrial products.

Despite the above-mentioned benefits, the functioning of the Customs Union was not frictionless. The tensions originated from many sources, such as Slovakia's less favorable economic situation which was reflected in the budget deficit, insufficient foreign exchange reserves (among other reasons as a consequence of amortizing the deficit in the Czech-Slovak clearing account) and higher unemployment. Slovakia understandably attempted to limit imports of Czech goods to possibly shield some segments of the domestic market, especially agriculture. Slovakia employed various measures to reach its objective and, due to the ambiguous formulations in the Agreement, it is hard to determine if they were or were not in direct conflict with the Customs Union.

A Slovak directive of 11 February 1994 not to allow any agricultural goods into Slovakia without a quality certificate issued by Slovak authorities was identified by the Czechs as the first serious breach of the Customs Union. However, it was not the first import-related problem. In the middle of September 1993, for example, the Slovak Central Inspection Institute for Agriculture discontinued imports of Czech potatoes for reasons of suspected infestation; on the other hand, in the middle of October 1993, the Czech inspectors of the Prague Inspection Institute terminated imports of Slovak sugar beets because of a viral infection.

Formally, the certificates introduced by Slovakia were not discriminatory against Czech exporters as the measure was binding for imports from all countries. After all, the Agreement permitted the taking of measures in order to protect human or animal health and vegetation. No hygienic, veterinary or other findings of such a nature were made. The unusually short time period (the introduction of the measure was officially communicated to the Czech party in the evening of 9 February and took effect on 11 February at midnight), the administrative disarray and customs officials' lack of information at the border crossings were very unpleasant for the Czech suppliers. The Czech officials accused Slovakia of unjustifiably abusing technical barriers to trade and declared that the measures were taken in order to protect the Slovak budget and not Slovak consumers. On 16 February after emergency Council session, Slovakia agreed to reinstate the status quo as of before 11 February. Nevertheless, imports remained complicated by various violations hidden behind equivocal bureaucratic conditions and rulings.

According to the Minister of Agriculture of the Czech Republic, the certificates were quite detrimental for Czech exporters since one quarter of the agricultural exports of the CR was funneled to Slovakia. As a consequence of the certificates, exports of agricultural goods to Slovakia in 1994 fell by almost 50 per cent; with some commodities it was even worse (margarine 96 per cent, pork 85 per cent, poultry 70 per cent and beer almost 50 per cent). In July 1995 Slovakia started monitoring imports of sugar, fats, alcohol, cigarettes, brown coal and other major Czech export articles. The SR also introduced quotas on the export of wood, recyclable metals and some agricultural goods, having been endangered by their possible re-export via the Czech Republic.

The introduction, by Slovakia, of a 10 per cent import surcharge which took effect on 3 March 1994 was another challenge to the functioning of the Customs Union. Although Slovak representatives had openly discussed the possibility of introducing a 20 per cent surcharge since mid-1993, the Czechs were surprised by its introduction shortly after the crisis caused by the quality certificates. The import surcharge was imposed on all consumer goods and on all goods imported for further use in services, and it applied to all importers of such merchandise from all countries. There was an exception made for goods relieved of import duties, reexports and goods designed for material consumption.

Slovakia justified the introduction of the import surcharge by the need to strengthen its balance of payments position, an act not in contradiction with the GATT regulations and, allegedly, not in conflict with the conclusions of the preliminary negotiations of the Customs Union Council. The Czech representatives, both at the Council and on different official occasions, expressed the conviction that the import surcharge was an internal Slovak affair which they did not want to and could not interfere with. The only failure was the inability of the Slovak party to have informed the Czech trade partners about the measure.

The Czech entrepreneurs criticized the attitude of the Czech government, seriously damaging the exporters' interests. Some experts claim that the Slovak activity was not in keeping with GATT and that it was not common even among parties to lower-level integrated entities than a customs union. It remained a question whether the main requirement for the approval of a surcharge was ever met - i.e. that there were problems concerning the balance of payments as such, not only vis-a-vis an individual country, and whether the unfavorable balance of payments development remained a problem even after sufficient measures were taken to change it (especially devaluation). The introduction of a surcharge formally requires the consent of the major members of GATT and the main trade partners, a condition which was not met in this case for Slovakia acquired the consent of the GATT Secretariat only.

For the Czech Republic, the import surcharge was a compromise, too. The clearing account balance was showing no signs of immediate or future improvement, so it was not reasonable to expect that the Slovak Republic, suffering from critically low foreign exchange reserves, could cover the millions of dollars overdraft as it did in December 1993 and January 1994.

The import surcharge was not without problemme for Slovakia either. On the one hand, it had the potential to help improve the balance of payments and protect domestic producers and jobs, but at the same time it represented a new inflation pressure, estimated by the Slovak Ministry of Finance to cause a 1 to 1.5 per cent increase in prices and it continued the Ministry's involvement in price controls. A number of imported products were difficult to replace in a short time or could not be replaced at all and therefore their prices had to go up. The protective shield created by the import surcharge strengthened domestic monopolies while impoverishing local markets and causing a negative international reaction to such an administrative infringement on the economy.

In the middle of May 1994, the Slovak media reported on the intention to impose tariffs on imports of so called 'sensitive' products from the Czech Republic. After the Customs Union Council emergency session on 18 May 1994, the Slovak representatives denied the reports, but they expressed an interest in concluding a special mutual agreement on 'sensitive' items not in conflict with GATT.

The Czech Republic did not avoid breaching the Customs Union Agreement either. The main Slovak criticism concerned delays in coordinating legal norms effecting Slovak producers. In the case of 'recycled paper', the Czech Parliament approved an amendment to the Value Added Tax Act on the import of sanitary paper produced with more than 70 per cent recycled paper. According to the Czech decision, passed without Customs Union Council approval, a Czech exporter was to pay a 5 per cent tax while a Slovak one 23 per cent. It was a strong discrimination against the Slovak producers of this merchandise who compose 30 per cent of the Czech market. Some technicalities of VAT collection were cited as deliberately trying to make Slovak goods more expensive on the Czech market.

Although the Czech representatives sometimes criticized the functioning of the Customs Union, they never cast doubt on its workability and the Czech political leaders often declared their interest in its preservation. The semi-official signs from Slovakia denouncing the Customs Union as disadvantageous for Slovakia became more outspoken in connection with the Czech withdrawal from the clearing payment system in July 1995, when the Slovak government approved the cancellation of an import surcharge for cars up to 1500 ccm. Czech politicians viewed this measure as a serious breach of the principles of the Customs Union, which prohibited the introduction of different taxes on imports from third countries, and as a resolution seriously damaging Czech interests.

5.4 Development of Czech and Slovak mutual trade

Although one of the main incentives for establishment of the Customs Union was to maintain mutual trade and to prevent the disintegration of important cooperative links and the supply of indispensable goods and services, the volume of trade between the two countries considerably decreased. The pessimistic forecasts estimating the decrease in the Czech and Slovak trade at about 50 per cent, which were based on inaccurate customs statistics from the beginning of 1993 and reflected the negative effects of the currency split, did not come true. On the other hand, the original government estimate of an approximate 10 per cent decrease was far too optimistic, and the statistics finally displayed a decrease of about 20 per cent. Although many question the accuracy of 1993 and early 1994 mutual trade data, the 20 per cent decrease seems realistic.

Although the decrease can be partly explained by past problems of cooperation, when relations between businesses were often motivated by 'production for production' and political objectives, we should not forget that almost all such excess capacities were removed during the first two years of reform. Already in 1992 there was a significant decrease in Czech-Slovak trade (the Czech exports to Slovakia fell by 8.3 per cent, and imports from Slovakia by 16.9 per cent compared to 1991). As a consequence, the active mutual trade balance increased almost 2 times in favor of the Czech Republic (from 10 billion CSK in 1991 to about 18 billion CSK in 1992).[38]

The specific developments in relations to Slovakia can be also illustrated by comparing them to the relations with other significant Czech trade partners outside the Customs Union. Czech exports statistics show that among the top ten export partners (by volume of trade), Slovakia was the only country displaying an unconditional decrease below first-quarter figures in the last quarter of 1993. Similarly, in the fourth quarter of 1993, of the top ten import partners only Slovakia fell below the figures of the second quarter (the development of imports and exports can be illustrated by a seasonal model which is characterized by culminating figures in the second and fourth quarters with the highest figures in the fourth quarter).

Table 3.12
Imports and exports from/to the Czech Republic

	1st Q.	*2nd Q.*	*3rd Q.*	*4th Q.*	*1-4 Q.*[a)]
	Imports to the CR (1st Q. = 100)				
Germany	100	144	127	171	92,12
Slovakia	100	118	103	114	65,017
Russia	100	121	86	127	36,118
Austria	100	137	136	164	28,312
Italy	100	156	165	190	17,184
	Exports from the CR (1st Q. = 100)				
Germany	100	105	103	121	100,137
Slovakia	100	110	93	75	74,678
Austria	100	109	126	130	22,916
Italy	100	120	75	113	18,868
Russia	100	109	103	146	15,539

Note: a) In billion of CSK
Source: Calculations are based on Statistical Data, no. 4, 1994

The loosening of Czech and Slovak mutual trade ws also reflected in the decrease of Slovak import/export share in the Czech foreign trade and vice versa. While in 1993 imports from the SR represented 17.8 per cent of total

Czech imports, in the first quarter of 1994 they fell to 15 per cent. A decrease was noticeable already in 1993; in the first three quarters the Slovak imports to the CRrepresented 18.7 per cent of total imports, while in the last quarter they represented 15.5 per cent. Czech exports to the SR followed the same course. In 1993, Czech exports to the SR represented 20.1 per cent of total exports; in the first quarter of 1994, they fell to 15.5 per cent. Again, the decreasing trend was noticeable already in 1993, when in the first three quarters Czech exports to the SR represented 21.7 per cent of the total exports, and in the last quarter they represented 15.3 per cent only. From the Slovak point of view, the decrease was the same for both Czech imports and exports, but the impact on the SR was much harder. In 1993, imports from the CR made up 35.5 per cent of total Slovak imports; in the first quarter of 1994 they fell to 30.4 per cent. In 1993, exports from the SR to the CR made up 42.2 per cent of total Slovak exports; in the first quarter of 1994 they decreased to 37.8 per cent.

Although there are necessary inaccuracies in the available data (especially in the first quarter of 1993 due to, introduction of new methods of collecting and processing customs statistics data, consistent circulation of customs documents, etc), the gradual decrease in mutual Czech-Slovak trade was so significant that it couldn't be reversed by any updates or statistical improvements.

The ongoing mutual trade decrease does not necessarily indicate that the Customs Union was not successful. If in general we expect the integration processes, aiming from lower to higher forms (i.e., from a free trade area to a customs union or from a customs union to a common market) to increase the volume of mutual trade among the parties involved, then, in a situation where the processes are oriented in the reverse as is the case of the Czech-Slovak Customs Union, it would be wrong to demand analogical outcomes. Logically, a transition from the common market of one country to a customs union between two successor states should result in decline of trade. The only way of finding a satisfactory answer to the Customs Union performance is to compare its results with the likely mutual trade decrease in the case of an absence of the Customs Union. However, such an experiment cannot separate the influence of other important factors such as the higher administrative costs of foreign trade transactions compared to the domestic ones, pressures to restore internal and external balance, administrative and technical barriers to trade, statistical inaccuracies, etc. Unfortunately, the national economy is not a good subject for such experiments.

A very rough estimate of the potential decrease in Czech-Slovak trade can be provided by a comparison of the absolute volume of Czech trade with some small states in Eastern, Central and Western Europe which, in 1993, was still considerably lower than the volume of trade with Slovakia.[39] The question is whether Czech-Slovak trade is going to reach this level. Does the Customs Union have the capacity to preserve the current level? Such questions will not be answered by anything else but the future.

Notes

1. The powers of the Federal Ministry of the Economy included complex obligations coming from the jointly managed enterprises, whose construction had been financed by the Federal budget. Their operations were sometimes linked with the foreign trading activities of the state (e.g. in the cases of the system of transit gas pipelines). The division of this property was one of the more complex problems.
2. The military personnel level in the Czech army was 105,857 persons as of 1 January 1993, 88,101 persons as of 1 June 1994, and should stabilise at around 65,000 persons in 1995.
3. Both central banks immediately after the break-up of the Federation recognised the licenses of the bank subsidiaries from the other Republic on the territory of their own Republic.
4. The CSA and Slov-air had come under the control of the Republic administrative authorities by the time the property was undergoing its division. The CSA was transferred from the control of the federation to the CR control as of 1 May 1991, and converted to a joint-stock company as of 1 August 1992; the same applies to Slov-air. At the time of property division, however, the flight supervision unit belonged to federal property, the value of its property was, however, low.
5. As further cases of investment projects abroad can be mentioned the Nickel combine Las Camariocos in Cuba, the Transpetrol, the Intermetal, the Participation of the CSFR in the International Centre for Technical and Scientific Information in Moscow, the share in the CMEA property.
6. See OECD (1994), page 115
7. As of 1 January 1993 when the common interbank foreign exchange trading was discontinued, the Czech National Bank and the National Bank of Slovakia started selling convertible currencies to Czech and Slovak banks only. Other common financial facilities continued operating until the currency separation; Slovak businesses continued taking loans from Czech banks and the central bank refinancing facility was not divided.

8. On 13 January 1993, the largest Austrian bank Bank Austria and other banks discontinued purchases of CSK due to increased offers of the currency from Slovak citizens. Hungarian banks suspended purchases of CSK at the end of January 1993 and so did Deutsche Bank and Dresdner Bank, leading German banks.
9. More precisely, payment conditions became gradually restricted according to the volume and nature of the imported goods.
10. The following paragraphs provide a systematic account of the preparation and realization phases of the currency separation in the Czech Republic. The most important facts and figures for the Slovak Republic can be found in the endnotes.
11. To be precise, the value of currency in circulation oscillated between CSK 94 billion (July) and CSK 112 billion (December). It reached its peak in December 18 and, before the end of the year, fell to about CSK 100 billion.
12. The new Slovak banknotes were distinguished by adhesive stamps. Next to 100, 500 and 1000 banknotes, the stamps were glued also on 20 and 50 denominations.
13. It was 40 million stamps for 1000 denominations, 50 million stamps for 500 and 70 million stamps for 100 denominations.
14. For example, a Czech speculator deposits the old banknotes only and withdraws new Czech banknotes from the bank. The new Czech banknotes then are exchanged for old banknotes supplied by a Slovak speculator. The Czech converts the old banknotes to new ones following the above scenario, and the vicious circle continues.
15. It was the Czech Post Office and the Czech Savings Bank which were given the task of establishing the exchange points for the public; Komercni banka which primarily stamped the banknotes; the Ministry of Internal Affairs and Police which guarded the exchange points, transportation and other specific aspects of the entire operation; and the Army which acted as a backup for transportation and, if necessary, the Police forces.
16. The Slovak Republic adopted very similar schemes and mechanisms and there were 2,300 exchange points established there.
17. In the Slovak Republic, the exchanges for the general public and corporate entities took place on 4-6 February 1993 (in the CR during four days) at exchange points set up by the Slovak Post Office, Slovak Savings Bank and in Vseobecna uverova banka. Slovak legislation allowed exchanges for persons above 15 years of age only (in the CR there was a limit of CSK 1,000 per person under 15). The limit for Slovak nationals of 15 years of age and over was CSK 4,000 (the same as in the CR). Entrepreneurs exchanged their money on 6 and 7 February (the old banknotes accepted by the businesses after the exchange could be deposited on the day of the currency separation - 8 February 1993 - unlike in the CR where exchanges for businesses kept taking place two days after the separation, i.e. until 10 February 1993). The total number of exchanges for the general public and corporate entities in Slovakia was 2.4 million with the total value of currency at SKK 4.8 billion (most of it

exchanged by the Slovak Post Office); for businesses it was 6,266 exchanges for a total of SKK 66.1 billion.

18. Time horizons of the validity of Slovak currency:

Denomination	*New currency issued as of*	*Old currency expiration*	*Old currency exchange deadline*
Coins			
0,01	-	31.07.1993	31.10.1993
0,05	-	31.07.1993	31.10.1993
0,10	29.10.1993	31.12.1993	28.02.1994
0,20	30.09.1993	30.11.1993	28.02.1994
0,50	30.06.1993	15.10.1993	31.01.1994
1,00	30.04.1993	15.10.1993	31.01.1994
2,00	30.04.1993	30.11.1993	28.02.1994
5,00	30.04.1993	30.11.1993	28.02.1994
10,00	8.02.1993	15.06.1993	30.09.1993
Banknotes			
10	-	15.06.1993	30.09.1993
20	30.09.1993	30.11.1993	31.03.1994
50	30.08.1993	31.10.1993	28.02.1994
100	30.09.1993	30.11.1993	31.03.1994
500	15.11.1993	10.01.1993	31.03.1994
1000	29.10.1993	22.10.1993	5.11.1993

19. *Analysis of the Monetary Separation and its Financing*. A report submitted to the Czech National Bank Council meeting on 5 June 1993.

20. The Czech Crown (CZK) and the Slovak Crown (SKK) became successors to the Czechoslovak Crown (CSK). Although the CSK was not a fully convertible currency, the economic transformation caused it to go through various phases of so called 'internal convertibility'.

21. For example, a Czech company claiming CSK 100 in Slovakia can result in two different payments depending on the chosen exchange rate; if CZK 1 = SKK 1 = CSK 1 it will be SKK 100; if CZK 1 = CSK 1 = SKK 1.10 it will be SKK 110.

22. Participants of the first meeting of the Czech-Slovak Monetary Committee on 8 January 1993 agreed to establish a working group which would prepare drafts for an agreement on the mutual relationship after the currency separation. There were two variants. The first one proposed mutual convertibility of the Czech and Slovak currencies and the second advanced the introduction of clearing. The second meeting of the Monetary Committee on 25 January 1993 recommended the latter.

23. Clearing agreements Czechoslovakia concluded with Afghanistan, India and Iran pointed at the viability of such a payment system even between countries with very different economic policies.

24. A Czech-Slovak transaction could be effected at a 1 to 1 ratio for payment within the old block, at the devalued or revalued clearing rate for payments of the new block, at a cross-exchange rate applicable for re-exports, and at a tourist exchange rate for non-trade payments.

25. Re-export is defined as a purchase of goods and services by a subject of one of the members to the agreement in a third country and a subsequent sale of these goods or services (unmodified and of unchanged quality) to a subject of the other member to the agreement. Packaging or mixing is not considered a change of quality.

26. The Czech National Bank data for the second half of 1994 show that the clearing center administered on average 7,000 clearing transactions a day. All payments were made within maximum three business days.

27. In compliance with the rules as of 1 September 1994, the turist limit was CZK 7,500.

28. The deadline for transfers of the Czech corporations' and physical persons' accounts from the SR to the CR was 15 May 1993; for transfers of Slovak corporations' and physical persons' accounts from the CR to the SR it was 9 June 1993. After these deadlines, transfers were subjected to the approval procedures binding for all international transactions.

29. The volume of claims which were to be redeemed within the old block was very difficult to determine. The Ministry of Finance estimated the volume of Czech businesses' claims in the Slovak Republic at roughly CZK 20 billion.

30. As of 1 September 1994, the exchange rate disadvantage of the Czech exporters to Slovakia in comparison with the situation under the Federal market reached 25 per cent (10 per cent official Slovak devaluation, 10 per cent import surcharge and 5 per cent clearing devaluation).

31. Deregulation in compliance with Article VIII means a full liberalization of transactions on the current account including the possibility to use the Czech currency for these transactions. A part of the deregulation is a commitment not to participate in discriminatory monetary measures or practise multiple exchange rates. To reach this objective, it might have been necessary to abolish the marginal credit (necessity of immediate, i.e. within 90 days, settlement of trade balance) and to narrow the difference between the official ECU and clearing ECU exchange rates (it shouldn't exceed 2 per cent).

32. See Čapek (1991)

33. On 4 May 1993 the Czech Republic and Slovenia signed agreements on mutual trade relations which served a base for an Agreement on Free Trade Area signed on 4 December 1993. Later, the Czech Republic also negotiated establishment of free trade areas with Mexico and Israel. In the CEFTA summit on 2 April 1994 the CR and the SR expressed their interest in concluding agreements on establishment of free trade areas with Turkey, Estonia and Rumania.

34. The agreement was signed on 21 December 1992 and took effect on 1 March 1993, even before the end of the ratification process. In 1993, there were further negotiations about an earlier introduction of liberalization of sensitive and very sensitive items in mutual trade in 1997 and 1998 respectively.

35. An interview with Jannis Sekellaria, a European Parliament Member, Mlada fronta dnes, 30 July 1993 and 11 August 1993.

36. See Šimůnek (1992)

37. Scharff, J. (one of the negotiators of the free trade agreement with CEFTA), 'Mistaken Signals to Slovakia'; *Hospodarske noviny*, 9 March 1994.

38. See Souček (1993)

39. While in 1993, the volume of the Czech-Slovak trade was 139,645 billion CZK, the trade with selected countries in the same period were as follows: Belgium 10,756 billion CZK; Denmark 6,617 billion CZK; Finland 4,159 billion CZK; Hungary 12,887 billion CZK; Austria 51,228 billion CZK; Slovenia 4,656 billion CZK.

Part Four
THE CZECH AND SLOVAK REPUBLICS AFTER THE BREAK-UP OF CZECHOSLOVAKIA

1 Macroeconomic development

The break-up of Czechoslovakia gave birth to numerous speculations on the future economic development of the successor Republics ranging from sober opinions to catastrophic visions of the Slovak Republic suffering major problems as a result of discontinued redistributions between both parts of what was once one state, and necessary investments into governmental infrastructure. The Czech economists feared narrowing of the domestic market and numerous internal trade relations becoming a part of international trade.

As shown in the following comparative analysis, the split of Czechoslovakia affected both succeeding Republics. The pessimistic visions, however, did not materialize. It was essential for both the Czech and Slovak Republics to minimize the immediate negative consequences of the split of an integrated economic entity. The responses to the newly emerged problems and the economic measures taken to fight them were often different partly due to the disparity between the initial conditions in the respective Republics.

The authors have analyzed many aspects of post-federation economic development in the previous chapters of this book, especially in the clearing payment system and the Czech-Slovak Customs Union sections. This part will therefore focus on analyzing basic trends of macroeconomic development and related economic measures. Proper attention will be paid to the privatisation process as it is an area in which major differences between the two Republics can be found.

1.1 Development of gross domestic product

In the year following the split of Czechoslovakia, the decrease of real GDP in the CR was 0.9 per cent; in the SR it was 4.1 per cent. For Slovakia, it was the worst relative decline vis-a-vis the Czech part of the Federation since 1989. In 1994, both economies marked an increase of real GDP -- a 2.6 per cent increase in the CR and 4.8 per cent in the SR (see Table 4.1). In the SR, 1994 only compensated for 1993's decline, while in the CR the GDP generated in 1994 was higher than in 1992 (by roughly 1.7 per cent).

Table 4.1
Growth of GDP and its components

	1993	1994
Czech Republic		
GDP	-0.9	2.6
Private consumption	2.9	5.3
Public consumption	-0.1	-2.3
Fixed capital formation	-7.7	17.3
Change in inventory [a)]	-2.7	-2.0
Export of goods and services	7.5	0.2
Import of goods and services	10.4	7.8
Slovak Republic		
GDP	-4.1	4.8
Private consumption	-0.6	2.5
Public consumption	-0.4	-3.5
Fixed capital formation	-3.4	-2.1
Change in inventory [a)]	-2.9	-
Export of goods and services	-1.9	12,4
Import of goods and services	1.6	7.8

Note: Growth in per cent, constant prices as of 1984; a) as a share of GDP from the previous year, in per cent

Source: Czech Statistical Office, Slovak Statistical Office and Infostat Bratislava

In 1993, the main differences between the CR and the SR were concentrated in the area of foreign trade. The major reason for the decrease of the real GDP in 1993 was the decline of mutual trade between the two Republics. Export of goods and services from the CR to the SR decreased by 23 per cent, and from the SR to the CR by 15 per cent.

Before the split, the share of exports from the CR to the SR in the Czech GDP was almost 15 per cent, while exports from the SR to the CR accounted for 33 per cent of the Slovak GDP. These figures indicate that the decline had much deeper consequences for the Slovak GDP. The CR compensated for the decline of exports to the SR with expansion to other markets while Slovak exports to other markets decreased.

In 1994, growth of the real GDP in both Republics was determined by completely different factors. The high growth rate of the Slovak output surprised many observers since it was expected to be negative or at least zero.[1] The GDP increase in the CR in 1994 was due to the growth of overall domestic demand while in the SR, where domestic demand slightly declined, growth was generated by accelerated foreign demand.

In 1994, the Czech domestic market marked a dynamic growth of private consumption and, in connection with the fall in 1993, an increase of gross formation of fixed capital. On the other hand, exports of goods and serviced slightly decreased. In the SR, private consumption increased only slightly while public consumption and gross formation of fixed capital declined. Decrease of public consumption reflected limited resources of the government budget. Export of goods and services was stimulated by a 10 per cent devaluation of Slovak currency in the middle of 1993 and by a devaluation within the clearing system by 5 per cent (in December 1993). The Slovak Statistical Office data indicate 12.5 per cent (in current prices) increase in export to the CR while the Czech Statistical Office figures claim a decrease of imports from the SR by 8.2 per cent (in current prices).[2]

In 1994, Slovakia's GDP growth was the third highest in Central Europe with Slovinia occupying the first position (5.5 per cent) followed by Poland (5.0), ahead of the Czech Republic (2.6 per cent) and Hungary (2.0 per cent).

1.2 Inflation rate

Inflation rate before the split of Czechoslovakia (measured in terms of the consumer price index) was almost identical in both Republics and remained so in 1993 and 1994.

In 1993, the inflation rate in the CR reached 20.8 per cent, in the SR it was 23.2 per cent. The increase of prices (roughly by 8 per cent) was partly due to the introduction of VAT. In 1994, inflation fell remarkably in both Republics; in the CR it was 10 per cent, in the SR 13.4 per cent (see Table 4.2). The 1993 and 1994 figures for both Republics were lower than for Hungary and Poland.[3]

The pressure to increase consumer prices in Slovakia was partly due to continued inflation of producer prices. In the SR in 1993, growth of industrial prices was 1/3 higher than in the CR; in 1994 industrial prices in the SR were twice those in the CR. In the SR, prices in agriculture rose twice as fast as in the CR. On the other hand, the rise of prices in construction was slower in the SR than in the CR (see Table 4.3).

Table 4.2
Consumer prices in the Czech and Slovak Republics

	1993	1994
Czech Republic		
Consumer prices	20.8	10.0
Food	16.6	9.3
Other goods	19.4	8.7
Public catering	27.5	7.6
Services	28.7	17.0
Slovak Republic		
Consumer prices	23.2	13.4
Food	21.3	16.2
Other goods	20.4	12.7
Public catering	35.5	13.1
Services	28.0	10.7

Note: Average annual increase in per cent
Source: Czech Statistical Office, Slovak Statistical Office and *Hospodarske noviny*, no. 24, 1995

Table 4.3
Producer prices in the Czech and Slovak Republics

	1993	1994
Czech Republic		
Industrial producer prices	13.1	5.3
Construction work prices	25.9	14.0
Agricultural producer prices	8.4	4.7
Vegetable products	14.4	- 4.4
Animal products	4.3	11.5
Slovak Republic		
Industrial producer prices	17.2	10.0
Construction work prices	24.1	11.0
Agricultural producer prices	14.6	10.8
Vegetable products	19.9	5.1
Animal products	10.6	15.4

Note: Average annual increase in per cent
Source: Czech Statistical Office, Slovak Statistical Office

1.3 Unemployment

After the split of Czechoslovakia, the unemployment rate was expected to rise in both successor Republics. Specialists forecasted faster growth of unemployment in the SR as a consequence of the anticipated more substantial decrease of the Slovak GDP. Hand in hand with the forecasts, the unemployment rate in the SR grew by 4 points and reached 14.4 per cent. In the CR, unemployment rose by less than one percent and the rate was 3.5 per cent.[4] In 1994, GDP rose in both Republics and unemployment rates marked almost no change; it was 14.8 per cent in the SR and 3.2 per cent in the CR.

Table 4.4
Unemployment rate in the Czech and Slovak Republics

	1992	1993	1994
Czech Republic	2.6	3.5	3.2
Slovak Republic	10.4	14.4	14.8

Note: In per cent
Source: Czech Statistical Office, Slovak Statistical Office

In the end of 1994, there were 371,500 job-seeking people in the SR and 166,500 in the CR. In the end of 1993, the SR registered 48 unemployed per one job vacancy, in the end of 1994 it was 28 per one; in the CR it was 3.4 (1993) and 2.2 (1994) unemployed per one job opportunity. In 1993, the Slovak unemployment offices reported 31.7 per cent of the unemployed had had no job opportunity for over one year; in the CR it was 19.5 per cent.[5]

In general, the unemployment rate in the Czech Republic after the break-up of Czechoslovakia remained the lowest in Central Europe, the Slovak Republic assumed the third position after the Czech Republic and Hungary but ahead of Poland.[6]

1.4 Labour productivity and wages

In 1993 and 1994, productivity of labour improved in both Republics (see Table 4.5). In 1993, the increase of labour productivity in the CR was relatively slow, with a faster increase in 1994; the SR, on the other hand, experienced a decrease in labour productivity in 1993 followed by rapid increase in 1994. Therefore, the final increase in both Republics was almost identical. In the CR in 1993, labour productivity in industry stagnated while in the SR it decreased. In 1994 figures rose in both Republics with the CR improving its productivity compared to 1992 and the SR just reaching the level of 1992.

In the first two years after the split, development of real wages in the CR accelerated and became faster than the growth of labour productivity. In the SR in 1993, real wages decreased faster than productivity while in 1994, they rose slower than productivity. This development partly levelled off the ratio between the productivity of labour and the average wage in both Republics which had been, before the split, relatively more favorable in the Czech Republic.

Table 4.5
Labour productivity and average wage in national economy and industry

	National economy		*Industry*	
	1993	1994	1993	1994
Czech Republic				
Productivity of labour [a)]	0.7	1.5	0.0	5.1
Nominal wage	25.0	17.1	23.8	15.7
Real wage [b)]	3.5	6.1	2.5	4.8
Slovak Republic				
Productivity of labour [a)]	-0.9	5.8	-7.3	7.5
Nominal wage	18.5	17.0	21.0	17.4
Real wage [b)]	-3.8	3.0	-1.7	3.3

Note: Growth rates in per cent; a) for national economy, GDP per worker; for industry, industrial output in constant prices per worker; b) nominal wage index divided by cost of living index

Source: Czech Statistical Office, Slovak Statistical Office

In the first two years after the split, real wages in both the CR and the SR rose faster than productivity of labour (with slightly faster growth of wages in the CR). Therefore, the SR partially retained its more favorable relationship between labour productivity and wages from the period before the split of Czechoslovakia.

The development of real wages in terms of producer prices in relation to labour productivity displayed similar trends. The main difference was in a significantly higher growth of real wages in terms of producer prices in both Republics (producer prices rose faster than costs of living) which resulted in decreased competitiveness due to labour costs. This phenomenon was more remarkable in the CR than in the SR.

1.5 Foreign trade and balance of payments

In 1992, exports to third countries (except for the SR resp. the CR) represented 31 per cent of the Czech GDP and 38 per cent of the Slovak GDP. In 1993, when trade between the Republics became a part of international trade, it increased to 40 per cent in the CR and 49 per cent in the SR.

Table 4.6
Foreign trade in the Czech and Slovak Republics

		1993	1994	
Export / import [a]				
Export to the other Republic	CR	-22.3	-18.9 [c]	-10.6 [d]
	SR	-18.0	-8.2 [c]	12.5 [d]
Export to other countries	CR	20.0	13.9	
	SR	-11.2	40.3	
Import from other countries	CR	2.7	17.6	
	SR	15,4	19.1	
Foreign trade balance [b]				
Total without the other Republic	CR	-7.0	-19.3	
	SR	-28.0	-13.3	
The CR with the SR		17.1 [c]	6.8 [c]	
		-1.3 [d]	-17.4 [d]	

Note: a) Growth rates in per cent; b) current prices, CZK and SKK; c) Figures of the Czech Statistical Office (country of trade); d) Figures of the Slovak Statistical Office (country of origin and destination)
Source: Czech Statistical Office, Slovak Statistical Office

In the first year after the split, the volume of exports from the CR to the SR fell by 22 per cent, but exports to other countries increased by 20 per cent. The decrease of exports from the SR to the CR was estimated at 18 per cent but, unlike the increase in the CR, exports to other countries fell by 11 per cent (see Table 4.6). Imports from foreign countries increased in both Republics, with higher figures for the SR. In the first year after the split of

Czechoslovakia, the CR managed to compensate for the decline of exports to the SR by finding other markets.

As a consequence of this development, the negative balance of Slovak international trade (excluding trade with the CR) increased and reached SKK 28 billion while passive balance in the CR was only CZK 7 billion. As far as mutual trade between the two countries was concerned, the Czech statistics displayed a CZK 17 billion surplus while Slovak figures showed a SKK 1.3 billion surplus (a discrepancy partly due to different methods of measuring the volume of international trade).

Measures Slovakia had introduced to support payment balance went into full effect in 1994. The export of Slovak goods and services to third countries (excluding the Czech Republic) which had fallen in the previous year, rose by 40 per cent, with imports rising less significantly by 19 per cent. The Slovak Republic displayed a notable increase of exports to the OECD members (56 per cent increase) and to the EU (also 56 per cent increase). As a consequence of these changes, the passive balance of international trade fell by roughly 50 per cent from SKK 28 billion in 1993 to SKK 13.3. billion in 1994.

Unlike in Slovakia, Czech exports to third countries (except for Slovakia) decelerated and imports increased with the deficit rising almost three times -- from CZK 7 billion in 1993 to CZK 19.3 billion in 1994.

Table 4.7
Balance of payments in the Czech and Slovak Republics

	Czech Republic		*Slovak Republic*	
	1993	1994	1993	1994
Current account	433	298	-698	-98
Trade balance	-609	-851	-1,095	-441
Balance of services	1,041	1,069	347	382
Balance of incomes	-128	-43	-24	-106
Unrequited transfers (net)	130	124	74	67
Capital account	2,639	2,106	488	505
Direct investments	517	842	144	179
Portfolio investments	1,059	819	244	263
Other long-term capital	528	501	478	524
Short-term capital	535	-56	-378	-461
Errors and omissions	-43	-32	268	608
Changes in reserves (-, increase)	-3,029	-2,372	-59	-1,015

Note: In million of USD
Source: Czech National Bank and National Bank of Slovakia

There were substantial differences in the territorial orientation of foreign trade and the composition of traded goods. Slovak foreign trade maintained its usual orientation on eastern markets and its trade with developed market economies remained less significant. Nevertheless, in 1994 the Slovak Republic experienced a relative increase in trading with developed economies. Compared to the CR, the SR has exported more chemical products and semi-finished products and less machinery products and equipment; data on Slovak imports display a relatively high volume of imported fuels (about twice more than the Czech Republic) and fewer imported machines and equipment.

In 1994, the Czech foreign trade deficit further increased. Nevertheless, both in 1993 and 1994 it was outbalanced by a relatively high surplus of services and therefore the current account of payment balance (in convertible currencies) in both years displayed positive figures. In Slovakia, on the other hand, services were not active enough to compensate for the deficit of trade balance. Nevertheless, its development contributed significantly to the decrease of the current account deficit (see Table 4.7).

Given the 1993-94 current account surplus in the CR and deficit in the SR, the main source of the overall surplus in both Republics was the inflowing capital. The inflow of capital was more dynamic in the CR and facilitated faster growth of foreign exchange reserves. Changes in the structure of capital flowing into the CR were characterized by decreased official borrowing and increased participation of private capital. In the SR, on the other hand, the main source of incoming capital became government and other official loans.

2 Development of fiscal and monetary policies

After the break-up of Czechoslovakia, policy makers of both succeeding Republics faced the task of maintaining macroeconomic equilibrium and managing adjustment processes as a response to the disruption of numerous economic relations which had existed in the Federation. Politicians believed in smoothing over the shocks by concluding numerous agreements which reflected the interests of both parties in coordinated activities in various areas.[8] Nevertheless, both sovereign Republics formulated independent although not dissimilar economic policies as a logical consequence of their common economic history.

2.1 Government budgets

In 1993, the fiscal systems of both Republics were exposed to several tests. Both the CR and the SR decided to sustain a plan (dating back to the times of the unified State) to introduce on January 1993 a new tax system (notably VAT), and to start financing health care via a network of health insurance agencies. It was hard to predict the consequences of such changes, including the impact of the Czech-Slovak clearing arrangement.[7] Government budgets of both Republics for 1993 were approved as balanced.

Unlike the Czech government budget which displayed, except for January 1993, a steady surplus throughout the whole year, the Slovak budget continued to suffer from a growing deficit. In the middle of 1993, after an agreement with the IMF, the Slovak Government revised its budget with the intention of reaching a SKK 16 billion deficit (5 per cent of the GDP). At the same time, Slovakia increased VAT rates from 5 and 23 to 6 and 25 per cent, respectively; consumer tax rates by roughly 6 per cent; and introduced a partial restriction of government expenditures. Nevertheless, these measures were not strong enough to meet the revised objectives.

The Slovak government budget deficit was caused both by underfulfilment of the planned revenues and by overdrafitng the planned expenditures. On the revenue side, the major underfulfilment was due to corporate taxes and social insurance contributions as well as consumer taxes, repayment of government loans, and VAT payments. On the expenditure side, overdrafting was due to interest payments to the National Bank of Slovakia (not counted upon in the approved government budget), installment payments to foreign banks, payments covering public and governmental needs and special government subsidies.[8] In 1993, the Slovak budget deficit reached SKK 23 billion, i.e. 6.8 per cent of the GDP (including the clearing account balance).

The final Czech government budget exceeded both revenues and expenditures and reached a CZK 1.1 billion surplus, i.e, 0.1 per cent of the GDP including the clearing account. The clearing account balance which, in 1993, increased revenues of the Slovak government budget by SKK 5.8 billion and the expenditures of the Czech government budget by CZK 4.6 billion was in fact a foreign loan. Without these figures, the Slovak deficit was SKK 28.8 billion, i.e. 8.6 per cent of the GDP and Czech surplus was CZK 5.7 billion, i.e. 0.6 per cent of the GDP (see Table 4.8).

Table 4.8
Balance of the Czech and Slovak government budgets

	Czech Republic		*Slovak Republic*	
	1993	1994	1993	1994
Government budget balance (in billions CZK,SKK)				
without clearing	5.7	10.4	-28.8	-8.9
including clearing	1.1	...	-23.0	-22.9
Government budget balance (in per cent of GDP)				
without clearing	0.6	1,0	-8.6	-2.3
including clearing	0.1	...	-6.8	-5.8

Note: From the beginning of October 1994, balance of clearing payments is not included in the government budget and represents a part of government financial assets

Source: Draft of final Slovak government budget for 1993, Bratislava, May 1994; *Finance a Uver*, no. 7, 1994, Bulletin of the Statistical Office of the Slovak Republic, no. 12, 1994

The Slovak government budget for 1994 was approved with a planned deficit of SKK 14.7 billion; the Czech government budget was outlined as balanced. Planned figures for both Republics were more or less followed. The Slovak government budget closed with a deficit of SKK 22.9 billion (including the clearing account balance with the CR). In 1994, when the SR granted the CR a SKK 5.8 billion credit, the situation in the clearing payment system changed substantially. If we deduct this sum from budget expenditures, the Slovak budget deficit would be only SKK 8.9 billion, i.e. 2.3 per cent of GDP (see Table 4.8) and the deficit would be lower than the previously agreed one. At the same time, total revenues were exceeded by 3.3 per cent and the plan for total expenditures without clearing was met out of 99.1 per cent (after incorporating the clearing balance it was exceeded by 8.5 per cent). The higher revenues were mostly due to overfulfillment of incoming tax payments except for VAT. On the side of expenditures, non-investment expenditures of governmental organizations were lower than planned (SKK 4.7 billion); investments were, on the other hand, exceeded by SKK 2.5 billion.

The Czech government budget for 1994 closed with a CZK 10.4 billion surplus (without clearing), i.e.,1 per cent of the GDP. Total revenues were exceeded by 1.3 per cent and the plan for total expenditures was met out of 98.6 per cent (after incorporating the clearing balance it was exceeded by 8.5 per cent). The higher revenues were mostly due to higher social insurance contributions (CZK 12.6 billion). On the side of expenditures, subsidies for businesses and governmental organizations were lower than planned (SKK 6.5 billion).

In conclusion, after the break-up of Czechoslovakia both Republics followed a strict budgetary policy. The Slovak budget deficit was not a surprise, for the split was expected to have deeper consequences for Slovakia. There were several causes for the deficit, such as Slovak aspirations to keep social security at the old 'Federal' level and the need to finalize the system of government agencies. The budget deficit decrease demonstrated positive attempts to suppress deficit financing of the Slovak economy but, at the same time, a departure from former intentions to use the government budget as an instrument for stimulating economic growth. Unlike in Slovakia, the surplus of the Czech government budget was an expression of the continuing observance of principles of prudential fiscal policies by the Federal government.

2.2 Character of monetary policy

After the break-up of Czechoslovakia, the succeeding Republics strived to maintain both internal and external monetary stability and to minimize price increases. The inflationary pressure of deficit financing made this a difficult task, especially in Slovakia.

The NBS monetary strategy for 1993 was based on an estimated 4 per cent decrease of GDP, a 17 per cent inflation rate and a 12 per cent growth in the money supply (M2). The strategy was revised in the middle of 1993 (due to a high government budget deficit) to a higher annual inflation rate of 25-30.4 per cent and a growth of net credit to the government. Consumer prices rose by 25.1 per cent (December 1993/December 1992) and money supply growth (M2) was 18.1 per cent.

The CNB monetary strategy for 1993 was based on an estimated 0-3 per cent increase of GDP, a 15 per cent inflation rate and a 17 per cent growth in the money supply (M2). The revised strategy prepared in the middle of 1993 was based on 0-0.5 per cent growth of GDP and an 18 per cent inflation rate. Finally, consumer prices grew by 18.2 per cent (December 1993/December 1992) and money stock (M2) grew by 20.2 per cent (see Table 4.9).

Table 4.9
Monetary development in the Czech and Slovak Republics

	Czech Republic		*Slovak Republic*	
	1993	1994	1993	1994
Money supply (M2) [a]	20.2	22.1	18.1	18.6
Credits to households and businesses [a]	18.7	15.1	10.5	-1.2
Discount rate	8.0	8.5	12.0	12.0

Note: a) Growth rate in per cent
Source: Czech National Bank, National Bank of Slovakia

As of 1 March 1993, the NBS limited the credit resources of commercial banks to control liquidity which resulted from deficit financing of the government budget. In the CR, the CNB used only indirect monetary instruments to exercise domestic monetary strategy. In the SR, the volume of household and business credits in domestic currency thus grew only by 10.4 per cent, while in the CR they grew by 18.7 per cent. Foreign exchange credits in the SR grew by SKK 4.4 billion (accounting for 3.1 per cent of total business and personal credits in December 1993); in the CR they grew by CZK 9.4 billion (3.7 per cent of total business and personal credits in December 1993).

The growth of net credit to government combined with an almost non-existent increase of net foreign assets had a significant influence on the growth of the Slovak money supply. Unlike in the SR, in the CR the net credit to government decreased with net foreign assets growing significantly, especially in the second half of the year.

The significant growth of net credit to government in Slovakia (by SKK 25.2 billion) was caused by the increasing government budget deficit, covered repeatedly by issuing Treasury bills. From the end of March on, the volume of these bills exceeded the purchasing potential of the commercial banks and the bills remained unsold in the NBS portfolio. From April on, the NBS financed budget deficits under more strict conditions (the interest rate reached 19 per cent). Close to the end of the year, the NBS extended direct credit to cover a major part of the budget deficit that contributed to the growth of money supply.

The discount rate in Czechoslovakia at the end of 1992 was 9.5 per cent. The NBS sustained this rate for almost a year before it was increased to 12 per cent in December 1993. In the CR, on the other hand, the discount rate decreased from 9.5 to 8 per cent. These opposing trends were reflected in the development of the interest rates market. The average commercial bank lending rate in the SR was roughly 1 per cent higher than in the CR; for interbank deposits the interest rate differential was 3-5 per cent, and close to the end of 1993 it was even 9 per cent.

A constantly growing trade balance deficit as well as the unfavourable development of foreign currency reserves forced the NBS to devalue Slovak currency vis-a-vis convertible currencies by 10 per cent. This devaluation and fresh official borrowing (IMF loan, World Bank loan and NBS bonds) stabilized and increased external reserves. In December 1993, Slovak currency devalued 5 per cent vis-a-vis Czech currency (within the framework of the clearing payment system) and in March 1994, Slovakia introduced a 10 per cent import surcharge. Altogether, these and other measures stimulated an increase in the inflation rate which, however, remained at an acceptable level for the entire year. The nominal exchange rate of the Czech currency vis-a-vis convertible currencies remained stable.[9]

The NBS monetary strategy for 1994 was based on 0-2 per cent GDP growth, 10-13.2 per cent inflation and 13.2 per cent money supply increase (M2) with an anticipated increase of household and business credit by 6 per cent. The actual GDP growth for 1994 was 4.2 per cent, the inflation rate was 11.7 per cent (December 1994/December 1993) and the money supply increased by 18.8 per cent.

The CNB monetary strategy for 1994 was based on an anticipated 1-2 per cent GDP growth, a 10 per cent inflation rate and a 12-15 per cent increase in the money supply (M2). Finally, the real GDP increase for 1994 was 2.6 per cent, the inflation rate was 10.2 per cent (December 1994/December 1993) and the money supply increased by 22.1 per cent.

To reach the declared objectives, the NBS in the first half of the year focused on siphoning off excess liquidity. Suspension of refinancing facility for commercial banks and introduction of credit limits caused a decrease in the money supply. Later, the credit limits were partly relaxed and resulted in the fall of the household and business credits in domestic currency by 1.2 per cent. Foreign exchange credits increased by SKK 2 billion (189 per cent) and represented 5.9 per cent of total household and business credits (in December 1994). The most important factor influencing the growth of the money supply was an increase in net foreign assets (positively influenced by the development of a clearing account with the Czech Republic). The money supply grew by 18.6 per cent for the entire year.

In the Czech Republic, domestic currency credits grew by 15.1 per cent while foreign exchange credits grew by CZK 16.8 billion (69 per cent) and represented 5.1 per cent of total household and business credits (in December 1994). With a decrease of net credit to government (CZK 9.8 billion decrease) and an increase in the net Fund of National Property credit (CZK 5.6 billion increase), the most important factor influencing the growth of the money supply was the increase of net foreign assets (CZK 90.2 billion increase). As a reaction to the growth of the money supply, the CNB increased minimum reserve requirements from 9 to 12 per cent (the 3 per cent rate for time deposits remained unchanged).

In 1994, the Slovak discount rate was 12 per cent while in the CR it rose from 8 to 8.5 per cent as a reaction to higher monthly inflation (in August and September 1994). Compared to the CR, the SR maintained higher interest rates on credits and interbank deposits.

A stable nominal exchange rate remained a CNB priority in 1994. The nominal exchange rate of Slovak currency also remained unchanged since the devaluation in July 1993. In both Republics, development of the capital account was promising and positively influenced the increase in foreign exchange reserves. Total volume of foreign exchange reserves in the CR increased from USD 6.2 billion at the end of 1993 to USD 8.9 billion at the end of 1994 (Czech National Bank reserves grew from USD 3.9 billion to USD 6.2 billion). Slovak foreign currency reserves increased from USD 1.4 billion to USD 2.9 billion in October 1994 (National Bank of Slovakia reserves grew from USD 0.5 billion to USD 1.6 billion).

The objectives and results of the monetary policy of both the Czech and Slovak Republics revealed similar precautionary approaches. The more restrictive policy of the NBS was partly due to Slovakia's more difficult starting position after the break-up and the restrictive measures introduced to prevent excess growth of the money supply and prices. A strong inflow of foreign capital soon precipitated a demand for a more active antiinflation policy in the Czech Republic as well.

3 Privatisation process

In November 1992, the Federal Assembly of the CSFR enacted an amendment to the Transformation Act, a piece of legislation which separated the privatisation process (including voucher privatisation) in the Czech and Slovak Republics. The amendment did not include shares purchased in the first wave of voucher privatisation. Nevertheless, it represented a legislative framework for independent preparation of the second wave of voucher privatisation which was, in both Republics, planned to follow immediately after the termination of the first wave.[10]

3.1 Transfers of assets between National Property Funds

Agreement on separation of the privatisation processes and on the break-up of Czechoslovakia retrospectively influenced numerous joint stock companies privatized within the first wave of the voucher privatisation. These businesses were established by the Ministry of Privatisation of one of the Republics (and therefore their privatisation fell under the jurisdiction of the Ministry of Privatisation and the National Property Fund of one of the Republics) but its business location was in the territory of the other Republic. Since the territorial principle assigned the ownership of a production facility to the Republic in which the facility was located, the compensation between the Republics was to adopt a form of transfer of corresponding volume of shares held by the National Property Fund of the Republic where the facility was established to the National Property Fund of the Republic where the business was located. Shares of the federal joint stock companies (especially those established after a reorganization of state financial institutions and foreign trade companies) held by the Federal National Property Fund were divided between the National Property Funds of the Czech and Slovak Republics in a 2:1 ratio (for figures on transfers see Table 4.10).

Table 4.10
Redistribution of shares of joint stock companies privatized in the first wave of voucher privatisation

	NPF CR	NPF SR
Transfer from NPF SR for shares of companies located in the CR	8,038	-
Transfer from NPF CR for shares of companies located in the SR	-	1,493,883
Transfer from Federal NPF	7,062,727	3,531,364

Note: Figures show number of shares (nominal value of one share is CSK 1,000)
Source: Statistical Yearbook

Division and redistribution of shares between the National Property Funds was not always so smooth. As late as two years after the break-up there remained unresolved cases (e.g. shares of the National Property Fund of the SR in Komercni banka, the largest Czech bank; and of the National Property Fund of the CR in Vseobecna uverova banka, the largest Slovak bank). In April 1995, a protocol on the division of the Federal National Property Fund was still waiting to be signed and therefore hindered trade on the capital market of roughly 2.5 million shares of businesses formerly owned by the Federation.

3.2 Privatisation in the Czech Republic

The break-up of Czechoslovakia initially decelerated the privatisation process in the Czech Republic. First, shares from the first wave of voucher privatisation had to be transferred to the Slovak nationals and Slovak investment privatisation funds (for details see Section 4 in Part Two). Secondly, participation in the second wave of voucher privatisation in the CR was limited to the Czech nationals only and therefore it was necessary (after the new legislation on nationality was passed in the Parliament) to allow time to grant Czech nationality to the Slovak nationals residing permanently in the CR. Registration for the second wave of voucher privatisation therefore started as late as 1 October 1993.

Regardless of the delay, large-scale privatisation followed the original scheme. Thanks to the experience gained during the first wave, the second wave of the voucher privatisation adopted a much faster course. In November 1994, i.e., seven months after the process was launched (11 April 1994), Czech investors had gone through all six rounds of bidding for shares.[11] Thanks to the repeated scheme, shares issued during the second wave of privatisation were traded on the capital market as soon as three months after the termination of the last round (1 March 1995).

Voucher privatisation became extremely popular. The number of people who registered for the second wave exceeded the participation in the first wave by 3.6 per cent (a total of 6.17 million people). The individual investors' success in the first wave, whereby they often made higher profits than those who relied on investment privatisation funds, led to an increased number of people investing individually in the second wave. A total of 63.5 per cent (i.e., 9 per cent less than in the first wave) of the investment points were entrusted in 353 investment privatisation funds, 220 of which were newly established. Next to the investment privatisation funds, established as joint stock companies, the administration of the second wave of voucher privatisation authorized registration of 38 open-end mutual funds and 120 closed-end mutual funds as new means of collective investing. There were in total 239 investment companies which helped manage or establish funds for the second wave of voucher privatisation.

The total nominal value of shares of 861 joint stock companies enlisted for the second wave of voucher privatisation traded in the second wave was CZK 155 billion, of which CZK 24 billion were shares of 185 companies not sold in the first wave. The volume of property per one voucher-holder was therefore slightly lower and its average book value was finally CZK 25.000 (i.e., about four times the average monthly wage in the Czech Republic in 1993). Unlike the first wave, the second one included fewer large companies but more state-owned enterprises in agriculture and forestry (41 per cent of the total offer) which were not restituted to the former owners. Finally, 96 per cent of the shares offered for bidding in the second wave were sold. Data show that investment funds collected only 28 per cent of the total number of shares and individual investors focused on purchasing more expensive shares of selected companies.[12]

Along with the preparation and execution of the voucher scheme, privatisation authorities were approving projects using standard methods of privatisation (see Table 4.11). From the beginning of the privatisation process until the end of 1993, privatisation authorities approved 7,533 projects for property of total value of CZK 871.6 billion.

Up to the end of 1993, the National Property Fund effected 62 per cent of the approved transformation projects (sale of property and shares, public tenders, restitutions, etc.). At the end of 1993, National Property Fund revenue from standard methods of privatisation was twice the revenue at the end of 1992 (an increase from CZK 26.8 billion CK to 54.4 billion). Most of the revenue was generated from the sale of shares and property to foreigners (43.9 per cent of the total revenue of large-scale privatisation up to the end of 1993).[13]

Since a substantial portion of the privatisation projects for the second wave of privatisation had been processed by the Ministry of Privatisation before the end of 1993, the volume of property approved by this Ministry transferred to the National Property Fund in 1994 represented only 1/10 of the 1993 volume (CZK 41 billion). In 1994, the National Property Fund earned CZK 33 billion from direct sales and public tenders.

Table 4.11
Privatisation projects approved in the Czech Republic in 1993

Privatisation method	*On 31 December 1993* Number	Value of property mil CZK	%	*In 1993* Number	Value of property mil CZK	%
Public auction	514	5,811	0.67	179	1,924	0.48
Public tender	502	19,188	2.20	201	9,067	2.25
Direct sale	1,680	46,284	5.31	707	19,787	4.91
Commercialization to a joint stock company and privatisation of existing ones	1,777	754,263	86.54	562	335,561	83.33
Vouchers [a)]	1,622	335,703	38.52			
Vouchers in the 2nd wave	861	155,000	17.78	455	98,466	24.45
Free transfers to municipalities, retirement funds and banks	2,318	30,013	3.44	1,284	20,354	5.05
Restitutions	742	16,004	1.84	742	16,004	3.97
Total	7,533	871,563	100.00	3,675	402,697	100.00

Note: a) Vouchers for both 1st and 2nd waves of privatisation approved on 31 December 1993

Source: Calculations based on Ministry of Privatisation of the Czech Republic data

From the beginning of the privatisation process until the end of 1994, the Ministry of Privatisation approved and transferred to the National Property Fund property worth CZK 912 billion (more than 92 per cent of the property submitted for the 1st and 2nd waves of large-scale privatisation). Approximately one-third of this was represented by property privatized in the

1st and 2nd waves of voucher privatisation. The completion of the transformation process should take the form of a much narrower third privatisation wave (the volume of property should not exceed CZK 5 billion).

In the Czech Republic, there were constant problems with transfers of ownership rights to new owners. In compliance with the approved privatisation projects, the National Property Fund was to retain only 7 per cent of all property. Nevertheless, at the end of 1994, almost 1/3 of the privatized property was temporarily held by the Fund.[14] This volume together with 6-10 per cent of the property not yet privatized added up to a total of 40 per cent of formerly state-owned enterprises which remained in the hands of state. Although the government made only marginal interferences into the business affairs of these enterprises, the 40 per cent figure prompted much criticism about the decelerating speed of privatisation.

3.3 Privatisation in the Slovak Republic

The privatisation process in Slovakia suffered from low visibility, and strongly reflected Slovak political instability. The Government Program of Prime Minister Vladimir Meciar of November 1992 proclaimed its intention to create a specific concept of privatisation to simplify the privatisation process, support the competitiveness of Slovak businesses and attract foreign investments.[15] This concept stressed standard methods of privatisation such as management buy-outs and public tenders with possible foreign participation. Voucher privatisation was downgraded to a subsidiary measure primarily to help distribute the shares left from the first wave. The Slovak Ministry of Privatisation preferred the standard methods because it feared that investment privatisation funds would assume majority positions in joint stock companies privatized through vouchers and then promote their own interests, mostly to the detriment of small shareholders.

A new concept of privatisation virtually put an end to the process of approving privatisation projects for the second wave of privatisation (see Table 4.12). By the end of October 1993, the Slovak Ministry of Privatisation had approved only 42 projects, half of which utilized public tender as a preferred method of privatisation.

Deceleration of the privatisation process, suspicious privatisation of selected state-owned enterprises and concerns of Meciar's political opponents about the top government executives commanding too much of the privatized property were among reasons that led to a fall of the Slovak Government in March 1994 and to early parliamentary elections.

Table 4.12
Structure of privatisation projects approved in the second wave of privatisation

Privatisation method	Number	Value of property mil SKK	%
Public auction	0	0	0.00
Public tender	21	1,635	6.54
Direct sale	0	0	0.00
Commercialization to a joint stock company and privatisation of existing ones	15	23,281	93.09
Vouchers	0	0	0.00
Free transfers to municipalities, retirement funds and banks	6	94	0.37
Total	42	25,010	100.00

Note: On 21 October 1993
Source: Czech Republic, Slovak Republic; OECD *Economic Survey*, Paris 1994

The new government led by Prime Minister Moravcik (March 1994-December 1994) decided to accelerate the privatisation process and proposed to offer 420 enterprises (SKK 220 billion) for the second wave of voucher privatisation. This plan recommended privatisation of large enterprises mostly through voucher privatisation, and of small and medium sized companies by standard method.[16] The Slovak government approved about 50 proposals for direct sale to previously agreed-upon buyers and, with the intention to nullify privatisation projects not made in compliance with law, decided to review decisions made by the former Government.

Property offered in the second wave of voucher privatisation was worth SKK 77 billion. Registration of vouchers commenced on 5 September 1995 (almost a year later than in the Czech Republic) with 3.42 million Slovaks finally deciding to participate (about 30 per cent more than in the first wave). The initially proposed share of property per one investor was almost SKK 23,000 (about four times the average monthly wage in Slovakia).

Moravcik's administration did not fully meet its promises. Slovak parliamentary elections in September 1994 and Vladimir Meciar's comeback to the post of Prime Minister again derailed the Slovak privatisation process. At midnight on 3 November 1994, the Slovak Parliament approved a new privatisation Act which nullified roughly 60 decisions related to privatisation made by the former Government after 6 September 1994 (i.e. after the election campaign was launched). In December 1994, although unsigned by the Slovak President, this Act was reconfirmed by the government coalition and became binding.

Meciar's new administration decided not to launch the zero round of voucher privatisation (a chance for individual investors to invest with privatisation funds) planned for 15 December 1994, due to alleged unpreparedness of the process and technical deficiencies.[17]

In July 1995, The Slovak Parliament passed an amendment to the Large-scale Privatization Act by which it canceled the second wave of voucher privatization. The voucher holders who acquired their vouchers in 1994 in turn had a right to receive bonds of a total face value of SKK 10,000 (issued by the Fund of National Property). These bonds can be exchanged for cash (either after their expiration on 31 December, 2000 or by selling them earlier for a market price), invested in purchasing shares of privatized companies, or used for the purchase of a state-owned apartment, or be included in retirement pension or health insurance scheme.

In another act the Slovak government declared the strategic interest in the privatization of important state-owned companies (there is a list of almost 30 strategic enterprises operating in the fields of electric energy, gas, telecommunications, water supply, the armament industry and banking sphere). This Act establishes a strong influence of the government on the decision-making processes in the given enterprises.

The development of privatization in Slovakia displays tendencies towards a formation of an ownership structure based on almost exclusive representation of domestic entrepreneurs, employees of the privatized businesses and direct involvement of the government.

Notes

1. The Institute for International Economic Comparison in Vienna forecasted a 2 per cent decline while OECD and IMF forecasted zero growth. See *Indicators of Monetary and Economic Development of the Czech Republic* (no. 24, 1993, Czech National Bank) and Jonáš (1994).
2. The paradox is caused mainly by different systems of data processing. Slovak Statistical Office distinguishes so called country of origin and country of destination while the Czech Statistical Office indicates country of trade. For example, if a Czech exporter re-exports Spanish oranges to Slovak markets, the Czech statistics put it down as export from the CR to the SR while Slovak statistics put it down as an import from Spain.
3. Inflation rate in Hungary was 23 per cent (1993) and 19 per cent (1994), in Poland it was 37 per cent (1993) and 29.5 per cent (1994).
4. Some forecasts (e.g. OECD forecast) predicted a 17 per cent inflation rate in the SR and 6-7 per cent in the CR.
5. National figures conceal high differences among counties in both the CR and the SR, some of which had had traditionally higher unemployment rate before the split of Czechoslovakia. On the one hand, counties such as Novy Jicin (7.5 per cent) or Bruntal (6.9 per cent) in the Czech Republic project unemployment rate much higher than the Republic average (3.2 per cent), on the other hand, unemployment in Prague was 0.3 per cent only. Selected Slovak counties such as Rimavska Sobota (29.4 per cent) showed much higher unemployment rate than the Slovak average (14.8 per cent), some, such as Bratislava (3.9 per cent) or Trencin (7.6 per cent), much lower.
6. Unemployment rate in Hungary was 13.2 per cent (1993) and 10.4 per cent (1994), in Poland it was 16.4 per cent (1993) and 16 per cent (1994).
7. For the relationship between the government budget and the clearing payment system see Part Three 4.
8. Household sector became the recipient of the benefits introduced as compensation for the increase in food prices in 1990 (as a consequence of withdrawal of government subsidies).

9. These other measures were especially the introduction of VAT and subsequent increase of VAT and consumer tax rates in the middle of 1993, deficit budget and withdrawal of wage control (reintroduced in 1994). In the Czech Republic, the policy of wage control remained in effect both in 1993 and 1994.
10. Separation of the second wave of voucher privatisation (regardless of the outcome of negotiations on future constitutional setup) had been agreed upon at the meeting of Ministers of Privatisation of the CR and the SR in Bratislava on 30 July 1992.
11. Higher number of rounds in the second wave of the voucher privatisation was partly due to the tactics of some investors which decelerated the process of matching the supply and demand and also due to the decision to terminate the wave after almost all of the investment points had been invested.
12. Based on *Voucher Privatisation* journal, volume III
13. Annual report of National Property Fund (1993)
14. *Hospodarske noviny*, 23 January 1995
15. Revitalization Strategy for Slovak Economy drafted by Slovak Government, Bratislava November 1992
16. Payments for this type of purchase were expected as follows: 15-20 per cent upon purchase and the rest in installments paid within 5-10 years.
17. There were 140,000 suspected cases of more than one voucher book registered per one person.

Bibliography

Bakeš, M. and Kočárník, I. (1992), *Fiscal Federalism - Experience of CSFR*, OECD Seminar.

Beneš, E. (1946), *Demokracie dnes a zítra* (Democracy, Today and Tomorrow) Čin, Praha.

Bofinger, P. (1990), *A Multilateral Payments Union for Eastern Europe?*, CEPR Discussion Paper, No. 458, London.

Brokl, L. (1994), 'Politická kultura a politický prostor České republiky' (The Political Culture and Environment of the Czech Republic), *Lidové noviny*, No. 265, Praha.

Čapek, A. et al. (1991), *Varianty vývoje česko-slovenských vztahů, jejich ekonomické implikace* (Possible Developments of Czech-Slovak Relations and the Economic Consequences), Economic Institute of the Czechoslovak Academy of Science, Praha.

Čapek, A. (1992), *The past and the future of Czecho-Slovak economic relations*, Program on Central and Eastern Europe, working paper series, No. 22, Harvard University.

Dědek, O. et al. (1992), *Otázky měnové spolupráce mezi nástupnickými státy ČSFR* (Monetary Cooperation between the Successor States of Czechoslovakia), IE ČNB, VP No.1, Praha.

Dornbusch, R., Helmers, F. and Leslie, C.H. (1988), *The Open Economy: Tools for Policy Makers in Developing Countries*, Oxford University Press.

Džmuráň, R. (1994), 'Zúčtovací centrum pro mezibankovní platební styk v ČR' (Clearing Center for Inter-bank Payments in the CR), *Bankovnictví*, No. 15, Praha.

Garguläk, R. (1993), *Třiletí prezidenta Václava Havla* (The Three Year Presidency of Vaclav Havel), Mezinárodní politologický ústav PFMU, Brno.

Gerloch, A. (1991), 'Nad variantami státopravního uspořádání československého státu' (An Overview of Possible Constitutional Setups for Czechoslovakia), *Právník*, No. 6, Praha.

Gerloch, A., Hřebejk, J. and Zoubek, V. (1994) *Ústavní systém České republiky* (The Constitutional Setup of the Czech Republic), Prospectrum, Praha.

Guba M. and Skolková, M. (1993), 'Transformace čs. ekonomiky a vývoj měnové politiky' (Transformation of the Czechoslovak Economy and Development of Monetary Policy), *Finance a úvěr*, No. 11.

Hübl, M. (1990), *Češi, Slováci a jejich sousedé* (Czechs, Slovaks and their Neighbors), Naše vojsko, Praha.

Jičínský, Z. (1993), *Problémy československé politiky* (Problems in Czechoslovak Politics), NADAS-AFGM s.r.o., Praha.

Jiroušek, P. (1993) 'Dvanáct tisíc spořitelních pracovníků za přepážkou' (Twelve Thousand Employees of the Savings Bank in Action), *Bankovnictví*, No. 4, Praha.

Jonáš, J. (1994), 'Slovenská ekonomika: lépe než se očekávalo' (The Slovak Economy: Better than Expected), *Lidové noviny*, 1 August, Praha.

Kay, J.A. (1990), 'Tax Policy: A Survey', *Economic Journal*, No. 3.

Kipka, R. and Vodička, K. (1993), *Rozloučení s Československem* (Farewell to Czechoslovakia), Český spisovatel, Praha.

Klvačová, E. (1993), 'Velká privatizace mezi dvěma vlnami' (Large-scale Privatization between the Two Waves), *Ekonom*, No. 7, Praha.

Kočarník, I. (1992), *The Problems of Fiscal Management in CSFR in the Time of Transition*, CERGE, Working Paper No.13, Praha.

Krejčí, O. (1994), *Kniha o volbách* (A Book about Elections), Victoria Publishing, Praha.

Křovák, J. and Zamrazilová, E. (1990), 'Analýza přesunu národního důchodu mezi republikami' (Transfers of National Income between Republics), *Politická ekonomie*, No. 8, Praha.

Kysilka, P. (1993), 'Příprava a realizace měnové odluky v ČR' (Preparation and Realization of Monetary Separation), *Finance a úvěr*, No. 9, Praha.

Lipianska, L. (1994), 'Privatizace v SR zatim ve skluzu' (Privatization in the SR Lags Behind), *Profit*, No. 14, Praha.

Mareš, J. (1993), 'Pro pracovníky bank akce pokračuje' (Bank Staff still in Action), *Bankovnictví*, No. 4, Praha.

Mataj, J. and Vojtíšek, P. (1992), 'Právní a ekonomické aspekty nového zákona o SBČS' (Legal and Economic Aspects of the New Act of the Czechoslovak State Bank), *Finance a úvěr*, No. 3, Praha.

Měchýř, J. (1991), *Slovensko v Československu* (Slovakia in Czechoslovakia) Práce, Praha.

Mikelka, E. et al. (1993), *Západoeuropská ekonomická integrácia v období prípravy jednotného trhu a jej vplyv na ekonomiku SR* (Western European Economic Integration during the Period of Preparing a Single Market and its Impact on the Slovak Economy), EU SAV, Bratislava.

OECD (1994), *Economic Surveys of the CR and the SR*, Paris.

Pavlíček, V. and Hřebejk, J. (1994), *Ústava a ústavní řád České republiky* (The Constitution and Constitutional Law in the Czech Republic), Linde, Praha.

Permanent Secretariat of the Customs Union Council (1994), *Colna unia Českej republiky a Slovenskej republiky v roku 1993* (Czech-Slovak Customs Union in 1993), Bratislava.

PFMU (1994), *Aktuální problémy Slovenska po rozpadu ČSFR; Budování státu* (Slovakia's Key Problems after the Break-up of Czechoslovakia; in: The Founding of States), Mezinárodní politologický ústav (International Institute for Political Science), Brno.

PFMU (1994), *Česko-slovenské vztahy a střední Evropa* (Czech-Slovak Relations and Central Europe), Mezinarodni politologicky ustav PFMU (International Institute for Political Science PFMU), Brno .

Prokop, L. (1994), *Příprava a průběh měnové odluky v České republice v roce 1993* (Preparation and Realization of the Currency Separation in the Czech Republic in 1993), IE ČNB, VP No. 28, Praha.

Scharff, J. (1994), 'Chybné signály vůči Slovensku' (Wrong Signals to the Slovak Republic), *Hospodářské noviny*, 9 March, Praha.

Souček, E. (1993), 'Česko-slovenský obchod' (Czech-Slovak Trade), *Ekonom*, No. 14, Praha.

Surga, L. (1993), 'Tuny nových peněz' (Tons of New Money), *Hospodářské noviny*, No. 67, Praha.

Surga, L. (1993), 'Výměna peněz za poločasem' (Money Exchange in its Final Stage), *Hospodářské noviny*, No. 169, Praha.

Surga, L. (1993), 'Rozdělení oběživa za měnové odluky' (Division of Currency in Circulation during the Currency Separation), *Finance a úvěr*, No. 9, Praha.

Šimůnek, P. (1992), 'Miliónová smlouva' (A Wonderful Treaty), *Mladá fronta dnes*, 2 March, Praha.

Škaloud, J. (1994), 'Trojí dělení Československa' (Three Divisions of Czechoslovakia), *Politologická revue* , No. 1, Praha.

Šmídková, K. (1993), *Exchange Rate System between the Czech and Slovak Republics*, IE ČNB, VP No. 16, Praha.

Tošovský, J. (1994), *The Role of the Central Bank in the Transition to a Market Economy*, paper submitted at: Central banks in Eastern Europe, Chicago.

Vintrová, R. et al. (1984), *Reprodukční proces v ČSSR v 80. letech* (Reproduction Process in Czechoslovakia in 1980s), Academia, Praha.

Vít, J. (1992), 'Jak lze dělit měnu' (Possible Ways of Dividing Currency), *Československé bankovnictví*, No. 12, Praha.

Vodička, K. (1993), 'Koaliční jednání: Rozdělíme stát!' (Coalition Talks: We're Dividing the State!') in: *Rozloučení s Československem* (A Farewell to Czechoslovakia), Český spisovatel, Praha.

Wawrosz, P. (1994), 'Konec kupónové privatizace' (The End of Voucher Privatisation), *Ekonom*, No. 51, Praha.

Willet, T. and Tower, E. (1970), *The Concept of Optimum Currency Areas and the The Choice between Fixed and Flexible Exchange Rates*, Princeton University Press.

Zajkr, B. (1993), 'Malá privatizace skončila, zapomeňte' (Small Privatization is over, Forget it), *Profit*, No. 6, Praha.

Zlý, B. (1993), *Mezinárodní ekonomická integrace* (International Economic Integration), VŠB, Ostrava.